SPATIAL BUSINESS

Competing and Leading with Location Analytics

SPATIAL BUSINESS

Competing and Leading
with Location Analytics

Thomas A. Horan, PhD | James B. Pick, PhD | Avijit Sarkar, PhD

Esri Press
REDLANDS | CALIFORNIA

Cover map by Karie Krocker DeLeon

Esri Press, 380 New York Street, Redlands, California 92373-8100
Copyright © 2022 Esri
All rights reserved.
Printed in the United States of America
26 25 24 23   2 3 4 5 6 7 8 9 10

Library of Congress Control Number: 2022938710
ISBN: 9781589485334

Contents

Part 2: Achieving business and societal value 67

Acknowledgments

The publication of *Spatial Business: Competing and Leading with Location Analytics* represents four years of work undertaken by the authors, who each made an equal contribution to the book. This book is part of the Spatial Business Initiative conducted in cooperation with Esri®. The partnership has been invaluable in providing a forum for investigating trends and developments in business location analytics. We are deeply grateful to Jack and Laura Dangermond for their support of this initiative. Special thanks to Cindy Elliott for her strong partnership as the designated lead at Esri as well as her insightful reviews of draft chapters. Nikki Paripovich Stifle and Karisa Schroeder provided expert input on several chapters, especially chapters 2 and 10. We are also appreciative of the guidance provided by so many at Esri Press, especially Catherine Ortiz, Carolyn Schatz, Stacy Krieg, Dave Boyles (in the early stages of the project), Alycia Tornetta, and Jenefer Shute. The book has also benefited from our participation in Harvard Business School's Microeconomics of Competition (MOC) network. Several key concepts in the book, including the location value chain, cluster mapping, and shared value, were inspired by materials, presentations, and collaborations made possible through the network.

During the book project, various forms of research and outreach were conducted to inform the concepts, methods, and cases outlined in the book. The most intensive of those efforts was the case study research, for which several private-sector leaders in charge of geospatial strategy and location intelligence provided keen insights about their respective organizations. We want to thank Gregg Katz, formerly of The Shopping Center Group; Ben Farster of Walgreens; Enrique Ernesto Espinosa Pérez of Oxxo; Kurt Towler of Sulphur Springs Valley Electric Cooperative; Joe Holubar of Travelers Insurance; Brian Boulmay, formerly of BP; Lawrence Joseph of KFC; Martin Minnoni of RapidSOS; and Andy Reid of Zonda. Each of them agreed to be interviewed as part of our spatial business research, shared nuanced insights on how location analytics is shaping competitiveness and strategies in their respective organizations, and was generous with their geospatial industry perspectives. Esri's Cindy Elliott, Helen Thompson, and Bill Meehan were instrumental in connecting us to several of these experts, and their roles are gratefully acknowledged.

We convey our thanks to several former and present graduate students who provided research assistance at various stages of the project. Anuradha Diekmann, Lauren Salazar, Simisoluwa Ogunleye, Jahanzeb Khan, and Burt Minjares helped record and transcribe case study interviews and collect relevant secondary information from various companies, businesses, academic journals, and business information databases. They distilled key findings and corroborated the findings with the research team members and knowledgeable business contacts and helped us procure permissions for the project's artwork. In addition to these talented students, we would also like to thank An Le for her graphic design work and Kian Nahavandi for her valuable administrative support for the book.

Finally, the University of Redlands provided a very accommodating environment for the project. We are grateful to colleagues at the university for their steadfast encouragement and support of this project.

To my wife, Ruti L. Abrashkin, with deep appreciation for providing a very supportive home life throughout the writing of this book.
—Thomas A. Horan

To my wife, Dr. Rosalyn M. Laudati, with heartfelt thanks for your encouragement, patience, and support.
—James B. Pick

To my wife, Sangita, and our daughter, Anoushka, with deep gratitude for your encouragement, endurance, wit, and unwavering support throughout this book project.
—Avijit Sarkar

Introduction

Technology and location

A quarter century ago, British economist, journalist, and academic Frances Cairncross (1997) proclaimed the "Death of Distance" and predicted a future not bound by location but connected via the electronic revolution. And to be sure, in the ensuing decades, individual lifestyles, the economy, and the world have undoubtedly been transformed by ongoing digital shifts.

Yet 25 years later, location is not dead but deeply intertwined with technology. We live in a global economy, but that economy varies widely by region and location. We live in a high-tech world that allows for unparalleled virtual connections, and yet these high-tech companies tend to cluster in certain regions of the world. We live in a world where shopping can be done entirely online, but these products are sourced through intricate global supply chains that deliver the product to your doorstep.

Location intelligence is embedded in these contemporary dynamics—that is, businesses need to know where to source, where to operate, where to market, where to grow, and so forth. This book is intended to inform business professionals as well as business students about this new world of location analytics and how to use this intelligence to achieve business success. It also aims to inform geographic information system (GIS) professionals and students about how location analytics can be considered and used within business functions and strategies. Indeed, the book unites these domains (business and GIS) into a sphere we call spatial business.

To support business progress in this expanding space, the geospatial industry is growing in its capacity to support location analytics, GIS, web- and cloud-based processing and display, satellite and drone imagery, lidar scanning, and navigation and indoor positioning tools. The total size of the geospatial industry is estimated to be US$439 billion by 2024 and at a compound annual growth rate (CAGR) of 13.8% (GMC 2019).

With this level of location digitization and growth, location intelligence has become foundational to business in its marketing, operations, services, risk management, deployment of assets, and many other functions. Through location analytics and location intelligence, a firm can use location information to make better-informed decisions and ultimately create value to the business and often to society as well. There are numerous examples of companies that have successfully built location analytics capacity and been able to use the ensuing insights to serve consumers better, operate more efficiently, and achieve competitive advantage. What has been needed is an integrated perspective on these developments, and that is the aim of this book.

Spatial business organization

This book provides a contemporary foundation for understanding the business and locational knowledge base to solve spatial problems, support location-based decision-making, and create location value. Our approach can be seen in figure 1, which provides an overview of the book's organization and key concepts. The opening segment (part 1, chapters 1–3) introduces spatial business foundations. Following these foundations, the book dives deeper (part 2, chapters 4–7) into achieving business and societal value in four areas: growing markets and customers, operating the enterprise, managing risk and resilience, and corporate social responsibility. The focus then turns (part 3, chapters 8 and 9) to the elements of management and strategy aimed toward spatial excellence. The book concludes (part 3, chapter 10) with a summary of key themes and a set of implications for practice for each of these themes.

What follows is a brief preview of key concepts, applications, and company cases that are examined in the book.

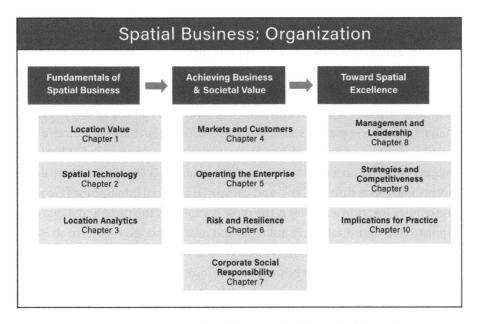

Figure 1. Organization of the *Spatial Business* book, showing how each of the 10 chapters fits within the three parts.

Fundamentals of spatial business

Spatial business refers to concepts, techniques, and actions that enhance the use of locational insights to achieve business and broader societal goals. Part 1 begins by considering the fundamental principles of locational value and how understanding location value chains can inform various business functions such as marketing, operations, and supply chains. Chapter 1 also outlines levels of a company's spatial maturity and the process of gaining maturity. The Shopping Center Group (TSCG) is provided as an example of a company with high spatial maturity and strategic use of location analytics.

These business and locational concepts provide an underpinning for describing the technology of spatial business architecture, which is outlined in chapter 2. As described here, the architecture begins with the business's goals and needs and then addresses business users and stakeholders who are responsible for addressing these business goals using location analytics. The architecture continues with a series of location analytics tools to apply to business areas, tools that depend on various forms of location data that are underpinned by geographic principles and scientific methods. Supporting all these functions are the various platforms that host spatial business processes, such as the cloud, the enterprise, or mobile services. The final component is the net consequence in terms of location intelligence that can be used to provide business insights, inform decisions, and have an impact on business performance. Companies such as Zonda and Walgreens are described as examples of effective architectural deployments.

Location analytics lies at the heart of spatial business architecture. Chapter 3 provides a deeper presentation of the use of descriptive, predictive, and prescriptive analyses. Descriptive location analytics provides exploratory spatial analysis of business patterns as well as visualization of patterns. Predictive location analytics encompasses spatial statistics to detect and predict business patterns and relationships, clusters, and hot spots. This can include spatial forecasting, space-time analysis, and geospatial artificial intelligence (GeoAI). Prescriptive location analytics is the most complex of the three and deploys sophisticated optimization, simulation, and related models to inform strategic decisions and actions. John Deere, Newton Nurseries, and CIDIU S.p.A. are provided as examples of business use of location analytics in chapter 3. Additional examples showcasing various facets of location analytics use across the organizational value chain appear throughout part 2 of the book.

Achieving business and societal value

Building on these spatial business fundamentals, part 2 explores the use of spatial analytics across business goals, focusing on growing markets and customers, operating the enterprise, and managing risk and resilience. It also considers the role of spatial business applications to understand and track a company's social responsibility or what has been termed the new "purpose of the business."

The role of location intelligence is evolving rapidly as organizations use geomarketing to generate deep locational insights about customers and markets. Chapter 4 analyzes the role of location analytics in market and industry cluster analysis to identify business opportunities, determine consumer preferences and buying patterns with customer segmentation, scrutinize geotagged social media streams to examine patterns and relationships between consumer sentiment and actual sales, and determine best locations for new facilities. The chapter also discusses the linkage of location analytics with the 7 *P*s of marketing. Acorn, FreshDirect, Heineken, and Oxxo are provided as examples of the use of location analytics for growing markets and customers.

Effective management of business operations is a highly varied, process-oriented part of an organization, and its functioning is critical to achieving business goals. Chapter 5 outlines how location analytics contributes situational awareness to facilities, ensuring business and service continuity and achieving efficiencies in supply chains and logistics. Los Angeles International Airport (LAX) and Cisco are given as examples of how to operate the enterprise.

Chapter 6 focuses on risk and resiliency. Using location analytics, companies can measure and initiate operational actions ahead of time, gaining the advantage of being proactive in managing risk. With improved visibility through dashboards, companies have the capacity to quickly adjust to events such as natural disasters and coronavirus disease (COVID-19)-related closures. General Motors (GM), CSX Corporation, and Travelers Insurance are provided as examples of location analytics using operational and risk management.

Corporate social responsibility (CSR) calls for companies to be socially accountable in ways that go beyond making a profit. These companies need to take a broader view of their goals, thinking not only of their stockholders but also of the benefits to their employees, customers, and community; the environment; and society. This expansive role of businesses to address social, racial, economic, health, and educational inequities has been heightened worldwide by the COVID-19 pandemic. As corporate leaders steer their businesses through increasingly uncertain business and geopolitical environments in the post-COVID world and are pressured to achieve growth, they are also being called to shape their organizations' role in confronting and addressing these issues. Chapter 7 outlines shared value strategies and actions by companies to use location analytics to address issues such as climate change impacts, sustainable supply chains, United Nations (UN 2022) 2030 Agenda sustainable development goals (SDGs), and economic advancement of underserved communities. Nespresso, Natura, AT&T, and JPMorgan Chase are provided as examples of how location analytics can contribute to these important societal goals.

Toward spatial excellence

A driving theme of spatial business is that location analytics should not be considered an isolated GIS undertaking but rather an integral analytical function for creating business success. Considering the importance of management and senior leadership in an enterprise's spatial transformation, part 3 details the application of management principles allied with spatial business strategies and building the location analytics workforce to accomplish this transformation. It concludes with implications for practice that serve as action items for those engaged in spatial business.

Chapter 8 outlines critical dimensions of spatial leadership needed to achieve spatial maturity, in which location analytics becomes intertwined with business strategies and business gains. The chapter discusses core activities such as demonstrating the value of location analytics to key business goals, championing spatial initiatives, and developing the workforce capacity to achieve these goals. Companies such as CoServ Electric and BP, formerly

British Petroleum, are provided as examples of effective spatial management and leadership.

Chapter 9 moves from leadership and management into strategic and competitive actions. Geospatial strategic planning is characterized as having both external and internal elements. The external element focuses on how location analytics can be used to strengthen the firm's competitive position or modify forces affecting competition, such as customer relationships or new products. Internal planning emphasizes improving the firm's own geospatial infrastructure and processes. The internal element focuses on alignment with the business needs, technological capacity, and human resource requirements to achieve desired location and business value. These strategic actions are demonstrated by examples of both a large company, KFC, formerly Kentucky Fried Chicken, and a small one, RapidSOS.

The concluding chapter, chapter 10, moves to implications for practice, gathered from all that has been presented in the book. This discussion is centered on 10 themes that can guide spatial business actions:

1. Identify and enhance the location value chain
2. Enable spatial maturity pathway
3. Match analytic approach to the business needs
4. Build a spatial business architecture
5. Use market and customer location intelligence to drive business growth
6. Measure, manage, and monitor the operation
7. Mitigate the risk and drive toward resiliency
8. Enhance corporate social responsibility
9. Develop a spatial strategy and capacity
10. Provide spatial leadership for sustainable advantage

A set of implications for practice is provided as specific steps to achieve an effective spatial business strategy and operations that will contribute to business success in today's complex and competitive environment.

We hope you will find the following chapters informative about the principles, concepts, and practices of spatial business. For leaders, it represents an important opportunity to use location intelligence for strategic leadership and competitive gain. For analysts, it is an exciting opportunity to deploy innovative location technologies and applications that can have a demonstrable impact. For students, it is a growing field of study and profession that complements and widens traditional business education and professions. For all, spatial business has elements that broaden the space of inquiry to consider related societal outcomes, challenges, and benefits for communities and the world.

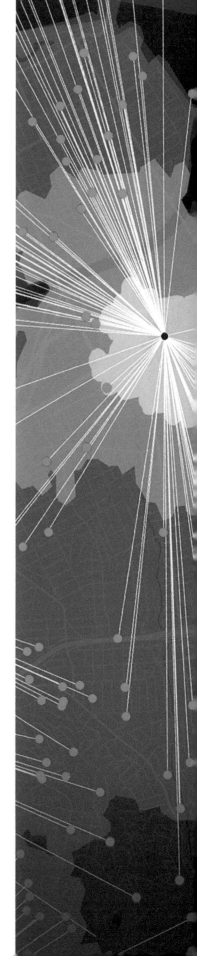

CHAPTER 1
Fundamentals of location value

Introduction

Creating value

If we begin with the premise that the purpose of a business is to create value, how do we identify specific value? In the private sector, this value is typically revealed in products and services that are successful in the marketplace. Technology companies provide products that are purchased, real estate companies provide homes and office buildings that are purchased or leased, and consultants provide advisory services that are procured. Every sector of industry, including government and nonprofits, has a range of specific value that it creates.

From a competitive perspective, this value is framed within the context of a company's unique "value proposition" to its customers. J. C. Anderson, J. A. Narus, and W. Van Rossum (2006) identified three types of value proposition: all benefits, comparative advantage, and resonating focus. An all-benefits value proposition represents the comprehensive set of customer benefits a company provides, whereas a comparative advantage value proposition highlights its value relative to the competition. A resonating focus value proposition—considered the gold standard of value propositions—identifies the key points of difference that will deliver the most compelling value to the customer.

The challenge of location analytics is to provide business insight into how location affects these value propositions, considering a host of geographic, economic, technological, environmental, and societal factors.

Sustainable value

Although many companies rightly focus on their value proposition to customers, broader value considerations affect their business activities and decisions. In the five decades since economist Milton Friedman famously proclaimed that the sole responsibility of business is to make a profit, there has been a growing recognition that the purpose of a company transcends its profit-making capacity. On August 22, 2019, in recognition of this expanded view of the role of business in society, the prestigious US Business Roundtable announced a revised articulation of the purpose of a business (Business Roundtable 2019). This broader perspective, backed by 181 of the top US companies, includes the following dimensions: delivering value to customers, investing in employees, dealing fairly and ethically with suppliers, supporting communities, embracing sustainable business practices, generating long-term value for shareholders, and engaging effectively with shareholders. As Darren Walker, president of the Ford Foundation, observed at the time of the announcement, "This is tremendous news because it is more critical than ever that businesses in the twenty-first century are focused on generating long-term value for all stakeholders and addressing the challenges we face, which will result in shared prosperity and sustainability for both business and society" (Business Roundtable 2019).

These developments are often framed within the context of corporate social responsibility, or CSR, and, more recently, environmental, social, and governance (ESG) factors. KPMG (2020), a British-Dutch accounting services network, has conducted an annual survey since 1993 on global corporate CSR/ESG activities and reporting. At the time of the 1993 survey, only 12% of the top companies (N100) in surveyed companies were reporting on their CSR/ESG activities. As of 2020, this reporting had grown to 85%. Moreover, the growth in ESG reporting in the top global corporations (G250), which KPMG started surveying in 1995, has risen to 90% (figure 1.1). Companies are clearly seeing the connection between their actions and the surrounding world and the need to track and address societal and environmental factors that could inhibit their success. For example, that same 2020 survey found that reporting on the threat of global climate change as a financial risk had grown dramatically for both groups, with 43% of top global companies (G250) and 53% of top national companies (N100) noting this financial risk.

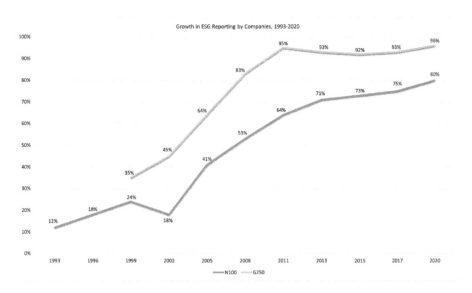

Figure 1.1. Growth in ESG reporting by top national and global companies. Trends for top national and global companies are displayed in dark-blue and light-blue lines, respectively. Source: KPMG 2020.

The COVID-19 pandemic has only served to intensify the interlinks between companies and societal conditions. During the pandemic, businesses have had to radically change employee work patterns and relationships with customers and do their part to safeguard the health and safety of all those within their business ecosystem—all of it amid dramatic economic and employment contractions and locational changes. It has become clear that the health and safety of employees is not only of great consequence when they are at work but also depends on the conditions of the environments and communities they live in and travel to.

Turning to the focus of this book, business location analytics also has a role in advancing this broad purpose of business in delivering value to customers, communities, and the global environment. Such a role can be best introduced by considering the spatial decision cycle that enhances business value.

Spatial decision cycle

Considering these various dimensions of value, ranging from a product to a societal impact, how can you start to think spatially about enhancing such value through location analytics? It is useful to consider a cycle of four elements in a spatial decision process: value, spatial thinking, location analytics, and data (figure 1.2). The cycle begins with understanding the value created by a company's products and services. It then considers the spatial dimension of the value created, followed by the appropriate location analytics suggested by this spatial thinking. The cycle then turns to the data requirement for achieving the desired location-analytics insights and concludes with the value added by these insights for business priorities.

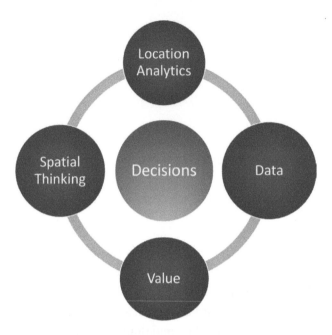

Figure 1.2. The spatial decision cycle, showing the links between its key elements: value, spatial thinking, location analytics, and data.

The spatial decision cycle

Element 1: Value (proposition)

From a strategic perspective, spatial decision-making begins with business goals to deliver a company's value proposition through market and customer growth, achieving competitive advantage in offerings, driving operational efficiencies, and managing risk and regulatory compliance. Considering the dimensions outlined by the Business Roundtable, these goals can also include upgrading employee skills, ensuring effective and sustainable supply chains, supporting local communities, and improving environmental conditions.

For example, the case of gourmet coffee company Nespresso (2021a) illustrates a business strategy that embraces these objectives and uses location analytics to achieve them. As the company notes in its business principles, its value proposition is to "promise consumers the finest coffee in the world that preserves the best of our world" (2021a). Similar to the Business Roundtable's new "Statement of Purpose of a Corporation" (Business Roundtable 2019), Nespresso notes, "If we are to be successful—not only as a business, but in delivering on this promise—we know we must earn the trust and respect of our people, our customers, our suppliers and wider society." As will be outlined in the Nespresso case study (in chapter 7), a key aspect of delivering on this promise is the use of location analytics to monitor and manage achieving a variety of business, environmental, and community goals under Nespresso's "Positive Cup" framework (2021b). Of course, not every company operates in the same context as Nespresso, but a key value proposition can usually be discerned, with priorities that set the stage for spatial thinking.

Element 2: Spatial thinking

This second stage of the cycle focuses on using spatial thinking to translate business objectives into spatial considerations. Spatial thinking is considered a form of intelligence, along with other forms of intelligence such as logical and interpersonal (Gardner 2006). The National Research Council (2006) noted that there are three components to spatial thinking: spatial attributes, spatial representations, and spatial reasoning. In spatial business, spatial attributes refer to the ways to measure and assess location dynamics in trade areas, supply chain transportation, and so forth. Spatial representations include various means of rendering spatial dynamics, such as customer cluster maps, business space-time trend lines, and supply network visualizations.

Perhaps the most important component is spatial reasoning. In spatial business, this calls for constructing a line of inquiry that reveals the influence of location factors on business success. For example, a hospital can examine its supplier network to determine where in the supply chain interruptions are occurring. A retail company can examine trends in sales across different customer markets to determine where new stores should be opened because such locales have a strong presence of desired customer profiles.

A classic example of strategic spatial reasoning is the case of the investment company Edward Jones. Edward Jones started as a small-town investment firm in Missouri. The company viewed its comparative value proposition as providing a single investment service to more rural communities, compared with Merrill, previously branded Merrill Lynch, which

provided full-service portfolios in large metropolitan areas (Collis and Rukstad 2008). In the early 1980s, Edward Jones conducted a series of analyses and consultations and discovered that its resonating value proposition was that it offered a highly personalized investment service to those individual customers who wanted to delegate investment decisions. It further discovered that it could competitively offer these services in select rural and metropolitan locales where such customer profiles were strongly represented. The company then proceeded to operationalize the new market mix. This spatial reasoning resulted in the rapid growth of Edward Jones from 400 to 1,000 locations in a seven-year period and remains its driving focus today (Edward Jones 2021).

Element 3: Location analytics

Clear spatial thinking drives the choice of location analytics. If a business is mostly interested in a general understanding of spatial trends in customers, assets, suppliers, and so forth, descriptive analysis can provide situational awareness through maps and infographics. If a business desires to carry the spatial analysis further, to understand how spatial insights can help achieve business value priorities, explanatory analysis can be conducted to help explain dynamics such as why growth did or did not occur or why certain sites or locations were or were not successful. If a business wants a predictive analysis of the likely success of a service, product, or location, it can conduct predictive spatial analysis. And if a business wants to know where to establish optimal new locations or serve new markets, it can conduct prescriptive analysis. These spatial analysis approaches are reviewed in detail in chapter 3.

Many industries are advancing their analytic capacities to move from descriptive analytics to predictive and prescriptive analytics. As one example, the insurance industry is rapidly evolving to adjust to the more extreme climate conditions brought on by climate change and other sociodemographic and economic changes. Companies such as Travelers Insurance (2021) now employ a full range of location analytics to assist a range of business-critical functions. These include predicting the location of natural disasters (for

The spatial decision cycle *(continued)*

underwriting purposes), analyzing damage locations (for claim purposes), and identifying high-priority locational impacts (for disaster response). These tools have been used with great success for recent hurricanes on the East Coast and wildfires on the West Coast (Claims Journal 2019).

Element 4: Data

The fourth element in the spatial decision cycle is data. As the expression goes, "You are only as good as your data." A business may have a driving need to use location analytics to enhance its success but will be hampered without the appropriate data. Typical data types include sales, profit, customer, cost, asset, and network data. In addition to this proprietary data, numerous governmental and commercial datasets can inform location analysis—for example, trade area analysis, business transactions, supply chain network data, and demographic, social, economic, and environmental trends. Companies are leaning toward digital transformation and so are aligning their business intelligence enterprises, which includes enhanced interoperability of these data sources. This data can be linked to location, often expressed as "georeferenced."

In addition to the need for "location stamped" data, three other data issues that deserve attention are the level of geographic specificity, the availability and consistency of data over time, and the policies surrounding data use. Regarding the first of the three, the greater the level of granularity, the better the analysis, although many publicly available datasets limit the granularity for reasons of privacy and anonymity. Regarding the second, temporal data is critical for looking at spatial changes over time, such as the growth or decline of customers, sales, inventory, and so forth. And third, various policies can affect the use of data within a company or its ability to share the results of the data. For some industries such as health care, these privacy conditions are well established, such as through the Health Insurance Portability and Accountability Act (HIPAA) of 1996, whereas for other industries such as retail, privacy issues are emerging around location-based services.

Element 5: Value (added)

The cycle concludes with the consequence of location analysis in contributing to business success. This may include value added to business priorities such as driving growth, improving operations, managing risk, and ensuring regulatory compliance. To the extent possible, this contribution should be documented in terms of the type and amount of value contributed and the stakeholders who received this value. There are several dimensions to consider in determining this value: depth, breadth, use, internal stakeholders, external stakeholders, and financial contribution, as summarized in table 1.1.

Beginning with depth, this value type refers to the value delivered to a specific business function such as marketing or operations. Breadth refers to the value delivered across business functions as the organization increases its spatial maturity. Then, there are different use values. These can include the value that location analytics has in informing stakeholders, through situational awareness; in decision-making; in contributing to business goals; and, ultimately, in contributing to the business mission.

Like beauty, value is in the eye of the beholder. There are internal stakeholders who perceive value, ranging from employees carrying out specific organizational functions to the ladder of middle, senior, and executive managers and leaders. There are external stakeholders who perceive value, including customers, partners, suppliers, distributors, and the public. Finally, there is the traditional estimation of value, often framed within the context of return on investment (ROI). This can be in the form of a formal or quantitative ROI or a more qualitative summarization of the value elements noted above. The former can be particularly appropriate when the costs and benefits can be easily parsed.

Most importantly, this version is but one iteration of the spatial decision cycle. The cycle should be considered ongoing and integrated into decisions regarding key business priorities. A case example of this tight integration is The Shopping Center Group, which we consider next.

Case example: The Shopping Center Group

The Shopping Center Group, or TSCG, is a leading national retail-only real estate service provider in the US. It has 20 offices in the US, 215 team members, and 28 GIS specialists (known as mappers). Over the last decade, the company has come to tightly integrate the use of business-focused location analytics that deliver business value to its customers and its organization (The Shopping Center Group 2021).

TSCG has four main service lines: tenant representations, project leasing, retail property sales, and property management of those retail properties. As TSCG's former Chief Strategy Officer Gregg Katz noted, "At the core of everything is GIS research. We consider GIS research to be the heartbeat of the organization. It allows all four of those service lines to tell a story" (Esri 2017). Each of the four service lines engages in ongoing spatial decision cycles—that is, what is the property in question? What are the business objectives for the property? What location analytics will inform decisions about the property? What data can be applied to this analysis? What recommendations come out of this cycle of analysis?

In this way, location analytics is providing considerable value to TSCG. Table 1.1 provides a summary of this value in terms of the dimensions described above. Beginning with value to key business functions, location analytics provides value to the company's marketing and sales support. This support features deep spatial insight into consumer and trade area markets. For example, an analysis conducted on behalf of Columbus Mall in Georgia combined trade area, drive-time, GPS, and psychographic analyses to pinpoint key market considerations to guide the selection of potential tenants for that commercial property.

Table 1.1. Value of location analytics for The Shopping Center Group

Value	Domain	Value to The Shopping Center Group
Depth	Value Within Marketing and Sales Support	Deep spatial insight on relative consumer and trade-area markets for commercial properties
Breadth	Value Along Key Business Priorities	Drives overall value proposition as an information-focused technology enabled commercial real estate company Success of brokers and growth of company
Use	Inform, Decide, Grow, Avoid	Used to inform brokers, decide on commercial selections, and avoid mismatches between commercial property types and surrounding markets
Who: Internal	Internal (Analysts, Managers, Sales, Operations, C-suite)	1:4 "mapper" to broker ratio C-suite vetting and management of commercial properties
Who: External	Clients and Partners	Multilayer commercial real estate maps for clients and partners
Results/ROI	Direct Input to Competitive Advantage and Growth	Key contributing component to 30% growth of company, and mission as an analytics-focused commercial real estate company

As table 1.1 shows, location analytics is part of the overall TSCG value proposition as an information-focused, technology-enabled commercial real estate company, and it spans a wide range of value types. It informs brokers and partners, it aids in their decision-making process, and it helps the company grow while avoiding costly market assumption errors in retail commercial transactions.

These location analytics insights and products are used by a wide range of stakeholders. Internally, brokers and other analysts have ready access to the 28 mappers who fuel the analysis. This utilization rises to the C-suite level, in which every major deal is required to have a location analytics review as part of the vetting process. Considering the highly integrated nature of location analytics in the TSCG mission, processes, and product lines, its ROI value is considered within the context of overall corporate success. In this case, company executives consider it to be a key contributor to TSCG's 30% growth and its emergence as a commercial retail and information company.

Location value chain

The use of location analysis across business dimensions can be considered the *location value chain*. The concept is a variant of Michael E. Porter's seminal *value chain*, which outlines the various business processes that combine to create value in terms of products and services delivered (Porter 1998b). A business's location value chain captures those business functions that benefit from location analytics and thus contribute to the overall value of the company.

Depending on the business value being pursued, location analytics can be deployed across a range of business functions (figure 1.3).

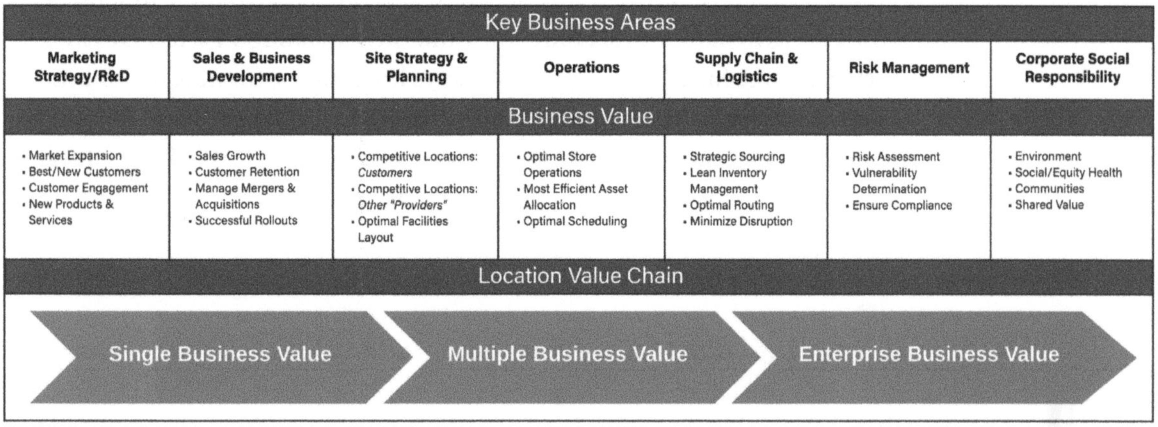

Key Business Areas						
Marketing Strategy/R&D	Sales & Business Development	Site Strategy & Planning	Operations	Supply Chain & Logistics	Risk Management	Corporate Social Responsibility
Business Value						
• Market Expansion • Best/New Customers • Customer Engagement • New Products & Services	• Sales Growth • Customer Retention • Manage Mergers & Acquisitions • Successful Rollouts	• Competitive Locations: *Customers* • Competitive Locations: *Other "Providers"* • Optimal Facilities Layout	• Optimal Store Operations • Most Efficient Asset Allocation • Optimal Scheduling	• Strategic Sourcing • Lean Inventory Management • Optimal Routing • Minimize Disruption	• Risk Assessment • Vulnerability Determination • Ensure Compliance	• Environment • Social/Equity Health • Communities • Shared Value
Location Value Chain						

Single Business Value → Multiple Business Value → Enterprise Business Value

Figure 1.3. Location value chain, comprising business functions and business needs within each function that prompt the use of location analytics.

Location analytics can be used across the following basic business functions:

- Research and development (R&D), including service and product development, new market development, acquisition due diligence, and location siting
- Marketing, including market expansion, customer segmentation, and customer retention
- Business development and sales, including product rollout, mergers and acquisitions, and sales growth
- Operations, including asset management and facilities management
- Site strategy, including trade area analysis, competitive analysis, and facilities layout
- Supply chain, including sourcing, operations, network analysis, tracking, and simulation
- Risk management, including risk assessment, management, recovery, and resiliency
- CSR, including employee health, social equity, community impacts, and shared-value creation

A variety of studies have documented the range of use for location analytics across this value chain. In 2018, the University of Redlands (2018) in

Redlands, California, conducted a survey of 200 businesses that had at least initial adoption of location technology to determine patterns of location analytics use. The survey found that an overwhelming majority (86%) of surveyed businesses report moderate to high use in more than one function (figure 1.4). Overall, 51% of businesses use GIS in one to three functions, 35% use GIS in four to six functions, and the remaining 14% use GIS in seven to nine functions. Figure 1.4 shows levels of use for nine major business functions, with GIS usage highest for R&D (58%), followed by operations (50%), services (48%), information technology (IT) (48%), sales and business development (47%), and marketing (43%).

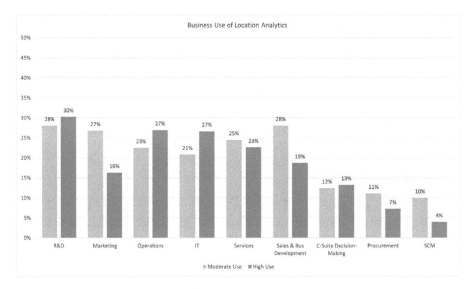

Figure 1.4. High and moderate use of location analytics in business functions along the location value chain (high use in dark blue and moderate use in light blue).

In terms of the overarching business motivations for using spatial analysis, 46% of the survey respondents reported moderate to high motivation for improving the competitive posture of the business. This was followed by GIS use to optimize business performance (39%), for effective risk and disaster management (31%), and finally for regulatory compliance (28%).

In a closer look at customer-centric activities, GIS use is highest for analysis of spatial patterns of customers (46% indicate moderate to high use) yet lowest for tracking and measuring sales activities (29%), pointing to a gap in GIS use for these purposes. In the middle are GIS use for customizing marketing strategies (38%), predicting future customer trends (36%), and optimizing sales territories (31%). Apart from tracking and measuring sales, GIS use for customer and sales activities seems to decline as the purpose of deriving location intelligence shifts from descriptive to predictive to prescriptive in nature.

Turning to operations, GIS use is highest among the following activities: space and location decisions (58% indicate moderate to high use), spatial field data collection (56%), tracking and managing asset allocations (43%), predicting future operational needs (36%), and managing logistics and supply chains (20%). As in customer and sales activities, moderate GIS use surpasses high use for operational activities.

Pandemic influences on the location value chain

The COVID-19 pandemic of 2020 profoundly influenced the location value chain of many businesses. With the disruption of operations, location analytics played an important role in assessing the challenges to business continuity, which varied by location. Businesses had to move quickly to close, modify, or continue with operations, depending on a variety of federal, state, and local conditions. The pandemic also had major impacts on business supply chains, most visibly on the health-care supply chain, in which the crisis exposed risks associated with the global, just-in-time systems that had come to dominate the medical device and supplies industry. In addition, businesses needed to have locational information on employees to ensure their safety and take appropriate action if they or their coworkers were exposed to infection.

As businesses enter a postpandemic era, new value propositions are emerging that will affect the location value chain of businesses. Within the retail sphere, online, on-ground hybrid models are being extended. McKinsey & Company (2020) reported that many customers have also tried new omnichannel models. For example, buy online, pickup in store (BOPIS) grew 28% year over year in February 2021, and grocery delivery was up by 57%. McKinsey further notes that many of these new engagement models are here to stay. Consumers report high intent to continue using models such as BOPIS (56%) and grocery delivery (45%) after the pandemic. As these business models evolve, they will create new opportunities to integrate location analytics into the new normal of business operations.

Drivers of spatial maturity

Spatial maturity involves the deepening of location analytics use across the location value chain. Looking at the range of use, the University of Redlands (2018) survey estimated that roughly one of five businesses (22%) uses GIS enterprise-wide, spanning multiple departments. At the other end of the spectrum, one of five businesses (20%) reports GIS usage to be very limited. In the middle, 28% of businesses report their GIS usage to be currently limited but poised to grow soon, whereas another 25% indicate GIS usage to be moderate and steady. Overall, business use of GIS has the potential to grow in the near term. However, charting a path for spatial business transformation is essential.

In determining the factors that contributed to achieving spatial maturity, the survey found five that played an influential role. The more advanced, spatially mature companies had (1) a perception of the value of location analytics, (2) a clear and coherent business strategy, (3) C-suite sponsorship and support, (4) availability of best-in-class technology, and (5) clear articulation of ROI.

Turning to inhibitors of spatial maturity, International Data Corporation (IDC) and Esri Canada (Lewin 2021) identified several factors as "challenges" to achieving deeper spatial maturity. Cost, culture, appropriate skill set, integration challenges, and data quality issues were identified as inhibitors that could impede the growth and use of location analytics in companies.

Various forecasting reports provide a generally bullish outlook on the future use of location analytics. This is due to at least these eight drivers of location analytics use:

- Growing geospatial ecosystem
- Deepening use across a range of industry applications and verticals
- Increasing availability of spatial analytics tools
- Integration of location analytics with business intelligence
- Widening range of location services
- Growing indoor location analytics
- Rise of associated advanced technologies
- Rise in global environmental, societal, and health challenges

Drivers of location analytics use

Driver 1: Geospatial ecosystem

Location analytics is part of a larger geospatial ecosystem that includes Global Navigation Satellite Systems (GNSS), GIS/spatial analytics, Earth observation, lidar, space-time visualization, augmented/virtual reality (AR/VR), and artificial intelligence (AI). The global geospatial solutions market is projected to reach US$502.6 billion by 2024 from an estimated US$239.1 billion in 2019, at a compound annual growth rate (CAGR) of 13.2% during the forecast period (Sreedhar and Bhatnagar 2019). The cornerstone of this industry is GNSS, which provides the technological backbone for the industry and accounts for approximately 59% of the total value. This has fueled the growth of GIS/spatial analytics as the second-largest segment of the industry, with growth expected to double by 2022 (GMC 2019).

Driver 2: Industry use

Consistent with the University of Redlands survey, other industry outlooks have documented deepening use across a range of industries. For example, the Dresner Advisory Location Analytics Survey (Dresner 2019) found that location analytics was viewed as critical or very important across a range of vertical industries. Some 93% of survey respondents viewed location analytics as having some importance to their organization, and more than 53% noted that it was critically or very important to their organizations. In terms of specific vertical markets, the survey found this to be especially true for health care, business services, financial services, consumer services, and manufacturing. Each of these sectors viewed location analytics as critical or very important to their organizations.

Driver 3: Spatial analytics tools

Spatial analytics tools continue to expand in their areas of application and their capabilities. In terms of broad solution sets, geocoding (and reverse geocoding), reporting and visualization, thematic mapping and analysis, and data integration/extract, transform, load (ETL) are each expected to grow substantially by 2024 (Sreedhar and Bhatnagar 2019). The ability to effectively geocode data is particularly helpful in making a

range of industry data available for location analytics, such as customer, business, product, and supply chain data. Thematic mapping and analysis growth will continue with the availability of increasingly sophisticated analytics. Reporting and visualization tend to increase demand both within businesses and from their external stakeholders. As the volume and value of data continue to grow, there is a strong need for integration across different systems, including business intelligence (BI) systems.

Driver 4: Business intelligence integration

Further fueling this growth is the increasing appetite for the business insights provided by location analytics. Dresner Advisory (2021) reports that R&D, marketing and sales, and executive management are expected to experience the highest growth for BI penetration (which includes location analytics) through 2024 and that "better decision-making" is the primary objective of BI use, followed by related key business areas such as (in descending order) growth in revenues, operational efficiencies, increased competitive advantage, enhanced customer service, and risk management. Increased integration into BI software suites and reports provides a natural path for location analytics to contribute to business growth and competitiveness.

Driver 5: Location services

The rise of location-based services (LBS) has provided unprecedented opportunities to customize offerings and customer experiences. The related rise of real-time location systems (RTLS) also provides unprecedented opportunities to track assets, personnel, and products. As an industry, LBS/RTLS services is expected to grow rapidly (CAGR of 20.1%) to become a US$40 billion market by 2024 (Sreedhar and Bhatnagar 2019). GPS-enabled mobile devices have spurred an entirely new dimension to retail marketing and customer services.

Driver 6: Indoor location analytics

Related to the growth of LBS and RTLS, indoor location analytics is growing rapidly as industries begin to appreciate its value, especially in operational

Drivers of location analytics use *(continued)*

efficiencies and risk management. For example, health care is considered a prime use of RTLS, and RTLS use in this sector is expected to grow by CAGR 18% to a US$6.84 billion market by 2027. Across industries, the COVID-19 pandemic has heightened the need to track and monitor personnel locations for health, safety, and other risk management measures. LBS/RTLS is also disrupting traditional distribution center workflows and processes, as evidenced by the innovative distribution center techniques deployed by such retail giants as Amazon, Target, and Walmart. As the penetration of the Internet of Things (IoT) and other location-based technologies deepens, new applications will emerge. At the same time, privacy and security threats will condition the extent to which such solutions are deployed, and this constraint could vary widely across regions and cultures.

Driver 7: Advanced technologies

A range of advanced technologies will provide numerous opportunities to extend and deepen the use of location analytics in business and contribute to the ongoing digital transformation of business. The IoT has already led to a pronounced rise in indoor GIS, particularly in the retail sector. The COVID-19 pandemic has heightened the need for and use of georeferenced IoT devices to track supply chains, analyze human travel patterns, and monitor health conditions. Advances in AI are enabling machine and deep learning across a range of business domains, such as analyzing and predicting customer buying patterns, operational improvements, and threats to business continuity. These and other AI applications make up what is known as GeoAI. Of course, IoT, AI, and related technological advances would not be feasible without continued advances in big data platforms and applications. Specific to location analytics, the geospatial industry is moving to highly cloud-based and Web GIS platforms with integration to big datasets and location analytics applications.

Driver 8: Global environmental, societal, and health challenges

The eighth driver is the changing environmental, health, and societal context in which businesses operate. In terms of the environment, the private sector is increasingly treating climate change as a contextual condition that can have a significant impact on business success. This impact is across the location value chain, affecting companies' ability to source sustainable suppliers and retain resilient supply chains through increasing volatile climate conditions. Societal issues range from racial equity, income disparities, and broadband access to other factors that can affect a company's performance and success in different regions and communities. The COVID-19 pandemic has raised awareness of the massive impact that such an outbreak can have on all aspects of the economy and the need to build resiliency into supply chains and operations.

At the macro level, M. Porter and M. Kramer (2016) have emphasized the concept of "creating shared value—pursuing financial success in a way that also yields societal benefits." They note: "Collective impact is based on the idea that social problems arise from and persist because of a complex combination of actions and omissions by players in all sectors—and therefore can be solved only by the coordinated efforts of those players, from businesses to government agencies, charitable organizations, and members of affected populations." There are many examples of such shared-value initiatives that rely on locational information. These include locationally targeted partnerships for economic development, training suppliers on sustainable practices relative to their local community, and public-private collaborations on relief during the COVID-19 pandemic.

Global location analytics outlook

These eight drivers, as well as other influences, are expected to result in considerable growth in location analytics across the globe. Location analytics as an industry is expected to rise from US$7.8 billion (2017) to US$22.8 billion (2024), representing 16.6% CAGR (Sreedhar and Bhatnagar 2019). This growth is expected to be worldwide. Currently, the major regional markets are North America (34.8%), Europe (28%), and Asia Pacific (20.4%). Leading to 2024, these will continue to be major markets with the largest growth (17.1% CAGR) expected in the Asia Pacific region. The Middle East and Latin America are expected to remain smaller regional markets, although each region is expected to have noteworthy growth (Sreedhar and Bhatnagar 2019).

The strongest growth (figure 1.5) is projected in supply chain planning and optimization (17.3%), sales and marketing optimization (17.1%), customer experience management (16.7%), remote monitoring (16.3%), and emergency response management (16.3%).

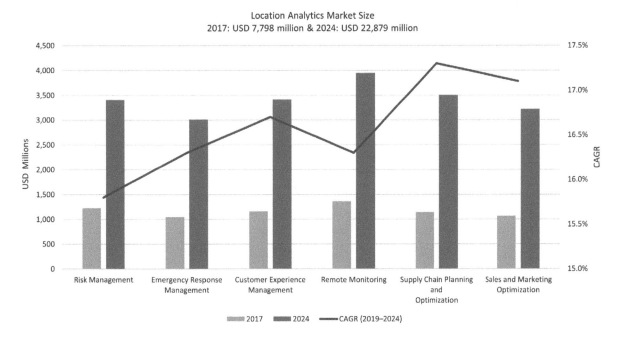

Figure 1.5. Global outlook for location analytics across business functions, with the base year (2017) in light blue and the forecast year (2024) in dark blue. Source: Sreedhar and Bhatnagar 2019.

In summary, the location value foundation outlined in this chapter serves as an organizing set of concepts, principles, and examples for understanding the business location value of any company, a value that includes organizational success within a societal context. As organizations broaden and deepen their use of location analytics to achieve business priorities and goals, location analytics can become more integral to a company's mission. Various market forecasts suggest that such deepening use will indeed be the case around the globe and across a wide range of industries and business functions. This growth, in turn, contributes to and benefits from the need to integrate across business intelligence systems, geospatial platforms, and various new technological systems and products as they arise. These technology issues are taken up next in chapter 2 in terms of a spatial business architecture and the technology needed to achieve it.

CHAPTER 2
Fundamentals of spatial technology

Introduction

Achieving location intelligence depends on a process that delivers valuable insights to business users. Although other technologies may specialize in informing who, what, and why, location intelligence makes information actionable by adding the element of where. Organizations increasingly focus on this location intelligence to drive strategic decisions at all levels of the enterprise.

This chapter defines the components of the technological backbone of location analytics by outlining the six essential elements of a spatial business architecture: business goals and needs, human talent, location analytics and its applications, data, platforms, and location intelligence (figure 2.1).

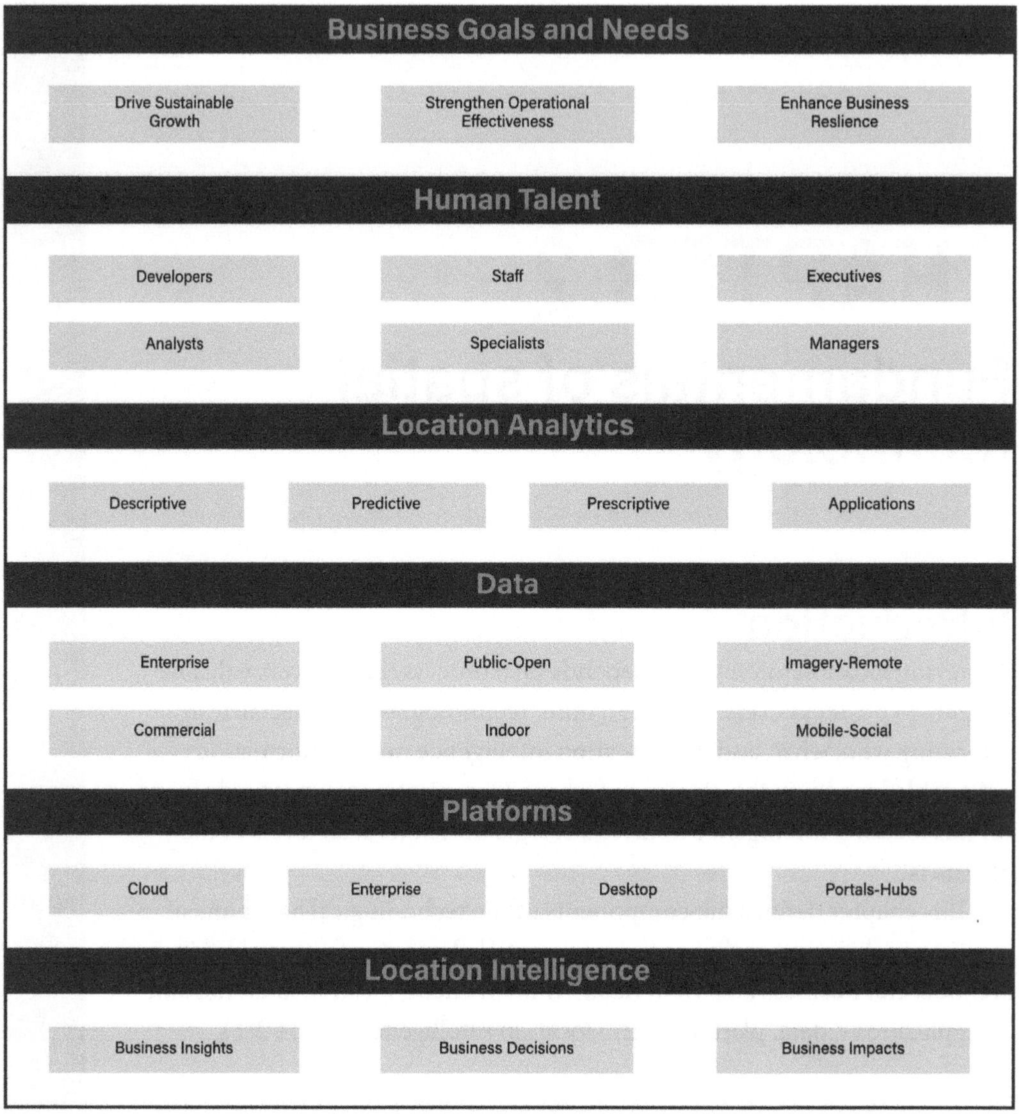

Business Goals and Needs		
Drive Sustainable Growth	Strengthen Operational Effectiveness	Enhance Business Reslience

Human Talent		
Developers	Staff	Executives
Analysts	Specialists	Managers

Location Analytics			
Descriptive	Predictive	Prescriptive	Applications

Data		
Enterprise	Public-Open	Imagery-Remote
Commercial	Indoor	Mobile-Social

Platforms			
Cloud	Enterprise	Desktop	Portals-Hubs

Location Intelligence		
Business Insights	Business Decisions	Business Impacts

Figure 2.1. The components of spatial business architecture include business goals, human talent, location analytics, data, platforms, and location intelligence.

Building spatial business architecture

The architecture begins with the business's goals and needs and the human talent needed to accomplish these business goals. The architecture continues with a series of location analytics tools and the data on which the analysis is performed. Underlying all these functions are the various platforms that host spatial business processes, such as the cloud, the enterprise, and portals. The final component is the net consequence in terms of location intelligence that provides insights, informs decisions, and impacts business performance. The following sections describe each of these components of spatial business architecture, with examples taken from case studies throughout the book.

Element 1: Business goals and needs

Location analytics is performed to enhance business value, in terms of the business goals and needs associated with achieving this value. Location analytics can contribute to diverse business goals, and they can be focused anywhere across the location value chain. The architecture highlights three goals that are generally central to any business: drive sustainable growth, strengthen operational effectiveness, and enhance business resilience.

Many factors are associated with sustainable business growth: having valued products and services, attracting and retaining customers, and operating in a socially and environmentally responsible manner, to name a few. The appropriate location analytics tools can contribute to business and broader goals. For example, John Deere (see chapter 3) is a leader in location-based precision farming that is responsive to climate changes and enables more sustainable farming practices.

A second goal is to strengthen operational effectiveness. Several factors are associated with achieving this goal, including operational performance, supply chain management, and logistics. For example, Cisco (see chapter 5) uses a customer location dashboard to ensure timely service support.

A third goal is to enhance business resilience. Factors associated with this central goal include risk management, risk recovery, and risk reliance. This can be seen in the locational risk and response algorithms developed by Travelers Insurance (see chapter 6) to predict hurricane directions and risk and by Mid-South Synergy's tree analysis (see chapter 6) to protect against power outages due to fallen trees.

Element 2: Human talent

The success of spatial business depends on having the human talent to accomplish the strategic and tactical actions needed to achieve business gains. Employees and stakeholders act in varying capacities at each stage of the spatial business cycle. To identify business needs, a variety of people contribute—business internal users of location-based systems, executives, managers, business and GIS analysts, and technical specialists. Trained developers design and build location analytics, consulting with managers.

Location-driven decision-making is carried out by managers, senior executives, and business unit managers. Staff at all levels, such as in sales, operations management, and service data collection, may use the applications.

This list is not exhaustive. The point is that the successful execution of a spatial business strategy depends on people at varied levels in the organizational hierarchy, with different skill sets and disparate levels of technical and business knowledge. Walgreens (see the closing case study at the end of the chapter) is an example of how technical and business unit managers collaborated to swiftly roll out COVID-19 pandemic testing applications and advance their overall spatial technology platform.

Element 3: Location analytics and applications

Location analytics may be divided into descriptive, predictive, and prescriptive tools. Descriptive analytics describes locational phenomena. For instance, a map of electric car-charging locations with car capacity and charging intensity is descriptive. Predictive location analytics predicts future business phenomena based on forecasting of georeferenced data and space-time prediction techniques. An example would be to predict in one year's time the locations of customers placing e-commerce orders based on trend analysis or geographically weighted statistical regression models. Prescriptive location analytics seeks to provide optimal locational and network arrangements to achieve a business objective. As an example, United Parcel Service (see chapter 9) developed a routing tool for optimized routing of deliveries that also produces considerable fuel savings.

Underlying location analytics are algorithmic techniques such as overlay, buffers, drive-time analysis, and sophisticated methods such as visualization, decision trees, text analysis, data mining, spatial cluster methodologies, spatial statistics, location-allocation modeling, network analysis, AI, and machine learning. The following represent a range of location analytics techniques.

Spatial visualization and hot spots

At a basic level, mapping is a form of visualization that simplifies understanding of geographic differences. For instance, the thematic map of the density of Airbnb properties in New York City (figure 2.2) visualizes the geography of the city and the density levels of Airbnb properties, indicating the highest levels in lower Manhattan and central Brooklyn. This visualization uses geography, colors, labeling, and scale to create impact and tell a story that the equivalent table of data would not do as easily.

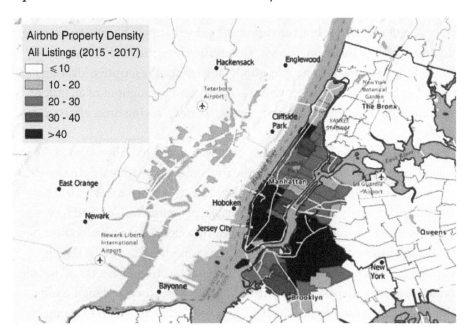

Figure 2.2. A thematic map exhibits the zip code areas of New York City by categories of Airbnb property densities, with the highest densities in lower Manhattan and central Brooklyn. Source: Sarkar, Koohikamali, and Pick 2020. ©2020 Emerald Publishing Ltd. All rights reserved.

Visualization offers a way to simplify massive data and its processed outputs to highlight the important overall outcomes and bring out cogent details, which might be overlooked in a tabular format. Visualization can help users identify patterns, such as density. For instance, perhaps an organization's marketing team is putting together an advertising campaign intended for tourists visiting the Manhattan area. Rather than canvas the entire metropolitan area, the marketing team can add value to the organization by spatially thinking about the solution. In running location analytics, the team can discover density levels of rental properties within Manhattan by visualizing location-enabled data. In the map in figure 2.2, it is not difficult to see the most effective place for the advertising campaign.

Cluster and hot spot analytics are the most advanced form of pattern detection. For example, cluster mapping can be done at industry locations to identify geographic concentrations of specific industry clusters, such as a medical device industry cluster. Hot spot analysis can track geographically concentrated events, as has been done extensively during the COVID pandemic.

Indoor analytics

Indoor analytics is a rapidly growing form of location analytics. The segment is estimated to grow from US$3.9 billion in 2019 to US$8.4 billion by 2024, at a CAGR of 16.5% (Sreedhar and Bhatnagar 2019). Indeed, maximizing the value of the indoor built environment is increasingly becoming a strategic differentiator for many businesses. Descriptive location analytics can track the indoor movement of people, goods, and assets. Prescriptive location analytics can be applied to improve productivity and throughput of an indoor space and provide navigation and routing services, saving time, effort, and money.

Consider the challenges inside a large warehouse to understand the spatial location of inventory, locate the movement of workers, optimize the movement of pallets of goods, coordinate arrival and departure of trucks, and adhere to safety regulations and social distancing from COVID-19. This indoor environment can be managed by a cloud-driven warehouse spatial intelligence (WSI) system (Zlatanova and Isikdag 2017). Data is entered from a combination of precise GIS 3D location of assets and people, radio-frequency identification (RFID) tags on inventory, and high-definition image and video feeds. The data goes beyond simple RFID tagging of inventory to identify the space-time dynamic movement of vehicles, people, and inventory (Pavate 2021). Such a system allows numerous location analyses. For instance, the location of warehouse inventory by product types can be studied by cluster analysis, visualization can be applied to understand complex spatial arrangements, and machine learning can aid in guiding the movement of warehouse robots.

Storytelling maps

Organizations looking to tell a data-driven story often look to maps to communicate with location intelligence. Including additional content alongside a map can help strengthen a map's persuasive storytelling. The ArcGIS® StoryMaps℠ app helps communicate a story by creating an interactive experience that features maps, text, images, and videos. Functioning in the manner of a templated website, the ArcGIS StoryMaps app includes adaptable blocks and other content elements that enable you to quickly build an information tool without having to learn code.

ArcGIS StoryMaps stories have become popular, with more than 450,000 published by 2021 (Semprebon 2021). The interactive capabilities of ArcGIS StoryMaps stories allow you to interact and engage with location information, unlocking possibilities otherwise impossible with static maps, tables, or charts. ArcGIS StoryMaps stories can be used internally for idea sharing, proof of concept, or financial reporting. Externally, ArcGIS StoryMaps stories can be branded and used to replace time-consuming web landing pages. You can even incorporate forms or survey links to enhance the storytelling engagement and continue to collect data within the organization.

One example is an ArcGIS StoryMaps story on corporate social responsibility, or CSR. Countries from around the world have committed to meeting the UN's 17 sustainable development goals, or SDGs, many of which have implications for industry actions. Ireland has published using ArcGIS StoryMaps online to explain progress in 2011–2018 toward the important goals of reducing poverty (SDG 1) and achieving decent work and economic growth (SDG 8) (Government of Ireland 2018). One section of this ArcGIS StoryMaps story shows unemployment in the Irish statistical regions in 2018 (figure 2.3). The ArcGIS StoryMaps narrative provides this and other mapping insights on the dynamics of changing unemployment over the seven years in relationship to the two UN SDGs.

The Changing Patterns of Unemployment and Poverty in Ireland, 2011-2018

According to the latest figures Ireland's unemployment rate stands at **5.4%** (2018 Q4). The figures are produced by the Central Statistics Office as part of the Labour Force Survey (LFS). The LFS is the official source of employment and unemployment statistics in Ireland.

The International Labour Organisation (ILO) Unemployment Rate (source LFS) is used for national reporting and is available at NUTS 3 (Regional) level. The map displays the ILO Unemployment Rate at NUTS 3 level across Ireland, 2018 Q4.

> 6.7

5.4

< 4.5

ILO Unemployment Rate 2018 Q4

Figure 2.3. A map image from an ArcGIS StoryMaps story of unemployment patterns in Ireland displays patterns of unemployment across the nation's regions.
Source: ©2018 Ordnance Survey Ireland, Central Statistics Office.

GeoAI

The speed of collection of big data has forced rapid adoption of AI and advanced analytic modeling. As the data has evolved, so have the tools needed to manage it. Big, unstructured, fast-moving data from a variety of sources has necessitated business investment in advanced analytics. GeoAI, or geospatial artificial intelligence, is an advanced form of location analytics designed to provide intelligence at scale. GeoAI may be streamlined from many structured and unstructured data sources. It can be used to identify real-time location-specific patterns, predict likely outcomes, and provide statistical projections. Such data analysis may be used to predict fluctuations in population, places, or environment and may be applied as a means of "knowledge work." The integration and embedding of AI with GIS technology has accelerated the pace of making predictions and business decisions at scale.

Companies are increasingly capturing new insights on their customers, which can provide deep intelligence on the lifestyle and preferences of various audience segments. By combining location-specific customer data—including web engagement, buying history, or common movement patterns—with news, social feeds, and current events, an organization can begin to define the unique attributes of their customers: Where do they go, what do they buy, and what influences them? This insight about a customer's mindset and behavior can help an organization identify other customers with similar behaviors. When modeled through GeoAI, consumer behavior can be used to identify new market opportunities. GeoAI aids in the discovery of loyal customer patterns. It also has related uses for financial AI services. For example, Visa's AI algorithm is used to detect unusual charges based on customer purchasing and geopatterns. Visa estimates that it has stopped or saved US$25 billion in fraud charges annually because of the model (Nelson 2021).

Digital twins

Digital twins can be used to predict space and time occurrences within a virtual replicated environment. A digital twin (Grieves and Vickers 2017) is a 3D virtual replica of physical assets, processes, or systems that bridges the gaps in both space and time between the physical and digital worlds. The lessons learned, issues observed, and opportunities uncovered within the virtual environment can be applied to the physical world, reducing time and expenses, minimizing disruptions and failures, and most importantly decreasing harm to users (Marr 2017). In construction, spatial integration technologies have elevated the electronic blueprint from 2D to 3D. Digital twin environments take real-world environments and create a digital world that can be used to plan and monitor a project over time. Digital twins can be used as a test environment to add different elements to a structure plan. As data comes alive within the digital twin environment, analysts can test and manipulate interior design or review different external scenarios, such as the placement of trees to avoid heat islands or the time and place of heavy traffic.

In a manufacturing setting, digital twin approaches are being used to inform product design and integrate it with actual factory environments to optimize production. Digital twins enhanced by location analytics can optimize warehouse management systems by providing decision support and comprehensive outcome analytics on workflows, energy and resource utilization efficiency, and overall plant management. Interactions between different parts of a dynamic production environment are visualized and analyzed using digital twins and location analytics and fed back to the design process of products (Lim, Zheng, and Chen 2019). Altogether, by fusing digital twins with GIS in innovative ways, businesses can create dynamic feedback loops in all stages between product and service design. Figure 2.4 illustrates an application in telecommunications, which allows for a digital twin virtualization of proposed 5G and fiber locations. The upper-left image is an example of an actual site, whereas the other images are digital twins that can be analyzed to determine proper cell tower locations (Esri 2019a).

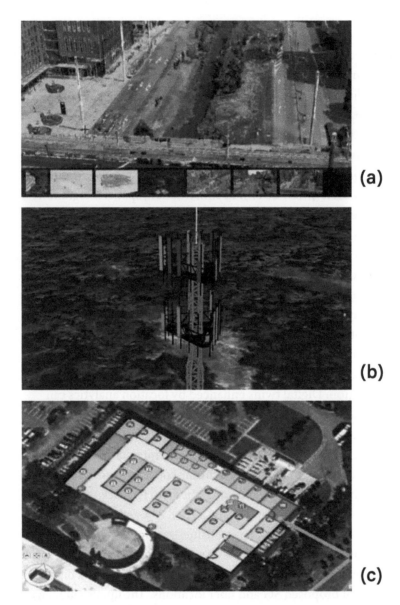

(a)

(b)

(c)

Figure 2.4. Digital twins for telecommunications, in which (a) shows the actual site of a 5G small-cell deployment, (b) shows a digital model of a proposed 5G cell tower, and (c) is a visualization of the internet service provider (ISP) center that the line would enter.
Source: Esri.

Element 4: Data for spatial business

A driving force in the growth of location analytics is the rise of big data. It is estimated that 181 zettabytes of data or information will be created, captured, copied, and consumed in 2025, at an annual growth rate from 2020 of 17% (Statista 2021). A zettabyte is equal to a trillion gigabytes. Most of this data is either already georeferenced or potentially able to be so. Businesses are increasingly using this big data. For spatial business, this enormous stream of data offers an opportunity to obtain value and competitive strength. Location analytics can use this data to describe, predict, and prescribe, using techniques that include visualization, data mining, clustering, network analysis, text analysis, machine learning, AI, and deep learning.

Location data is pervasive and growing, in size and type. Spatial business architecture includes all forms of customer, demographic, business, financial, social, and environmental data. Table 2.1 provides a summary of primary data types used to conduct location analytics for business. The sources of this data are discussed next.

Table 2.1. Summary of spatial business data

Type	Dimensions	Locational Use
Customer	Psychographics Lifestyle Preferences Satisfaction	Customer data includes attributes on lifestyle, brand preferences, and spending habits, informing marketing, sales, and customer growth and retention.
Points of Interest (POIs)	Places Nearness Relatedness	Business POIs include business and supplier locations, providing locational information for business planning, and operations and supply chain management.
Movement	Human Cargo Networks	Movement data looks at the physical movement of people and cargo from place to place, facilitating business location services and resilient supply chains.
Community	Demographic Community	Demographic, community data can inform business community strategies and impacts in areas such as social and racial equity.
Imagery and Remote Sensing	Aerial-Satellite, InSAR-Street Level Remote Sensing	Provides intelligence showing emergency situations in business facilities and locations, movements of assets, movement of supply chain materials, and understanding the geography and players in markets.
Environment	Climate Change Air Quality Land Use	Environment data provides authorities indicators of key environmental conditions and can inform corporate social responsibility actions.

Business data—enterprise

Many companies already have a vast network of geographically enabled data available internally for location analytics and discovery. A cornerstone of business data is customer data. When customer data is analyzed by location, new opportunities are presented, indicating by analysis exactly where behaviors are occurring and when. For example, it may be common for a suburban family of four to frequent the movie theater, whereas a young professional in a nearby downtown neighborhood may rarely visit the theater, opting for live music venues instead. Deep understanding of customer demographics, behaviors, and lifestyle preferences presents substantial business value by opening the door to build products that resonate and launch go-to-market strategies that are embraced by consumers and extend a product's life cycle far beyond the average sunset length. Location intelligence aids in understanding who the customer is, what product is desired and where, and where demand is highest.

Technology advancements enable the deployment of location-based applications to understand indoor spatial patterns such as foot traffic and dwell time. As a customer makes their way in a pathway of locations, their movement data can be tracked and assigned to the customer's device ID. This device ID then indicates the behaviors of the customer and indicates willingness to buy a product and respond to promotions. Other examples of business data include revenue and sales metrics, employee profiles, customer profiles, asset logs, and logistics. Asset management relies on private business data, and in times of crisis, the transparency of this data helps overcome risk. Knowing which assets are in a location, how many trucks are en route near a hazard, or how much revenue may be lost if a route is not fulfilled are all spatial questions that a business can answer with spatial technology and business data.

Business data may also include product data, research data, and supply chain data. Everyday business processes and functions also produce spatial data. The business value of this data is high because it directly contributes to product development, asset tracking, customer loyalty, and revenue gains. Some business data may be automated—for example, automated data from customer, supplier, or facility movements. Other data may come from transactions that are reported. With the rise in automated collection methods, what may previously have taken a business several weeks, months, or even years to capture and store within a company's database may now be immediately streamed into business applications. It is the size and fluidity of this data that enables decision-makers to add business value to the organization in real time.

Business data—commercial

To make location intelligence more powerful, many organizations seek third-party private commercial data to enhance first-party business data. By augmenting enterprise data with third-party data, organizations create enriched portfolios of location data. For example, a company may combine its customer data with commercial geodemographic data not only to understand where its customers are located but also to examine where potential customers who are similar to its existing customers are located. This can help determine a market growth strategy.

The emergence of data marketplaces has made commercial data more readily available. These self-serving e-commerce platforms have enabled the data industry to sell commercial data at scale. Commonly used data marketplaces include Snowflake and Teradata Vantage, which reside on cloud providers such as Amazon Web Services (AWS) and Microsoft Azure. Data-as-a-service (DaaS) solutions are now easily accessed, with streamlined integration and pricing models. With DaaS, data can be streamed into organizational databases and dashboards, bringing in up-to-date data and speeding the process of pushing out location intelligence. Beyond demographics, massive files on human behaviors are often exchanged through data marketplaces. This includes movement data, which matches device IDs to locations. When a user opts for location sharing on a mobile device, the device will aid in time-stamping the user's pathways. For example, over a four-month period in the New York City area, location data from a single user's smartphone was recorded more than 8,600 times, once every 21 minutes (Valentino-Devries et al. 2018).

Community and environmental data—public/open

Like commercial data, public/open data may be used to augment an organization's existing database. Open data is public data often made available through a Creative Commons license from government sources or open-crowdsourcing communities. Many familiar authoritative US government agencies provide public data as open data to maintain an open government status. For example, the US Census is a source of public demographic data made available as open data; it provides authoritative demographic data yearly and every 10 years through the decennial census. Other authoritative US government agencies providing business-related public data include the Department of Commerce (DOC), Environmental Protection Agency (EPA), and Department of Labor (DOL). These agencies and others provide essential community and environmental data that can be used to track CSR actions and outcomes.

Open data can also be crowdsourced. It may come from community contributed data, as part of an open data initiative to share data openly and freely in the name of a common cause. Many organizations choose to use hubs to host open data initiatives, which is discussed later in the chapter. Crowdsourced data can be added via web or desktop apps, but the validity of the data is not always cross-checked. In some cases, open data may be the only type of data available. When this is the case, an organization must evaluate the risk of the data's accuracy and consider whether other methods can be used to vet or quality-check the open data contributions. Many foundational GIS maps use a combination of authoritative and crowdsourced open data. This helps keep maps up-to-date by allowing users to contribute changes to the map in real time and allows for changes that may otherwise be overlooked, such as the addition of a streetlight, road, or detour.

Imagery and remote sensing data

Remote sensing refers to imagery that is not collected directly but at a distance away from the object. Devices that perform remote sensing include satellites, planes, and drones. These devices tend to have digital image collectors, including radar collectors, lidar, multispectral collectors, and digital cameras. Each mode of collection is appropriate for certain business applications, and each mode has advantages and disadvantages (Sarlitto 2020). Digital cameras are user-friendly but limited to the part of the electromagnetic spectrum that covers the range of the human eye, whereas radar can sense large areas from high altitudes and penetrate through cloud barriers but has limited resolution and is expensive. Local overflights by small planes or drones with digital cameras are a less expensive but widely used imagery-gathering approach in extractive, agricultural, and environmental industries.

The imagery sector is enriching spatial business by providing basemaps, point clouds, space-time imagery, AI-enhanced map imagery, and raster analytics and modeling (Dangermond 2021). The rapidity of imaging means that information can be provided daily or under refresh mode, yielding timely business intelligence showing emergency situations in business facilities and locations, movement of assets, or movement of supply chain materials. Imagery also yields greater understanding of the geography and players in markets.

Today, the earth has thousands of daily satellite overflights and image gathering by dozens of governments, international organizations, large, well-known imagery companies, and small firms (Sarlitto 2020). For instance, in the US, NASA has been collecting imagery in its Earth Observing System (EOS) satellite program for two and a half decades, including its planetary land surface imagery from the Landsat series and its Sentinel-6 in collaboration with the European Space Agency to measure global sea level rise. Large Earth observation businesses such as Descartes Labs and Planet Labs in the US, Skyrora in the UK, and Axelspace in Japan create commercial satellites for Earth observation, whereas smaller specialist companies such as Zonda design and manage small satellites and provide location analytics services.

Case example: Zonda

Zonda produces business intelligence, advanced imagery, and analytics solutions for the business needs of home builders, land developers, and financial institutions. Zonda brings a location analytics approach to the monitoring of residential investment properties and construction sites (Reid 2021).

Traditionally, most residential real estate construction monitoring researched the stages of building construction. Before the COVID-19 pandemic in early 2020, Zonda's field crews would visit home sites quarterly to observe and record the stage of construction, using simple commercial mapping software. COVID, however, put a stop to the field visits because of the health threat to the crews.

Because of the business need created, the company's analytics team developed machine learning algorithms that can be trained with data to recognize which construction stage a new home is in. Subsequently, during the pandemic, Zonda rapidly grew its satellite-based monitoring in both scale and capabilities. It has now set a standard that 80% of its home monitoring be performed by automatic satellite observation and only 20% by the traditional driving to sites.

Element 5: Platforms

Location analytics is not limited to a single type of platform. Depending on the needs of an organization, spatial technology may take shape through a variety of platform solutions, ranging from cloud-based software to enterprise system deployment to geoenabled hubs. Organizations of all sizes, budgets, and scalability may find success in deploying spatial solutions. As diverse as the nature of business, spatial technology is adaptable and can be personalized based on desired results and intelligence goals.

The cloud

The evolution of cloud computing software has accelerated major advances in spatial technology. GIS software can support a software-as-a-service (SaaS) model. This revolution of GIS as SaaS has opened new opportunities for organizations looking to establish a spatial infrastructure. Within this infrastructure, the organization can use a variety of spatial tools to perform day-to-day business functions. With the connections enabled through the cloud, these tools can work in tandem with one another, enabling a network that supports an interconnected workflow among processes and people within different areas of the organization.

The architecture within the cloud has the capability to manage all aspects of a geospatial system, from maps and data to analytic tools and applications. The connection of tools within the cloud environment enables location intelligence sharing at scale. Millions of active interactions can take place at any time. Organizations functioning within the cloud benefit from the fluidity and open access of data sharing and management. Open sharing within a department or across the organization enables users of varying job titles to access and build on one another's work. Additionally, SaaS-based GIS software is intelligently designed to provide seamless updates, removing the necessity of downloading the latest features and updates.

Though data security within the cloud may be of top concern, the evolving geospatial architecture alongside advances in cloud-secure environments has helped alleviate this concern among stakeholders. In many cases, the benefits of the cloud outweigh the risk, especially as organizations build infrastructures that connect workers on-site to home office workers. By automating processes and streamlining the data flow through other emerging technologies, such as IoT sensors, vehicle sensors, social media, and web data, geographic information can be obtained in real time.

Enterprise

Enterprise integration is a process of expanding location analytics and intelligence to serve spatial needs across the organization. It must serve all departments in the organization that need locational systems (Woodward 2020). Stand-alone spatial systems in separate departments that have their own separate databases create obstacles to the consistent and rapid sharing of data. These separate systems may serve a department well in the early spatial maturity stages of an organization when the users are limited and mainly interested in data from their own department. Moving to enterprise integration of data has many advantages, including eliminating redundancy in the data and enabling users in diverse areas of the organization to be consistent in their use of location analytics and intelligence. Having a common platform can also be helpful from an information security standpoint because security protection can be strengthened for one central database rather than being scattered to the separate silos.

Another advantage of an enterprise system is that any user of location analytics throughout the company has the potential to access all the spatial data available across the organization. The user may not have a present need for all this data, but if future needs arise to add data from a distant department, it will be easily accessible. Because of an increase in spatial users, expanded data, and consistency of enterprise GIS software, having an enterprise spatial system adds to the competitiveness of the company.

An enterprise GIS offers decision-makers options because an enterprise platform connects with the full set of company GIS solutions. Leaders are increasingly choosing to base the enterprise system in the cloud or retain it within internal infrastructure for security and control reasons. Users looking to perform advanced spatial analysis through desktop or mobile apps can benefit greatly from an enterprise system.

Desktop

GIS started with a strong desktop (stand-alone) component, but the massive movement to the cloud over the last two decades has substantially altered the use of this platform. Although desktop provides essential high-end GIS computing to skilled individuals or teams of professionals, its weaknesses include challenges in scaling the number of users and increasing the capacity of desktop or local servers, challenges in providing simplified user interfaces to the business nontechnical user, and vulnerability of desktop systems to physical failure.

The desktop can be enhanced at low cost through connections to Web GIS. This Web GIS platform provides GIS software, data, and processing on the web, so you are freed from devices and installations and need only a web browser for access. This setup has several advantages: it is available worldwide, there is a low cost of implementation, it has minimal requirements for the desktop, and a large variety of related web services and libraries can be integrated (Fu 2022; Longley et al. 2015).

Portals

A spatial portal is a public or private location to share applications across designated users that can range from small groups to the entire organization (Tang and Selwood 2005; Esri 2016a). The portal is useful for organizing information and making it available to groups of users. Private and restricted information can be excluded from the portal or made accessible to approved users only. The overall philosophy behind the portal concept is to make as much information as possible open and easily accessible. A portal is designed to share the information across mobile devices, social media, Web GIS, and servers.

An example of a business portal is Portal for ArcGIS, which can be installed, along with its applications, on a company-owned server or in the cloud (Esri 2016a). Commonly available apps include cloud-based GIS (ArcGIS Online), a user-friendly mobile app builder (ArcGIS Web AppBuilder), a dashboard creator and operator (ArcGIS Dashboards), two apps for collecting information with a mobile device (ArcGIS Collector and ArcGIS Survey123), software that supports users in creating imagery such as point clouds (ArcGIS Drone2Map®), and an app to encourage teamwork and coordination for the field workforce (ArcGIS Workforce). These apps can be supplemented with other applications available commercially and proprietary ones developed by the company.

A spatial portal aims to foster collaboration among the users within a business. A company can offer private portals restricted to segments of its workforce and public portals for invited customers or open to the public (Tang and Selwood 2005; Esri 2016a). For the portal user, the portal provides a web-based set of apps, flexible and accessible across devices, to address a problem, develop location analytics solutions, and support research or decisions. The web positioning of the portal raises potential security issues but security measures can mitigate or largely eliminate the risk.

Hubs

Organizations looking to center their workforce on collaborative initiatives may find interest in the cloud-based hub platform. Hubs are much broader in reach than a portal, providing a centralized location for people, data, and tools to reach common goals. The platform enables a single place to communicate and collaborate on key initiatives within the organization, including planning activities, sharing projects, and setting goals. Often used for community engagement, a hub can also be used for a variety of business functions, including spearheading a new product launch, strengthening company culture, or onboarding new employees. Hubs support the hosting of geoenabled databases, allowing quick access to mapping layers, prepared visualizations, raw datasets, and ArcGIS StoryMaps stories.

Functioning much like a website, a hub grants unlimited possibilities for building its contents, allowing components and structure to take shape around business needs. Templates are adaptable to brand personalization and unique initiative aspects. Analytic components of a hub also allow for the tracking of views and interactions within the platform. This added value can help decision-makers evaluate content engagement and stakeholder interaction.

With hubs, organizations enable open sharing of location intelligence across the globe while centralizing common themes that connect people and places on a unified platform. The Los Angeles GeoHub exemplifies a community hub with intensive use (figure 2.5). The hub has publicly available maps, downloadable data, and documentation on more than 1,000 features for citizens and businesses alike, including analyses of job accessibility and a range of demographic analyses (Marshall 2016). The hub also has features to create customized experiences, contribute data to the hub, and participate in work being done on initiatives by internal, external, or combined teams (Esri 2021a).

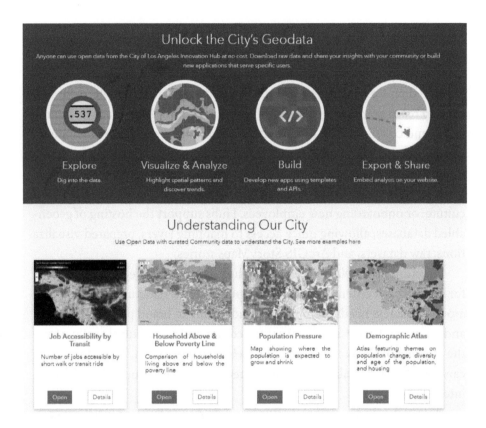

Figure 2.5. Los Angeles GeoHub's "Understanding Our City" page includes sets of features the public can access to explore, visualize, analyze, build, export, and share maps, with an example of a web app for job accessibility by transit type (*far left*). Courtesy of City of Los Angeles.

A datacentric business that seeks to interact with the public can install a hub to improve sharing and collaboration of its own teams inside the company, provide easily accessible maps and data to customers or the public, and encourage collaboration between the company's workforce and outside existing and prospective customers. The firm as a profit-making organization could maintain a portion of its data on the inside for commercial sales. For instance, the hub may be appropriate for government data providers, statistical data providers, environmental consulting firms, or think tanks.

A general point for platforms and applications concerns data protection of private information. Recent movements in consumer data protection have shifted the use of location services to include permission-based options. Many applications now require opt-in services, mandating that you have the choice not to consent to provide personal data at the time of entering a software service. These changes have been important to protect the rights of consumers and in many ways also have been crucial to alleviating the ethical dilemma that organizations often face in using consumer data tracking.

Keeping consumer data private and permission based helps protect personal information. Ethical data practices protect both the consumer and the organization. Companies should have a sound ethical policy and data implementation strategy to help minimize this risk for an organization looking to implement spatial technology.

Element 6: Location intelligence

Location intelligence is a broad concept of using the outputs of location analytics and mapping to contribute to business goals, strategies, and tactics. Three levels of influence affect location intelligence: (1) insights, (2) decisions, and (3) impacts.

Location analytics can lead to locational insights and create intelligence across the value chain. For example, these techniques can be used to understand customer patterns, assess the potential of new geographic markets, and monitor economic, social, and environmental conditions of various business locations. More operationally, this includes creating situational awareness of complex networks and systems. For example, utility companies, such as energy and telecommunications, have a strong need for situational awareness across their networks. Geospatial dashboards are often the means for achieving such awareness.

The second level of location intelligence includes decisions based on location insights. Location intelligence can inform decisions to increase competitiveness, foster new products and services, and provide new ways to strengthen ties with suppliers and buyers. For instance, KFC (see chapter 9) provides its franchisees with rich and varied social media and demographic information at the micro level for decision-making on competitive locations of retail units. Decision-making also benefits by group collaboration, big data, and anytime/anywhere availability of location analytics (Sharda, Delen, and Turban 2018). The wide dispersion of location analytics capability in companies means that dispersed team members can be informed by location analytics and collaborate on decisions.

A third level of location intelligence includes the impacts resulting from location analytics. These impacts include the performance of a company on many dimensions, such as market share growth, customer satisfaction, operational efficiencies, supply chain reliability, and societal benefit. As seen in this chapter's Walgreens closing case study, impacts occur at the operational level as well. In this case, it was the quick development of an application to provide testing and vaccines equitably to the public that also served to enable a broader enterprise solution.

Closing case study: Walgreens

Walgreens is one of the two largest pharmacy firms worldwide, with 2020 revenues of US$140 billion and assets of US$87 billion. It operates 9,000 drug stores throughout the US and in 2014 acquired a majority interest in Alliance Boots, one of the largest pharmacy firms in Europe and parts of Asia. It acquired 1,000 Rite Aid stores in 2017. Walgreens has intensive competition and must drive sales volume to achieve its profit margins (Morningstar 2021). The firm also faces regulatory constraints on its drug products and pharmacy activities.

GIS has been present in the firm for more than 15 years, and its principal use is for planning and operations of Walgreens's store network throughout the US. Walgreens has a spatial enterprise system for its US stores and employs simpler cloud-based spatial solutions for certain special projects. The corporate GIS team for operations in the US consists of the director of enterprise location intelligence, several GIS power users, and specialists who focus on external-facing provision of spatial data, statistics, and maps. The team participates in designing the GIS features for consumer mobile apps that are used to access the varied product channels of the firm, including visiting and purchasing from stores.

Figure 2.6. Regional middle managers at Walgreens discuss how to solve a spatial problem, which is being displayed on a large screen using the firm's WalMap software.
Source: Esri 2015a.

The leading GIS applications are WalMap and WalMap Pro, locally tailored software that supports middle and upper-middle management corporate-wide in group analytics and decision-making. In regional offices throughout the firm, conference rooms have large screens displaying Walgreens's and competitors' store locations, demographic features, and market indicators (figure 2.6). The enterprise system supports WalMap on mobile devices and the web, making it device-independent and centrally controlled. WalMap provides solutions for (1) deciding the locations of stores and the optimization of the geography of groups of stores; (2) giving broad demographic and marketing information to the middle ranks of management firm-wide; (3) maintaining and displaying competitive data on a monthly basis so merchandising can tell whether a store location is competitive; and (4) offering a range of other mapping, such as pharmacy information, market share, and aerial imagery. WalMap Pro provides advanced tools to a select group with the market planning and research group.

The systems development of these two critical applications was accomplished through the coordination of four system development teams: the corporate GIS team, information technology (IT), an offshore outsourcer, and Latitude Geographics, based in Canada. The project success is ascribed to a talented director of enterprise location intelligence, who kept everything moving. This key manager reflected that "the team had to have patience and set reasonable expectations. They said it's going to take a little bit longer to make sure we get it right and that's okay, with the payoff at the end" (Walgreens 2018). The same team also launched a spatial enterprise project.

Walgreens's relatively slow and deliberate improvement steps were interrupted by the start of the COVID-19 pandemic in March 2020. A White House meeting led to an urgent request to Walgreens's location intelligence director to decide where testing sites would be set up. Within hours, the director created a web app that could choose testing locations and shared it with other key leaders, a rapid exchange that led to a prototyped solution. It was later refined by the spatial team, who within weeks began designating COVID-19 testing sites throughout the nation, eventually designating a national set of thousands of locations. By the following winter, the team was doing a similar designation for stores providing vaccinations (Walgreens 2021).

In this rapid and successful site selection, the team was helped by an existing robust database of store locations and attributes and demographic and other information. In the process, the team emphasized equity of distribution and set up distribution for socially vulnerable communities first.

An offshoot of this emergency intervention in the COVID-19 crisis is that the GIS leadership pushed forward rapidly to complete the spatial enterprise system that was on a slow track before the pandemic (Shah 2021; Walgreens 2021). The firm's location enterprise portal resides on a cloud platform provided by a leading vendor. The user can enter the portal through an enterprise location intelligence home page, which provides access to all the enterprise modules, including the latest versions of WalMap, WalMap Pro, and the Asset Protection mapping module, which provides location analytics for sustaining and protecting assets from environmental and other threats (figure 2.7). The portal entry page reinforces that varied personnel have different mapping needs. Here, middle managers use the simple and data-rich WalMap app, GIS analysts and company planners use the full-featured WalMap Pro, and emergency and security personal depend on the specialized asset protection map. All the interfaces draw on the centralized enterprise data and analytics.

An example of WalMap Pro's capabilities is a real-time display of customers, in a time slice, for three Walgreens stores in the Inland Empire of Southern California, showing a tendency for clustering of customer residences around each of the three stores, with relatively little cannibalizing of sales (figure 2.8). This exemplifies the power of cloud-based, real-time situational analytics. Using the cloud platform, Walgreens's GIS team can better integrate mapping and location analytics for employees accessing mobile devices, remote workers, and group decision-making in regional offices and headquarters while communicating through integrated web mapping across the company.

Walgreens's GIS management estimated that the company has moved 80% of the way toward full GIS maturity. Although the location enterprise portal has been the centerpiece so far, GIS management sees several projects needed in the future to move toward maturity, including supporting IoT and introducing AI and machine learning analytics.

In summary, Walgreens illustrates the dimensions of a spatial business architecture. Business goals drive its use, and a strong technical team collaborates with management to address needs with solutions. As such, they demonstrate the development of an enterprise-level spatial platform that responds to business needs, attends to a pressing societal issue (a pandemic), relies on human talent, and creates strategic value for the company.

Figure 2.7. A diagram of the Walgreens Enterprise Portal shows its major components of WalMap Pro, Enterprise Location Intelligence, Asset Protection Mapping, and WalMap Lite. Source: Walgreens 2021.

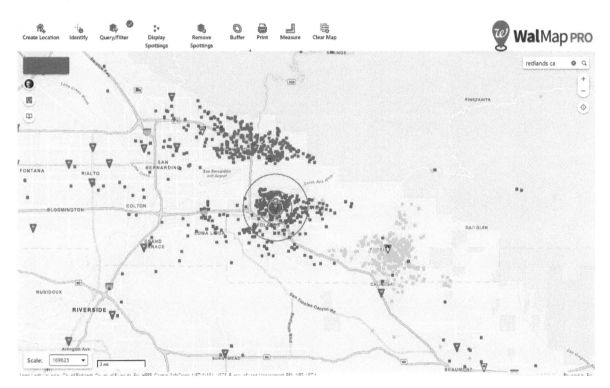

Figure 2.8. WalMap Pro mapping of a time slice of customers' affinities for three neighboring Walgreens stores in San Bernardino County, California. Source: Walgreens 2021.

CHAPTER 3
Fundamentals of location analytics

Introduction

To achieve competitive success, organizations are increasingly placing analytics at the heart of the business. Business analytics has been defined by Thomas Davenport as the "extensive use of data, statistical and quantitative analysis, explanatory and predictive models, and fact-based management to drive decisions and actions" (Davenport and Harris 2017, 26). Davenport's definition not only highlights the importance of data and analytic modeling in contemporary organizations but connects it to decision-making and actions. This connection is key. Clearly, the analytic process of transforming data into insights has a purpose: to provide evidence and support for decision-making. By using analytics to make better decisions, organizations generate value that manifests in the form of business benefits, both tangible and intangible. These include cost savings, revenue growth through increased share of wallet, uncovering business opportunities and untapped markets, increase in productivity, process improvements resulting in asset efficiency, enhanced brand recognition, increased customer satisfaction, and benefits to the environment and society. In digitally mature organizations, analytics is not just an add-on to existing processes and practices but is fully integrated into the company's strategies and business functions.

This chapter dives deeper into the location analytics element introduced as part of the spatial business architecture in chapter 2 and explores its use throughout the location value chain. Location analytics can inform where companies should locate new stores, stock facilities, and enhance infrastructure. It can guide employee recruitment, optimize sales territories, and maximize loyalty programs. It also helps companies appraise risk emerging from threats such as competitors, the natural environment, changing business patterns and trends, and unanticipated events such as weather emergencies, pandemics, and social unrest—information that is critical to a proactive response, mitigating threats to business continuity and improving business resilience. Finally, location analytics helps companies direct their philanthropic endeavors and shape CSR strategies and initiatives.

Principles of business location analytics

Business location analytics, which recognizes the critical importance of location in business, helps organizations make decisions informed by data, using sophisticated analytic methods and spatial analysis techniques.

Underpinning business location analytics are the following four principles of location:

- Location proximity and relatedness
- Location differences
- Location linkages
- Location contexts

Location proximity and relatedness

As businesses seek ideal customers, their own locations relative to the locations of prospective customers and competitors become paramount. For example, a bakery and coffee retail chain seeks customers with certain consumer preferences and wants to ascertain where these customers live, work, and shop. What are their usual routes as they travel from work to school or from home to work, and how far do they live from various points of interest (POIs), such as grocery stores, gyms, libraries, and restaurants? What are their demographic, socioeconomic, and psychographic characteristics?

The first principle of location proximity and relatedness stems from W. R. Tobler's (1970) first law of geography. This seminal law states: "Everything is related to everything else, but near things are more related than distant things." "Related" and "near" are the cornerstones of this first principle of location. In business decision-making, proximity—whether to customers, suppliers, competitors, complementary businesses, assets, or infrastructure—is the basis of important strategic, tactical, and operational considerations. Proximity implies relatedness, or spatial heterogeneity, and suggests that local factors can make one area significantly different from others. In a business context, nearness or proximity is often measured in terms of driving distance, driving time, or walking time and is fundamental to the delineation and description of trade areas and service areas, discussed later in this chapter.

For example, consider a full-service insurance company. To determine premiums, an insurer would factor in population density, crime rates, and proximity of businesses and customers to coastal areas that are prone to flooding, among many other factors. Insurance premiums of two similar properties, located in the same neighborhood, close to each other and equidistant from the coast (nearness), are more likely to be comparable (relatedness) than properties located in a different neighborhood (dissimilar population density and crime rate) farther inland.

For location analytics modeling and decision-making, nearness and relatedness have several implications. Nearness and proximity are often measured for business locational decision-making using distances that are factored into various models for description, prediction, and ultimately decision-making. However, nearness can potentially introduce spatial bias into location-based analytic models, which stems from a pitfall of spatial data known as spatial autocorrelation. These factors, particularly the issue of spatial autocorrelation (Longley et al. 2015), have methodological implications for location analytics models.

Location differences, linkages, and contexts

The next three principles that inform business location analytics are location differences, location linkages, and location contexts (Church and Murray 2009). The first principle, location differences, indicates that some locations are better than others for a given purpose. The second principle, location linkages, means that an optimal multisite pattern must be selected simultaneously rather than independently, one site at a time. The third principle, location context, indicates that the context of a location can influence business success (Church and Murray 2009).

The principle of location differences can be illustrated through the lens of industry clusters—geographic concentrations of interconnected firms and institutions in a particular field that are known to be engines of economic development and regional prosperity (Porter 1998a). For example, Napa Valley in Northern California is a leading wine production cluster worldwide because of a climate that is conducive to grape production and, consequently, the presence of hundreds of independent wine grape growers, among many other factors. On the other hand, Carlsbad near San Diego in Southern California has a specialized cluster of golf equipment manufacturers that has its roots in Southern California's aerospace industry, which spawned manufacturing businesses specializing in metal castings and other advanced materials. Because of location differences between the two regions, businesses engaged in sports equipment would have more affinity for the Carlsbad region, whereas manufacturers or parts suppliers of irrigation and harvesting equipment would be more likely to find the Napa region more attractive. Regional economics uses a measure known as the location quotient (LQ) to measure this industry concentration of a region.

Next, to understand location linkages, consider the medical device manufacturing industry, which is linked to nine other industry clusters: biopharmaceutical, distribution and e-commerce, jewelry, recreational goods, electrical wiring, plastics, IT, production technology, and downstream metals (Harvard Business School 2021). A recent study (Munnich et al. 2021) has shown that Minnesota is a national leader in medical device manufacturing. The development of the medical device cluster in Minnesota originated in the greater Minneapolis metropolitan area because of the presence of Medtronic, a leader in medical device innovation. Now, in Minnesota, almost 500 medical device companies statewide are complemented by more than 6,000 businesses in the nine linked industries (Munnich et al. 2021).

In terms of location context, Minnesota's medical device cluster relies on a robust professional, scientific, and technical service workforce as well as a reliable transportation network that enables efficient goods movement. Alongside the Mayo Clinic, with 63,000 employees in the academic medical center, the greater Minneapolis–St. Paul metropolitan area is home to the University of Minnesota, a flagship university producing a readymade workforce comprising medical, business, engineering, IT, and computer science professionals, analysts, and researchers for medical device and other companies that offer high-paying jobs. In addition, from the perspective of location context, Minnesota's medical device industry benefits from the presence of the Minneapolis–St. Paul International Airport (MSP), which acts as a gateway for high-valued and often critical medical devices and equipment exported to various parts of the world.

These principles have the following implications for business location analytics. To develop an effective location-based business strategy, it is essential to adopt a clear understanding of how locations affect business success. Locations can provide a competitive advantage because of their distinctive physical, environmental, and human characteristics. Locations can have vital business linkages for talent, customers, and supply chain and logistics networks. This configuration creates a location context that, if properly understood, can be a key factor in business strategy and success. Location analytics provides the tools to assess such factors.

Hierarchy of location analytics

Just as business analytics is broken into three main categories—descriptive, predictive, and prescriptive—the hierarchy of business location analytics consists of descriptive location analytics, predictive location analytics, and prescriptive location analytics, as shown in figure 3.1. Each step of the hierarchy is informed by increasing levels of sophistication of analytic (mathematical and statistical) methods. The hierarchy of spatial analysis techniques—spatial data manipulation, spatial data analysis, spatial statistical analysis, and spatial modeling (O'Sullivan and Unwin 2014)—informs the hierarchy of business location analytics. As the sophistication of mathematical and statistical modeling as well as spatial analysis increases, the extent of location intelligence and, consequently, location-based insights increase as well. A business can use this modeling and analysis to design spatially aware business strategies that yield competitive advantage.

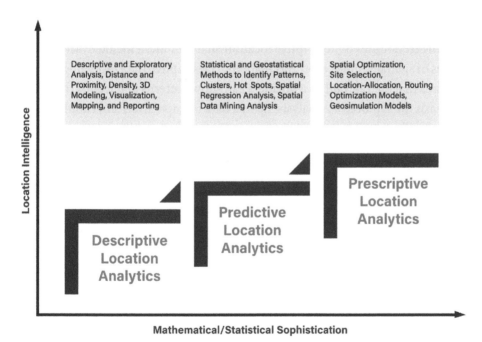

Figure 3.1. Hierarchy of business location analytics, comprising descriptive, predictive, and prescriptive location analytics.

Descriptive location analytics

Descriptive location analytics is often used to analyze current or historical business data to understand what has occurred or is occurring and where. Descriptive location analytics is characterized by spatial visualizations such as maps, reports, and dashboards. These visualizations show where customers, employees, stores, competitor locations, suppliers, distribution centers, transportation hubs, critical infrastructure and assets, and POIs are located, often relative to each other. They also reveal spatial patterns and changes in important business key performance indicators (KPIs), such as sales, profits, revenues, and consumer preferences, as well as geographically referenced characteristics of areas of interest, such as socioeconomic attributes of trade areas.

In other contexts, maps, reports, and dashboards may show important parts of a supply chain. These features may include connections, linkages, and routes between customers, suppliers, and distribution or transshipment hubs, as well as territories vulnerable to business disruption—for example, because of a natural disaster or other emergency such as the failure of critical infrastructure. Descriptive location analytics provides important visual cues, uncovers patterns, and reveals location-specific insights previously unknown to a business.

The techniques of descriptive location analytics often include various forms of spatial visualization and mapping. Descriptive data modeling of features that are relevant to a business can show patterns and trends that form the basis for exploratory analysis. Spatial data manipulation and rudimentary spatial analysis functions such as intersection, union, overlay, querying, and basic summary statistics characterize descriptive location analytics. Apart from these techniques, distance and proximity analysis, buffering, density analysis, and 3D modeling are often part of descriptive location analytics. As mapping provides visual cues of change, descriptive analysis is an efficient way to turn large, complex datasets into effective visualizations. These maps bring valuable spatial context to decision-making. In many cases, descriptive analytics may be the greatest depth needed to draw a statistically backed conclusion.

The process of moving from exploratory to more advanced analytics is considered "enrichment" and can introduce several layers: a customer layer, a geodemographic layer, a facilities layer, and so forth. Visual patterns may emerge as obvious or may necessitate descriptive spatial statistics such as hot spot and cluster analyses.

Descriptive analytics may be used to further prepare data for predictive and prescriptive analytics. It is often a manual process and may be seen as a first pass of data discovery. A series of spatial layers may be overlapped to observe correlations among varying datasets. Additionally, spatial layers may be used as the foundation for deeper analysis. The information products created in descriptive analysis can then be applied as the foundation for predictive and prescriptive analytics.

Case example: Newton Nurseries

Consider the example of Newton Nurseries, a wholesale nursery serving professional landscapers which is considering business development and expansion in the Houston Metropolitan Statistical Area (MSA) market. To examine market saturation and analyze opportunities, it has created a web map that comprises several layers, shown in figure 3.2.

Alongside existing Newton Nurseries locations, the map shows locations of major competitors, such as Home Depot, Lowe's, and Houston Garden Centers stores. The layer of competitors includes garden centers at other retailers as well as other nurseries. The web map also includes locations of garden center farm supply businesses and landscaping companies. The Houston MSA market around Newton's existing locations, as well as those of its competitors, is broken down by discretization into 1,000 × 1,000 foot cells, and each cell's market potential is scored based on several factors, including demographics, economics, competition, and accessibility. Demographic factors include current population, projected five-year population growth, median age, and population density. Economic factors include median household income and average home value. Newton also analyzes consumer preferences for lawn care by estimating average annual lawn spending. Based on these and several other factors including the accessibility of Newton's own locations and those of its competitors to professional landscapers (for example, within 15-minute drive times as shown in figure 3.2), each 1,000 × 1,000 foot cell is assigned a market potential score. In figure 3.2, dark red represents cells with higher market potential.

Geoenriching the map are some of the external variables, such as major shopping center locations with attributes including gross leasable areas, anchor stores, cotenancy opportunities, year opened, and annual sales, as well as various population and demographic variables. The market potential layer is examined for canvasing and site selection in the Houston MSA in the context of market opportunities that are represented in five categories:

(1) proposed locations of new stores (red circle with a number), (2) locations with ongoing negotiations, (3) areas of interest for business development, (4) locations of interest but no opportunity to develop at the present time, and (5) locations that have been evaluated but ultimately not selected for development. By clicking on any such location, Newton's business development team can readily access additional information such as proximity to other shopping centers, their anchor stores, proximity to freeway on- and off-ramps, and availability of parking.

These map layers work in tandem to provide a holistic view of business development opportunities for Newton Nurseries. In terms of descriptive location analysis, the map layers are rich with possibilities. For example, drive-time buffers can produce trade areas to be analyzed for market potential. Analysis of proximity to competitors, nearby shopping centers, and retail locations; demographic and economic factors; and consumer preferences can inform sales forecasts. Overall, this example illustrates the potential of descriptive location analytics to provide valuable business insights and inform decision-making.

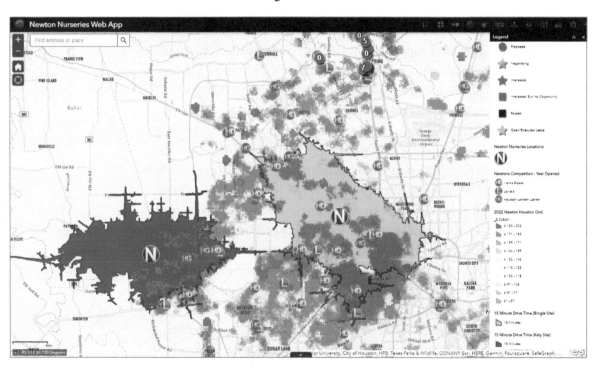

Figure 3.2. Web map layers of Newton Nurseries locations and opportunities for business development in the greater Houston, Texas, metro area. Source: Newton Nurseries 2022.

Predictive location analytics

Descriptive location analytics provides organizations with location intelligence about the current state of business or past business patterns. Although insightful, descriptive location analytics only scratches the surface of what is possible with location analytics. Predictive location analytics provides a deeper understanding of what is happening in current and past states, while simultaneously detecting meaningful statistical patterns to predict future business outcomes. Through the identification of spatial patterns, business outcomes may be forecast, which can help decision-makers see opportunities for growth, profitability, and risk.

With the availability of large and timely datasets, many organizations increasingly rely on predictive location analytics to discover meaningful, statistically significant spatial patterns, spatial clusters, and outliers, related to the prediction of business outcomes such as profitability, growth, risk of customer defection, and incidences of fraud. Whereas standard (nonspatial) predictive analytics determines what is likely to happen in the future, predictive location analytics determines not only what is likely to happen in the future but where. In this way, predictive location analytics provides guidance to organizations about the likelihood of future events, contingent on location.

Predictive location analytics methods are more sophisticated than descriptive location analytics. These techniques involve the application of traditional statistical and geostatistical approaches to analyze spatial clusters that may become evident from descriptive mapping. For example, clustering models may confirm the importance of a region of parts suppliers in an organization's supply chain. Analysis of spatial clusters of internet users in a region may provide insights about a region's preference for e-commerce; this has implications for an organization's business development strategy. Statistical models may show hot spots and cold spots of customer activity on social media. For example, the use of social media data may be used to discover pockets of expressive sentiments about companies and their products across the US. Geotagged sentiments can be mined to uncover a range of customer experiences and emotions and predict regions where customer churn (rate of change based on loss or addition) is likely, and therefore where customer retention efforts need to be initiated or redoubled.

Another form of spatial statistical analysis involves regression-based modeling that establishes associations between a dependent variable of interest and several independent predictor variables. For example, an insurer may model insurance premiums based on location, type of client, type of insurance, proximity to risk factors, and so forth. However, such models that include variables subject to location relatedness, nearness, and differences may be prone to spatial bias. Diagnostic tests that measure spatial bias are essential for such models.

With the increasing availability of geospatial big data, spatially mature organizations are deploying data mining and GeoAI-based predictive models that use machine learning to explore spatial relationships among dozens of factors and an outcome of interest for a business. For example, GeoAI models can uncover potential threats to a firm's supply chain in the event of a natural disaster or an emergency.

Illustration of predictive location analytics

In the agriculture sector, effective weed control that minimizes damage to crops spread over tens of thousands of hectares is essential. To accomplish this, farmers need to know the precise location of each crop. They also need to accurately pinpoint the application of herbicide, as well as fertilizer and fungicide. Growers need information on the types of weeds, as well as their number and location, so that herbicide programs can be tailored accordingly. Each crop has its own set of conditions, and spraying herbicide outside precisely defined buffers can not only destroy crops but render entire fields unfit for farming.

To address this problem, cameras and sensors outfitted on tractors capture geotagged images every 50 milliseconds from different angles, creating enormous volumes of spatiotemporal big data on crop and weed growth. The cameras and sensors on these See & Spray–outfitted machines (figure 3.3) use deep learning algorithms (Peters 2017) that are in many ways similar to facial recognition.

Figure 3.3. Blue River Technology (acquired by John Deere) LettuceBot using See & Spray technology in a field in Salinas, California. Source: From "See & Spray: The Next Generation of Weed Control," by Ben Chostner (2017). ©2017 ASABE. Used with permission.

To distinguish weeds from crops, deep learning–based neural networks are trained by tens of thousands of images—unstructured big data—stored in huge image libraries (Chostner 2017). With sufficient training, these systems can recognize different types of weeds with a high degree of accuracy. Matching weeds to locations, See & Spray machines spray precise amounts of herbicide within precisely defined crop buffers. Deep learning algorithms are enriched to account for other location variables such as hillside gradients. This deep learning–based location intelligence approach has been shown to save tremendous amounts of herbicide compared with conventional spraying technology, enabling farmers to grow more with less. The automation of weed control also results in cost savings for labor, especially on large farms.

Prescriptive location analytics

Prescriptive location analytics is the most advanced form of location analytics. Reliant on historical data and trained models, prescriptive location analytics can calculate the probability of events occurring, which consequently produces a suggested course of action. Whereas predictive location analytics generates a forecast or predicts the likelihood of an event occurring, the output of a prescriptive model is a decision, much like a prescription written by a doctor to treat an ailing patient. Viewed through a spatial lens, prescriptive location analytics models business scenarios by factoring in locational attributes and constraints of specific locations to prescribe the best course of action for optimal business solutions and outcomes. Prescriptive location analytics satisfies business objectives by factoring in mathematical equations that connect data based on proximity, relatedness, and calculation of spatial differences.

Prescriptive location analytics is widely used in facility location decisions, supply chain network design, and route optimization. It is particularly relevant for optimally siting manufacturing facilities relative to the locations of suppliers, customers, and transportation options, factoring in environmental considerations, and siting retailers' warehouses, fulfillment centers, and distribution centers in coordination with complex or shifting demand patterns. Spatial objectives may include the minimization of transit costs, maximization of population coverage, or a combination of several objectives. Nonspatial constraints may include schedules of deliveries to be made, delivery time windows, trucking capacity, and regulations imposed by state and federal departments of transportation. Spatial constraints may occur because of barriers imposed by the physical geography of a region (for example, mountainous terrain or temporary road closures), street attributes (for example, one-way streets in central business districts, historical traffic patterns, or speed limits), and distance or travel time restrictions.

Prescriptive location analytics can support organizations in addressing strategic, tactical, and operational problems and can be especially helpful when problems are repetitive. Often underpinned by optimization approaches that are grounded in operations research and enriched by spatial analysis, prescriptive location analytics can provide optimal or close-to-optimal solutions for large, complex problems. Apart from site location analysis and distribution system design, such models are used for routing optimization, demand coverage, analysis of cannibalization, and informing relocation strategies in myriad settings.

Illustration of prescriptive location analytics

Consider the example of CIDIU S.p.A., an Italian company that works in environmental services, dealing with all aspects of the waste management cycle—collection, treatment, disposal, recycling, and energy recovery—using integrated sophisticated optimization modeling with GIS to schedule weekly waste-collection activities for multiple types of waste.

The company's main objective was to generate efficient weekly shifts of garbage pickup by reducing operational costs and minimizing total service costs, including environmental costs. Main decisions to be made included the weekly assignment of a vehicle to a garbage type and the daily route of each garbage pickup vehicle for each shift (Fadda et al. 2018).

By innovatively using the IoT paradigm, the company outfitted dumpsters and garbage pickup vehicles with sensors to monitor the capacity of garbage in dumpsters and vehicles. As soon as the capacity of dumpsters approached 80%, depending on the type of trash, an appropriate vehicle from the company's daily operational fleet, working three shifts of six hours each, would be routed (or rerouted) to pick up the trash, depending on location proximity, capacity of the truck, and several other factors. The service area was an urban area near Turin, Italy. By integrating IoT, GIS, and optimization modeling and using a location-aware approach (figure 3.4), CIDIU S.p.A. was able to eliminate the third shift for the entire service area. In addition, the number of vehicles used during a test period decreased by 33%, reducing waste collection operational costs and increasing the company's competitiveness (Fadda et al. 2018).

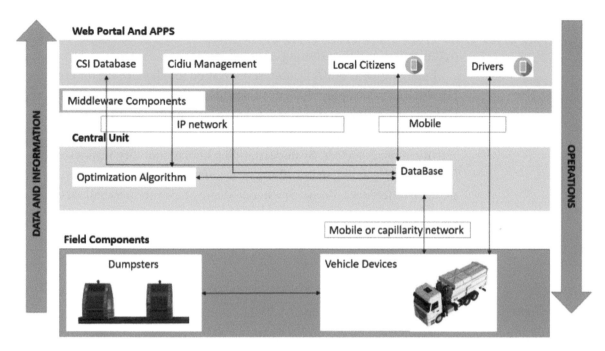

Figure 3.4. CIDIU S.p.A. solution architecture comprising field components, middleware, the route optimization algorithm, web portals, and apps. Source: Republished with permission of The Institute for Operations Research and the Management Sciences (INFORMS) (Fadda et al. 2018). Permission conveyed through Copyright Clearance Center Inc.

Location analytics across the value chain

The application of descriptive, predictive, and prescriptive location analytics is spurred by specific business needs. Table 3.1 and the subsequent descriptions serve as an overview of various types of business needs that necessitate the application of location analytics. They are offered as a starting point for assessing an organization's value chain and how different parts of the value chain can benefit from the deployment of location analytics.

Research and development

Recent location intelligence market studies have revealed that location intelligence is critically important for the R&D function, more so than for other organizational functions such as operations, marketing, and IT (Dresner 2019; University of Redlands 2018). Drivers of this trend include the proliferation of mobile geolocation data and the development of mobile-friendly location-based services. Such studies have also shown that R&D interest in location intelligence is highest for data visualization purposes, followed by moderate interest for conducting real estate investment and pricing analysis, geomarketing, site planning and site selection, territory management and optimization, and fleet routing and tracking.

Emerging areas of R&D interest in location intelligence are for business purposes such as supply chain optimization, indoor mapping, and IoT. Unlocking location intelligence from massive mobile data to understand patterns of human movement is another critical contemporary area of R&D activity in many sectors. By understanding human mobility, businesses can forecast supply and demand efforts to account for locational preferences and seasonal differences. Knowing when to deploy new products and services is just as important as knowing where.

Table 3.1. Applications of location analytics along the organizational value chain

| | LOCATION ANALYTICS | | |
VALUE CHAIN	Descriptive	Predictive	Prescriptive
R&D and Market Research	Customer Preferences: Mapping of customer behaviors to understand product preferences.	New Product Prediction: Analyzing demographic, income, and spending behaviors to predict the likely success of a product in different locations.	Feature Segmentation: Use of telemetry data to understand feature and functionality response, which is funneled into a dashboard to indicate where to first launch a new product feature.
Marketing and Sales	Audience Targeting: Identifying target areas for the purpose of marketing to select audience types, developing sales territories to service the needs of a region.	Customer Prediction: Identifying common consumer behaviors over time to predict where you will find more customers like them to increase lift to a retail location.	Campaign Attribution: Discovering the right advertising channel to focus marketing efforts on location-based target audience behavioral response to different media types.
Location Planning and Real Estate Strategy	Expansion Analysis: Comparative analysis of economic, talent, customer, community attributes of business sites for expansion.	Site Selection: Trade Area analysis to determine location of new facilities. Analysis of supply chain network to determine location and needed capacity of a new distribution center.	Virtual Site Creation: Creation of a digital twin that mimics the characteristics of the real-world site that can be manipulated with varying datasets to analyze design and implementation plans and identify risks.
Operations	Monitoring Dashboards: Dashboard that monitors activities across key business locations.	Employee Safety Management: Analyzing employee safety trends to improve health and safety management in high-risk locations.	Supply Chain Optimization: Projecting incremental store traffic lift to aid in procurement efforts to keep shelves stocked with product during seasonal high demand.
Corporate Social Responsibility	Diversity Progress: Mapping business and community data to tell a story of diversity and the impact on the local community.	Environmental Impacts: Dashboards that visualize and predict environmental impacts of operations to assess needed changes.	Health Targeting: Understanding the likelihood of a population to receive a vaccine, deploying more communication efforts in areas where response may be low.

Descriptive location analytics may look at store locations with consumer attributes attached, such as overall sales, distance to store, and so forth. Predictive location analytics may take this a step further, by using historic consumer behavior data, such as demographics, purchase behaviors, and foot traffic, to predict the likelihood of a consumer buying a certain product within a certain market. Prescriptive location analytics will project consumer behavior data while estimating the likelihood of certain outcomes to help the business hone new product features to defined market segment and locations.

With location at the forefront of decision-making, R&D efforts can sway with the ebb and flow of different trade areas while also considering consumer demographics, behaviors, and store proximity. This can also help retailers understand which areas' customers are more likely to buy online versus brick-and-mortar sales, how to advertise to audiences en route to a location, and how to restock supply based on shelf replenishment needs in the quickest, most efficient ways possible. Beyond retail, urban mobility patterns can also be used to determine risk—particularly in the insurance industry, which may be experimenting with new terms and policies based on location. By performing location intelligence research and analyzing data through the various location analytics techniques, businesses can keep up-to-date in understanding how to deploy critical business developments in the right place at the right time.

Other areas of R&D inquiry include strategic location planning at scale, involving networks of stores, competitors, traffic, demographics, psychographics, urban mobility patterns, and other factors. Beyond location planning, manufacturers and utility companies are using digitized representations of facilities and critical infrastructure to create digital twins. A GIS can then simulate movements of people and parts and track the use of machinery, equipment, and other assets using sensor data. This data can help predict equipment breakdowns and facilitate preventive maintenance.

Marketing and sales

Taking customer data a step further, businesses that seek to understand their markets and audiences for expansion find great insights through location analytics. Descriptive mapping of an organization's customer data provides insights about customer segments that may otherwise be locked up within customer relationship management (CRM) databases and customer data platforms (CDPs). By enriching demographic data with socioeconomic attributes and business data, businesses can segment customers into audiences based on consumer and lifestyle preferences. This information can be combined with trade area analysis to determine locations of new facilities.

Considering the typical data a business collects on its customers in relation to place, many outcomes are possible, depending on how the data is joined. Through geoenrichment, location data can be enriched with attributes such as customer demographics, ability to pay, basket size (the number of products sold in a single purchase), time of purchase, and product upsells (purchases of higher-end products). When tied to marketing and sales efforts, such data enables businesses to deploy trackable advertising campaigns—from the moment a target audience sees the advertising to the moment the audience crosses a store threshold to the moment the audience purchases a product.

All marketing and sales outcomes can be measured and tied to marketing campaigns by using geoenriched location data to understand consumer behavior. This information is then funneled back to the organization to analyze market behaviors. As research has shown, market behaviors are not always fixed to regional location but may sometimes shift based on proximity to similar population characteristics, environmental surroundings, and overall neighborhood tendencies. Geoenriched data can help businesses identify new customers based on existing customer behaviors, consider whether to cross-sell (sell related or complementary products) or upsell, and predict the risk of churn. With these insights, a company can decide how to optimize the prices of products and services based on spending and income or wealth profiles, determine hyperlocal product assortments, and develop mitigation strategies to retain high-risk yet profitable customers.

Real estate and site selection

Location analytics can assist in understanding current and future business locations. One of the significant objectives of business development is to estimate the future sales potential of markets. Forecasts of sales or any other business KPIs can be modeled using statistical regression models. Such models consider demographic and psychographic attributes of sites, population density, past sales, and foot traffic and use them as independent variables to explain and predict current and future site performance.

At a more advanced level, sophisticated GeoAI-based machine learning and deep learning models can be used to predict risk exposure and related KPIs. Location intelligence derived from such predictive models is critical to executive leadership in making decisions on capital-intensive business development projects. Such models can also be used to make merger and acquisition decisions and accelerate strategic expansion in both domestic and international markets. Advanced techniques such as digital twins can create a virtual replica of the physical entity or network, allowing for virtual simulations and assessments. Creation of such a virtual site that mimics the characteristics of the real-world site can be manipulated with varying datasets to suggest how to develop blueprints, landscaping, wayfinding, indoor navigation, and emergency evacuation.

Operations

Operational activities rely heavily on spatial monitoring systems. Tied closely to the location value chain, operational intelligence allows businesses to understand business needs on large-scale enterprise levels and also within more granular segments of day-to-day business function. Dashboards inform operations strategies, with descriptive analytics communicating data through mapping and visualizations. Whereas in the past, managing decision-making for multiple business locations may have been a more manual process, spatial technology has enabled a new generation of business management practices. As operational data is geovisualized and analyzed, operational awareness is heightened, facilitating timely decisions to ensure consistent operational performance.

This data also enables predictive and prescriptive decision-making. To support employee safety and comply with regulations, data can be tracked over time to predict future incidents. Operations managers may see safety violations regularly occurring within a specific time frame within a specific area; perhaps spills are occurring regularly on a platform, or equipment is consistently damaged when accessing a route, lowering productivity. Spatial manipulation of data can predict the likelihood of such occurrences and can help estimate the exposure to related risks, thereby laying the foundation for risk mitigation and enhancing situational awareness. Predictive analytics can demonstrate the likelihood of reoccurrence, and prescriptive analytics will inform the optimal solution.

Supply chain network visualization, transparency, and product traceability are often informed by detailed network maps, while supply chain resilience—an issue of great importance considering the COVID-19 pandemic—can be modeled using geostatistical approaches. Modern supply chains are complex and consist of a network of facilities. Facility locations along a supply chain and overall supply chain network design can be informed using optimization approaches that can also facilitate efficient routing and navigation of people and assets. This is critical for businesses considering the rapid growth of e-commerce deliveries. Businesses also require spatial mapping and modeling of risk for situational awareness, as well as real-time tracking and monitoring of assets, people, processes, and potential hazards. Business disruption can be prevented by accurately and spatially modeling risks, fraud, and other disruptive events. This can help generate risk mitigation strategies that ensure business continuity, maintain regulatory compliance, and enhance disaster preparedness.

Corporate social responsibility

The value of the company in the community is a critical component of contemporary business environments. For CSR, timely information is needed across a broad range of areas, including diversity, community impacts, and environmental performance. Business and community data can be mapped to tell a story of the business's economic impact in various locations. Diversity data can be spatially analyzed to track diversity in the company relative to surrounding communities. Dashboards can be used to understand and predict the level of corporate environmental sustainability. And prescriptive analysis can guide efforts during a public health crisis, as has been experienced during the COVID-19 pandemic.

Although aspects of CSR require data beyond the company's data, when such data is integrated, the output may be informative and groundbreaking. Spatially understanding a business's impact on a local community, exploring matters at the heart of employee culture, or deploying location solutions according to an ethical standard can positively impact customer sentiment, which will affect brand loyalty or may even create positive change within a community.

Achieving value with location analytics

It may feel as if a microscopic lens were placed on the behavior of twenty-first-century businesses. However, this lens has forced necessary change, which has affected the planning and management of operations. Whether addressing issues such as climate change or weather hazards, changes in economic security, or changes in overall resources to support public health and human services, businesses have an opportunity to create shared-value solutions to these challenges.

Overall, the value proposition of location analytics depends on the breadth and depth of applications. Broad applications, spanning multiple business priorities, and deep analysis, using sophisticated, context-appropriate combinations of descriptive, predictive, and prescriptive location analytics, are likely to maximize the value of location analytics. This, in turn, can shape decisions and actions in different parts of an organization, spanning multiple levels of the organizational hierarchy and facilitating enterprise-wide spatial transformation.

The analytic methods underpinning these applications are key. They may range from simple descriptive mapping-based visualizations, smart mapping, and geoenrichment with external data to sophisticated dashboards that enable reporting, disclosures, or organizational deliberations. Predictive models that range from traditional time series regression models to more sophisticated GeoAI-based machine learning and deep learning models are increasingly popular as data science teams mine structured and unstructured geospatial big data to uncover and decipher patterns and relationships among dozens of variables. Finally, optimization models such as location-allocation, demand coverage, product mix, and vehicle routing are informing site selection, last-mile logistics, supply chain optimization, and related strategic, tactical, and operational decisions. For example, in location-allocation modeling, multiple facilities such as warehouses and distribution centers are located in continuous space, and discrete demand (sometimes estimated by population) is optimally allocated to facilities, whereas, in other contexts, the objective of a business may be to maximize demand coverage using the minimum number of facilities located strategically through demand coverage models. Location data (both internal and external to the organization) plays a critical role in framing, developing, testing, and validating these location analytics models and approaches.

Closing case study: John Deere

As the global population continues to expand, sustainably growing enough food to feed every person on the planet is a fundamental challenge. The challenge of increasing farming productivity while at the same time addressing climate change and extreme weather conditions confronts not only farmers but also manufacturers of farming equipment, such as John Deere.

Founded in 1837, John Deere is well known as a global manufacturer and distributor of a full line of agricultural, construction, turf, and forestry equipment (Deere 2021). Headquartered in Moline, Illinois, and operating in 27 countries with a corporate presence in 19 US states, John Deere operates 23 manufacturing plants, with more plants overseas. Deere products are sold by its vast network of dealers in more than 100 countries (Deere 2021).

A cornerstone of John Deere is the use of advanced location analytics across its range of products and services (Esri 2020a).

A major area of development has been precision farming (Deere 2022a). Now, with IoT sensors embedded in John Deere equipment, customers within the global farming ecosystem are more connected than ever, with the ability to produce enormous volumes of geographic data and imagery. With John Deere equipment primed and ready for the collection and management of massive data streams, the company can derive location intelligence to build better products, provide customers with the tools to streamline farming operations, and support the farming community with sustainable development efforts (Kantor and van der Schaaf 2019; Deere 2022a). Agribusiness intelligence translates to increased efficiency and productivity to farm and cultivate crops, with attention to granular details for process improvement and product enhancements.

Location intelligence for R&D in precision farming

As with all spatial problems, having access to timely and relevant data can make all the difference in running location analytics. Data as it is streamed to a dashboard will provide descriptive location intelligence, but data that is collected over time and enriched with additional attributes can advance agribusiness through predictive and prescriptive location intelligence (Esri 2020a). With John Deere integrating data collection into farming equipment, data collection can be automated in the field and efficiently managed to make better business decisions. A connected equipment network aids farm customers in planning and managing growing seasons, from precisely planting seeds to maximizing harvest yields (Deere 2022b). John Deere Operations Center (figure 3.5) is activated by field data that can indicate overall equipment performance and inform research and development efforts.

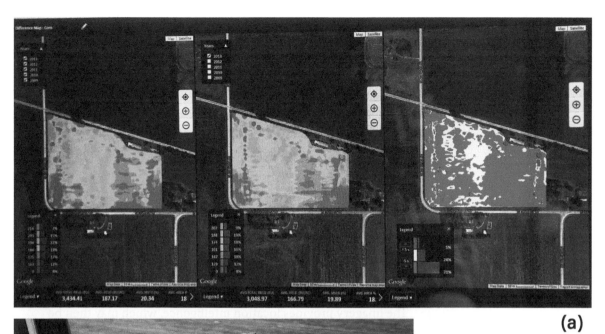

(a)

(b)

(c)

Figure 3.5. (a) A difference map shows changes in corn yield in a particular field in the year 2013 compared with average yield over a five-year period (2009-13), as part of Deere's Field Analyzer tool. (b) Data taken from within the cab of a Deere tractor enables real-time tracking, prescriptive decision-making, and collaboration with Deere's Operations Center. (c) Collaborative work in the field using computers and handheld devices can produce customized plans for unique zones, prioritize work, and direct operators on what to do. Courtesy of John Deere (2022b).

In today's sustainable precision farming movement, farmers need access to reliable georeferenced information. A variety of data is brought into GIS to analyze and make descriptive, predictive, and prescriptive decisions. This data may focus on the weather and environment. It may look at soil type and nutrients, precipitation, groundwater level and runoff, air pollution, and other factors (Deere 2020). Farmers can use the data to make informed choices to maximize limited budgets and predict change over time across vast areas of farmland. To help farmers georeference field data, analysts at John Deere collect Landsat satellite imagery for understanding changes in the land over time. Every few days, farmers can see, for example, if flooding from a rainstorm has damaged a crop or determine whether additional fungicide should be applied in a certain area (Esri 2018a).

John Deere Operations Center then uses immense volumes of satellite imagery and weather data to enrich the customer farming data (Deere 2022b). The imagery provides location intelligence, which may then be mined using AI and deep learning algorithms. As data is mined, intelligence that is uncovered may include optimal planting time and growing time for a given location. This intelligence may indicate which type of crop to grow each year and help determine the type of farming equipment that may be required to produce a quality harvest. Farmers can intuitively act based on their location, knowing the precise level of nutrients to put in the soil; the correct amount of water to release; how much fertilizer, seed, and tillage is needed; and when the optimal time is to act. This ensures sustainable use of resources, maximizes productivity, and minimizes soil erosion and chemical damage to the subsurface, thereby protecting precious farmland for future generations (Esri 2018a; Deere 2020).

Location intelligence also facilitates predictive maintenance of farm equipment. Deere's equipment and machinery consist of parts sourced from various plants all over the world. Its advanced telematics systems remotely connect agricultural equipment owners, business managers, and dealers to agricultural equipment in the field, providing real-time alerts and information about equipment location, use, maintenance, and performance (revolutions per minute [RPMs], oil pressure, and so forth). In a breakdown, locations are determined. For example, did the equipment break down over a steep hillside? Is a cluster of breakdowns tied to a location? In one such instance, there were repeated issues with fuel pumps. After analyzing location data, analysts determined that fuel coming from a local refinery was the culprit, adversely impacting a critical component within the pumps (Esri 2020a). Accordingly, measures were taken to service equipment proactively.

Location intelligence for business development and sales

John Deere is a technology and data company as much as it is an agribusiness company (Deere 2021). Using a location-scientific approach, Deere's data science team examines thousands of variables during the early stages of market studies to identify geographic areas of potential growth (Kantor and van der Schaaf 2019; Esri 2020a). This includes land cover analysis using satellite imagery, which helps decision-makers estimate how various grasslands, crop fields, or lawns correlate with consumer purchases in rural communities. Ultimately, about 20 variables such as land cover, historical customer sales, income, demographics, existing dealers, competitive dealers, and distances to all those features are incorporated into an AI-driven regression model to predict the commercial potential of US Census blocks. The predictive AI models also factor in market characteristics—for example, the presence of more lawns than crop fields in a target market—to refine sales forecasts (Esri 2020a).

Location intelligence for real estate strategy and store operations

To help dealers expand their retail footprint and build additional dealership locations, Deere's data science team provides a wealth of psychographic insights for target locations. With products that range in price from $1,600 to $600,000, customer segmentation is a must—both in the private-user segment (lawn and garden maintenance) and the commercial-customer segment (golf clubs, sports facilities, and so forth) (Kantor and van der Schaaf 2019). Psychographic analysis is deployed to determine the lifestyles of potential consumers so that dealers can make site selection decisions and determine appropriate marketing channels for their potential customers. For instance, online marketing campaigns can be targeted at consumers living in higher-acreage homes in affluent areas versus direct mail to target customers who prefer to pay bills in person and avoid using the internet for financial transactions.

In addition, depending on location-based psychographic intelligence, dealers can stock appropriate products and product mix in stores. Because any given Deere product line can be arranged into tens of thousands of configurations, detailed location intelligence about consumer preferences can help Deere's product marketing group, sales leadership, and dealer council steer customers toward an optimal set of product configurations for the local market. This can help dealers avoid inflated overhead costs due to expansive product lines without disappointing customers or sacrificing profits (Yunes et al. 2007).

Environmental and societal elements

Climate change is one of the greatest threats of the twenty-first century. Scarce rainfall, extreme droughts, and shrinking farmland are becoming increasingly common. Despite slowing population growth, the UN projects global population to approach 10 billion by 2050. To combat challenges to food security and prevent hunger and malnutrition, smart precision agriculture that is environmentally sustainable is critical to maximize crop yield and produce enough food while preserving the land for future generations of farmers.

Location intelligence at John Deere is poised to catalyze innovation in every part of the company's value chain, impacting farmers, dealers, and consumers while transforming the company into a technocentric sustainable agribusiness (Deere 2020). As farmland contracts worldwide and farmers age, spatial intelligence is central for a newer, younger, and technologically savvy generation of farmers to ensure that their farms are operating at maximum potential at sub-inch accuracy with optimal use of scarce natural resources and minimal use of fertilizer, fuel, herbicides, and pesticides. Among other benefits, location intelligence is expected to help the new generation of farmers meet the challenges and needs of the business of modern-day farming in which they must wear multiple hats—those of broker, banker, chemist, agronomist, and technologist, all at the same time (Esri 2018a). In each of these roles, John Deere is using GeoAI-based modeling approaches to help farmers improve yield, increase productivity, lower costs, and achieve more precision while factoring in shifts in weather patterns and other uncertainties such as commodity prices and grain prices, sometimes a year or more in advance of the growing season (Deere 2022a).

While advancing precision farming and agriculture, GeoAI-powered innovations are helping farmers become stewards of the land through data-driven decision-making. Using location as a guiding principle, with advanced location analytics, John Deere is enabling sustainable precision farming that is integrated with the environment while driving growth and profitability for all stakeholders.

CHAPTER 4
Growing markets and customers

Introduction

Understanding customers and markets has always been a key to business success. Whether a firm's customers are individual consumers or other businesses, understanding their needs, preferences, attitudes, value propositions, priorities, challenges, and purpose provides insights about customers that can inform the development of a differentiated business strategy compared with peers and competitors.

Many of these attributes of customers are tied to location. In the case of individuals, where they live, work, shop, and engage in professional or social activities provides location-specific insights to companies about their lifestyles and consumer preferences. This is especially important at a time when there is an unprecedented acceleration in the growth of e-commerce, resulting in a shift from physical stores to online shopping. This digital-first shift is impacting many consumer-facing industries, creating competitive advantage for some.

When the customer itself is a business, the geographic locations of a business's operations; key business assets such as personnel, spare parts, and inventory; and critical facilities along the supply chain (for example, warehouses and distribution centers), relative to service and fulfillment territories, provide clues about processes and workflows, allocation of resources, prioritization of key business objectives, risk tolerance, and overall business resilience. During the COVID-19 pandemic, the lack of a location-based view of business operations, supply chain locations, network connectivity, and other contributing factors has exposed loopholes in business strategy and severely disrupted business continuity in organizations across several sectors and industries.

Understanding business markets

As introduced in chapter 2, industry clusters play a critical role in individual business growth as cumulated growth of the regions they operate in (Porter 1998a, 1998b). The Porter cluster theory, named after Michael E. Porter, a professor at Harvard Business School, is based on competitiveness of firms within a geographic unit, which could be a state, region within a state, or metropolitan region. Clustering is dynamic—clusters sprout up and do not necessarily last forever. Internal or external forces can lead to the decline or death of a cluster (Porter 1998a).

Industry clusters are defined as a geographic agglomeration of firms and institutions in a similar economic sector, interconnected in multiple ways (Porter 1998a, 1998b). Businesses and institutions in clusters share infrastructure and often a pool of human resources. They relate upstream to a common set of suppliers and downstream to related companies and institutions, such as universities, think tanks, trade organizations, and specialized government offices. Porter's regional cluster constitutes an agglomeration of firms of regional, national, and worldwide impact of such strength overall that the cluster is considered a world leader.

A variety of cluster mapping tools have been developed to help businesses understand where certain clusters are developing. This includes a cluster mapping tool developed by the Harvard Business School in collaboration with the US Economic Development Agency (Porter 2021) (figure 4.1).

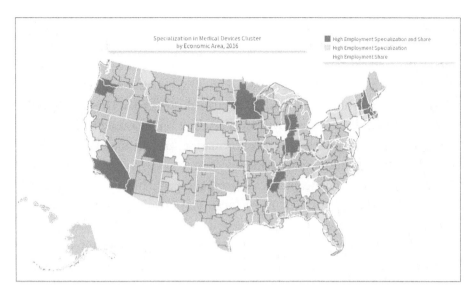

Figure 4.1. Specialization in Medical Devices Cluster in Economic Areas, United States, 2016 (blue indicates economic areas with high employment specialization and share, cyan indicates counties with high employment specialization, and yellow indicates high employment share). Source: Cluster Mapping 2021.

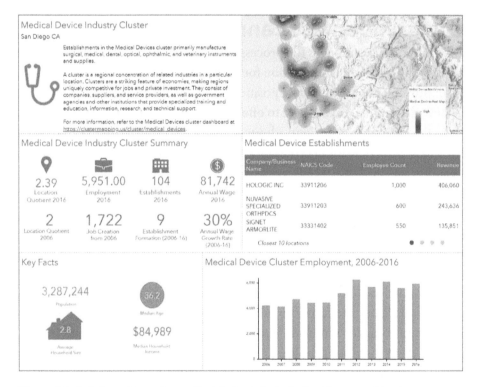

Figure 4.2. An infographic on the medical device industry in San Diego, reaching from Oceanside to near the Mexican border, in 2021.

PART 2 ACHIEVING BUSINESS AND SOCIETAL VALUE

Data from this tool can be enriched by other locational data. For example, the University of Redlands has created an enriched infographic of the San Diego medical device industry cluster using ArcGIS Business Analyst™ (figure 4.2). This enrichment provides demographic insights as well as additional information about the medical devices cluster in San Diego, including data on individual firms, employment specialization measured by Location Quotient, job creation, establishment formation, and the longitudinal trend in medical devices cluster employment.

The Porter cluster concept has a bearing on spatial business. First, spatial business involves decision-making on locations of companies, and that is influenced by the draw of being in or near an industrial cluster. Among the reasons to locate is the marketing benefit. Marketing may gain potency by emphasizing, for example, "Silicon Valley firm" or "Hollywood talent agency." Second, for leading businesses located in a cluster region, spatial business marketing can be strengthened by the dynamics, visibility, and expanded customer target pools associated with the cluster.

Environmental scanning

Environmental scanning is the process of obtaining, examining, and disseminating marketing information for tactical or strategic objectives, such as improvement of competitive position by analyzing competitor supply chains, determination of where to offer insurance by examining insurance risks throughout a region, and advancement of R&D by deciding where and why to locate a new R&D center by assessing labor markets. Environmental scanning can be done once, several times, or continually. It is achieved using descriptive analytics, often involving location analytics, as described in chapter 3. Companies justify environmental scanning as providing a view of the status of markets, yielding information that can be applied to company strategy and decision-making.

Figure 4.3 shows three levels of scanning: internal to the organization, in the immediate industry environment, and in the macro environment of external factors and forces broader than the industry (Kumar 2011). Scanning a company's industry environment includes gaining current information on the firm's stakeholders, such as customers, suppliers, partners, and investors, as well as its competitors.

Environmental scanning extends to the macro environment within which the company does business, including political, economic, social, and technological factors (Kumar 2011). Scanning all these elements can involve location.

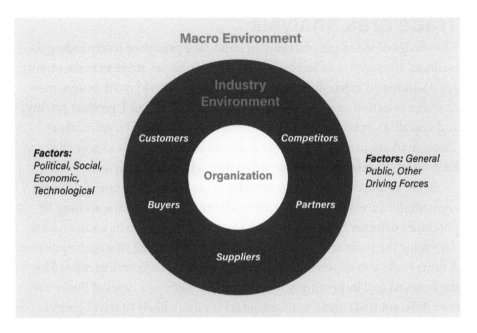

Figure 4.3. Environmental scanning situates the organization at the central core, surrounded by a ring of the industry environment, outside of which appears the macro environment of political, social, economic, and technological forces. Source: adapted from van der Heijden et al. 2002.

Environmental scanning is also used by firms in developing nations to expand their customer base. For instance, in India, location-based environment scanning is done by companies that seek to send goods into India's rural villages. Dabur is the dominant world provider of Ayurvedic goods related to the traditional system of medicine in India and also markets consumer product staples, mostly in India but also in 120 other nations. It uses GIS mapping for its environmental scanning of Indian demographic data from government sources and private vendors, surveys of indicators of community wealth, and data on different groups' values, attitudes, and behavior (Kapur, Dawar, and Ahuja 2014). In this way, Dabur has identified 287 well-off rural districts in 10 Indian states as having potential for markets. Each month, the firm focuses its marketing on a new rural district, and deliveries are optimized using the routing features in GIS software (Kapur, Dawar, and Ahuja 2014). Dabur has been successful in introducing its goods to rural areas, topping its original goal of providing service to 30,000 villages within a year and a half of commencing marketing to the rural districts. The initiative has benefited the firm, which now has more than 40% more business in rural areas than in urban (Kapur, Dawar, and Ahuja 2014).

Trade area analysis

Knowledge of the target market is an important precursor to expanding the business. Irrespective of sector or industry, businesses strive to make important decisions on expansion, such as site selection, store layout design, merchandise selection, customization, ability to fulfill demand, product pricing, and available workforce, based on intimate knowledge of target markets. Target markets, in turn, lead to the question of trade areas and how they can be delineated, described, and modeled through spatial analysis.

In the context of business geography, trade areas define specific market segmentation areas and help businesses better understand the existing or potential customer base. What are the factors that need to be considered to determine the trade area of a business that is considering strategic expansion? A firm's trade area depends on the variety of goods and services offered by the business and its proximity to competitors. Different types of businesses have different trade areas, and customers are more likely to travel greater distances to purchase certain types of goods and services or buy online with home delivery. To strategically expand, businesses need to estimate the market or trade area of a store or fulfillment center at a specific site by factoring in the geographic distribution of existing customers, potential customers within a defined service or delivery area that encompasses the site, and potential competitors.

Popular and intuitive methods of delineating trade areas involve radial distance-based concentric rings and irregular travel time–based trade area polygons, as shown in figures 4.4 and 4.5. Such trade areas are based on customer spotting (Applebaum 1966), and a business's trade area can be divided into primary, secondary, and tertiary (or fringe) areas, which are determined by the distance from the firm's site. From the standpoint of a business, the primary trade area is key. To statistically evaluate revenue performance with respect to opportunity, the primary trade area is thought of as the geographic core in which at least 50% of the business's customers live and work (Church and Murray 2009). This is the area closest to the store or center of the trade area, as measured by driving distance or automobile driving time, and is expected to contain the highest residential density of the store's customers and the highest per capita sales by residence locations. Adjoining the primary trade area is the secondary trade area, from which a store anticipates visits by approximately 25% of its customers, followed by the tertiary area.

In figure 4.4, two restaurant locations of a quick-service restaurant (QSR) chain have a reasonably significant difference in daytime population density in their primary and secondary trade areas, defined by 1- and 2-mile distance buffers. Daytime populations in the proposed location's primary and secondary trade areas, shown on the left, are significantly higher compared with those of the existing store, shown on the right, whereas daytime population in the fringe areas is not significantly different.

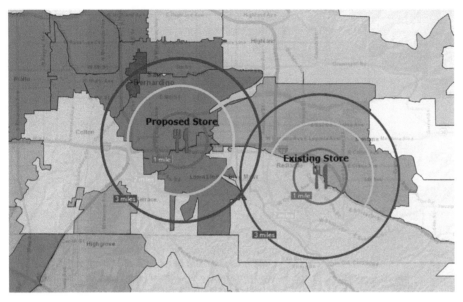

2021 Daytime Pop Density (Pop/Sq. Mile, ZIP Codes)

9,142.2	to	11,535.8
4,668.3	to	9,142.1
2,708.1	to	4,668.2
1,012.6	to	2,708
3.9	to	1,012.5

Figure 4.4. Existing and proposed store locations are mapped, each surrounded by 1-, 2-, and 3-mile distance rings representing trade areas, which are superimposed on a thematic map layer of daytime population densities for 2021.

Figure 4.5 shows trade areas for the same two restaurant locations, defined by 3-, 6-, and 10-minute drive times. These drive-time buffers are distorted in certain directions because travel speeds vary, depending on the time of day or even day of the week. In fact, in modern GIS software packages, it is possible to refine such drive time–based trade areas and model them, based on historic traffic data, for times of the day and days of the week, along with direction of travel. This information can be valuable for analysis of densely populated, high-traffic urban markets.

As with distance-based trade areas, drive time–based trade areas may overlap. For example, in figure 4.5, the 3-minute drive-time trade areas of the existing store and proposed location of a new store do not overlap; however, there is slight overlap of the 6-minute drive-time trade areas and significant overlap of the 10-minute drive-time buffers. Overlap can alert the manager of the proposed store to strong competition and cannibalization (loss of sales) if both stores belong to the same company.

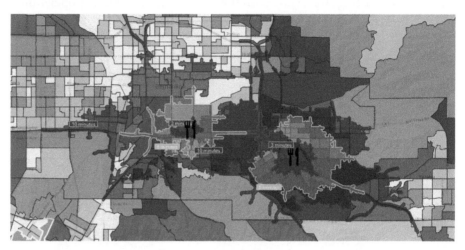

2021 Median Household Income by ZIP Codes

$86,531	to	$114,295
$69,774	to	$86,530
$51,924	to	$69,773
$28,649	to	$51,923
$0	to	$28,648

Figure 4.5. Drive-time buffers of 3, 6, and 10 minutes are mapped for two nearby stores to represent trade areas that are partially overlapping, which are superimposed on a thematic map layer of median household income for 2021.

A firm can approximate the customer base within each travel time zone—for example, in terms of demographic attributes such as daytime resident population—and characterize them—for example, in terms of economic attributes, such as median household income—using simple spatial analysis functions within a GIS, such as overlay, union, intersection, querying, and summary statistics.

Often internal organizational data, such as spatially referenced sales transactions, or external third-party data, such as live traffic feeds, can be incorporated within a GIS for efficient analysis to geoenrich trade area zones. The resulting trade area reports and map visualizations can provide location-based intelligence that informs business strategy. Trade areas can also be compared with each other, based on the demographic, psychographic, and socioeconomic attributes of customers in those areas or in other local, state, and national geographies and benchmarks. Such comparisons can inform and guide senior leaders as they consider strategic expansion opportunities in competitive markets.

Such environmental scanning of trade areas constitutes exploratory analysis and descriptive location analytics, often the first, foundational step in analyzing trade areas. As the next step, a statistical analysis using regression-based models can incorporate the following:

- Demand factors, such as population density of trade areas and extent of competition in trade areas
- Site characteristics of an existing or proposed site, such as square footage, number of employees, available parking, easy roadway access, and signage
- Demographic, socioeconomic, and psychographic attributes of customers in trade areas
- Geographic attributes, such as distances, directions, and elevations

Regression models can predict the brand share of wallet, overall sales, revenue, and profit potential of trade areas, providing guidance for business growth.

Trade area analysis can also play an important role in prescriptive analysis of site location. Consider the QSR with one of the existing restaurant locations shown descriptively in figures 4.4 and 4.5. That QSR is interested in opening a new location. By factoring in business constraints such as KPI benchmarks (for factors such as labor costs), supply capacity constraints, demand requirements, and local zoning regulations, plus geographic constraints such as those imposed by natural barriers (for example, mountains or rivers) that impact mobility and travel times, the QSR can optimize a specific business objective—for example, market potential measured by sales—and select an optimal location for a new restaurant. Prescriptive modeling, using operations research methods, can aid such sophisticated optimal location modeling and is incorporated within contemporary GIS software.

Growing customers

Market research and analysis is a critical function across the value chain. The purpose of marketing is to identify, attract, and retain the customer, a goal abetted by today's technologies, which provide a multifaceted and continually updated view of the customer. This is seen in contemporary customer relationship management, or CRM, systems, in which the customer can be an individual or a business.

Location-based marketing, also referred to as geomarketing, uses an array of datasets and analytics to gain a multifaceted understanding of customers. The insights gained on customer segments, interests, and location contexts can both inform new products and services and fine-tune current strategies. This platform for location-based marketing can also be used to reach new markets and customers. At the same time, some forms of location-based marketing raise ethical privacy considerations that businesses cannot afford to ignore.

Market segmentation: Geodemographics

Customer segmenting has been a cornerstone technique in marketing for several decades. There are various ways to define segments. Five common segments are demographic, geographic, psychographic, behavioral, and firmographic. The first four are segments for business to consumer (B2C) marketing; the last refers to firm characteristics for business to business (B2B) marketing. Technological advances coupled with the rapid advance of large data sources have allowed companies to combine elements of these segments for a desired one-to-one B2C marketing that closely connects with the customer's journey (Elliott and Nickola 2021).

One approach to this integration is geodemographics. The foundation for geodemographics was the 1970 US and UK censuses, which produced, for the first time, massive amounts of computerized information. As censuses have improved over time, so has the availability of accurate and extensive geodemographics, not only for the US and UK but for Canada and several other nations. Today, software can characterize every census tract in the US, making it possible to use geodemographic mapping and further enrich it with social and economic variables for a more refined view of potential customers.

There are more than 10 major geodemographic products in the US—several developed in the UK, such as Acorn and Mosaic, and others suitable for developing nations. Commercial geodemographic software will often have from 50 to 80 neighborhood types; Esri Tapestry™ Segmentation has 67 distinctive neighborhood market segments, which are estimated by cluster analysis and other statistical methods, based largely on census data. The segments can be mapped at the zip code, census tract, and block group levels. An advantage of having census tracts of 5,000–10,000 people is that individual identity can be suppressed, protecting personal privacy.

In the US, census data that underpins such categories is mostly accurate but is only collected every 10 years, so a weakness of geodemographics is the aging of data as the decennial census period nears its end. The model for Tapestry is rebuilt at every decennial census, but the demographic balance and set of constituent neighborhood segments change yearly. Updates to the base data imply that a neighborhood may have a shifting geodemographic composition and dominant segment over time.

Another example of a geodemographic tool is Acorn, which provides classification of consumers for segments in the UK by postcode. The postcode had an average population in 2020 of 533,000 (CACI 2020). The data sources for the tool are open data, government data, commercial data, and data collected by the Acorn firm, CACI. Acorn classifies each postcode into one of 62 types, which can be aggregated into 18 groups. Groups include such categories as city sophisticates, successful suburbs, comfortable seniors, student life, striving families, and modest means.

An example of a type is Semiprofessional Families, Owner-Occupied Neighborhoods. It applies to 1.2 million adults, which is 2.3% of UK adults. This type belongs to the category Successful Suburbs. The typical location is "found in villages and on the edge of towns" and "more than average of these couples are well educated and in managerial occupations, while the neighborhoods will contain a broad mix of people" (CACI 2020). The geodemographic profiles offer a richer characterization than is possible with a single variable. As shown in figure 4.6, this type's annual household income is £47,000 (US$32,082), which is above the UK average, and the typical adult age range is 25–34, with two children per household. The profile also provides average financial, digital-attitudinal, technology, and housing information. For instance, 42% of households stream TV services, and 59% indicate, "I am very good at managing money" (CACI 2020). This segment can be compared with 61 other types in the full Acorn set.

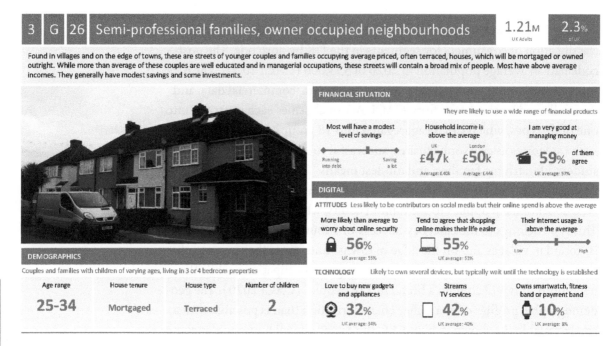

Figure 4.6. An Acorn geosegmentation dashboard displays a photo of a typical dwelling for the segment of semiprofessional families, as well as the segment's indicators of the average family financial situation, digital capabilities, and demographics. Source: CACI Ltd. 2019.

As a marketing tool, geodemographics provides considerable insights to businesses and allows for geotargeted campaigns to customer segments. At the same time, geodemographics has limitations (Dalton and Thatcher 2015; Leventhal 2016). Specifically, in addition to the public data update only once a decade, outlier residents are obfuscated. Emphasis on the average profile of a neighborhood misses the outliers at either end of the scale. This prevents the full perception of a neighborhood. A further subtle issue with geodemographics is commodification. Naming and branding a neighborhood followed by broadcasting the profile may itself affect the neighborhood's composition. A neighborhood branded and marketed as "City Sophisticates," for instance, subtly encourages outlier persons to leave and new arrivals to resemble the branded image (Dalton and Thatcher 2015).

In addition to geodemographic marketing, businesses now are devising and implementing more personalized, "relationship" marketing approaches. A business may prefer to segment its customers through its own customer feedback and survey inputs. Another approach is to use the firm's internal business transaction data and customer relationship information to segment its customers into "loyalty" categories. Psychographic analysis can also be applied to characterize the behavior and attitudes of customers, yielding an alternative customer segmentation. Some firms combine these segmentation approaches: for instance, Nike segments its customer base by demographic categories, geographic variables such as metropolitan/nonmetropolitan, and behavioral variables that emphasize customer feelings about the firms' products (Singh 2017).

Location analytics across the 7 *P*s of marketing

For B2C marketing, the well-known 7 *P*s of marketing apply: product, price, place, promotion, physical evidence, people, and process (Investopedia 2019). For B2C, the 7 *P*s connect with location as follows:

- **Product.** GIS and location technologies are embedded in many products and services, adding to their value—in services such as delivery and in products such as cars, cell phones, consumer-level drones, and wayfinding devices, among others. This added value, in turn, enhances the marketing potential of those products and services.
- **Price.** The pricing of a product or service is based on the real or perceived tangible value. Spatial features of the product or service can enhance or lower value, depending on user perception. For instance, for a wholesale store, location-based inventory and distribution may marginally lower cost, enabling a comparable decrease in pricing.
- **Place.** Predictive locational analytics can be helpful in choosing where to place a product or service. For instance, some fast-food companies, including KFC, employ geospatial tools to assist in physical placement of a new outlet, considering the locations of competitors, traffic flow volumes and directions, signage of competitors, and socioeconomic attributes of the area.
- **Promotion.** Promotion is how the customer becomes aware of the product or service. It can occur through public relations, advertising, direct marketing, media attention, or an item going viral on social media, all of which can focus on getting the word out to target markets across geographies.
- **Physical evidence.** This refers to the physical spaces where customers interact with business representatives. Although such spaces were restricted during the COVID-19 pandemic, they generally include retail stores, customer field visits, meetings, conferences, and other venues. For many companies, the use of Salesforce and other customer relationship software provides tracking of physical interactions. CRM software

can be linked with GIS software, which can then apply spatial analytics to better understand where a customer has touch points with a company's employees and other channels of physical interaction with the firm.

- **People.** Marketing professionals who include location intelligence and location analytics in their knowledge and skill set are better prepared to conduct marketing and customer engagement. This enhances the company's ability to incorporate geographies to better identify, engage, and serve the customer.
- **Process.** This consists of well-designed steps in the process to provide goods and services to customers and influence the customer experience. A process can be made faster, more efficient, and more satisfying to the customer by including steps that use location analytics. For instance, express delivery services by FedEx optimize the process of routing using location analytics, which results in faster delivery and, at the same time, provides the customer with the current tracking location of the package. The same process enhancements occur with B2B deliveries. As a result, location intelligence has become a competitive aspect for local niches—as in the following example for at-home food delivery in New York City. This example emphasizes the *P*s of product, price, and place.

Case example: FreshDirect

In the nine boroughs of New York City, citizens live in a dense urban setting and often prefer not to own personal vehicles for transportation. It is difficult for many to shop for groceries at full-size stores, so they use local corner markets and small venues instead. FreshDirect was first to market as a citywide fresh food delivery firm in New York City, and it holds about 63% of the market (Boyle and Giammona 2018).

Founded in 2011, the firm 11 years later has more than $750 million in annual revenue and a 400,000-foot distribution facility in the South Bronx. It dispatches a fleet of delivery trucks that are GPS-enabled (figure 4.7) and monitors the fleet through a GIS-based control room that serves to optimize routing and maintenance.

During the second half of the 2010s and beyond, the market heated up. Rearing their heads as competitors to FreshDirect in delivery of perishable food are Instacart, Shipt, and Amazon Fresh. Together, the perishable competitors currently have 23% of the market and are chipping away at FreshDirect's lead. Instacart started up with $1 billion in funding and is taking the tactic of partnering with large supermarket chains in the city (Boyle and Giammona 2018). Shipt, founded in 2014 in Birmingham, Alabama, and now part of Target, focuses on vetted reliable shoppers who partner with local retailers to procure items for delivery (Shipt 2022). Amazon Fresh, with huge resources, is aggressively seeking to grow in the fresh food market. Because New York City is so densely populated, refrigerated delivery trucks are not always needed, so competitors seek to deliver in under two hours to the market of 9 million people. Spatial technologies are used by all three competitors.

Figure 4.7. A GPS-enabled FreshDirect delivery truck rounds a corner in New York City. Courtesy of Kendra Drischler.

FreshDirect's new fulfillment center includes a control center for inventory and smart routing of its truck fleet, kitchen facilities, nine miles of conveyer belts (as shown in figure 4.8), robotic order picking, and rooms set at temperatures for different product types (Wells 2018). The center also is linked upstream to a distribution and production network. All is calibrated to satisfy projected daily market demand (Wells 2018).

FreshDirect exemplifies how the *P*s of product, place, and process are affected by location analytics. Location is embedded in the product's servicing—that is, location-based home delivery. Place concerns the location intelligence determining the location of the fulfillment center and the geographic boundaries of the service area. Process is the supply chain process, which includes the location-based navigation steps in B2B delivery of food by suppliers to the fulfillment center, and after sorting at the center, the B2C location-based navigation in delivery to the customer.

Figure 4.8. FreshDirect's automated order fulfillment facility shows automated conveyers, which sort inbound logistics supplies for placement on GPS-enabled delivery trucks. Courtesy of Haruka Sakaguchi.

Amazon Fresh constitutes the most powerful competition, with automated fulfillment centers, offering New York customers two-hour delivery times through Instacart. Many dimensions of competition exist between these rivals, one of which is competing in spatially driven delivery, which depends on integration of each rival's fulfillment center with inbound distribution networks of available foods. Ultimately, the customer will make the decision. Effective marketing, assisted by knowledge of customer locations and tastes in this densely distributed and sophisticated customer base, is crucial.

Location-based marketing

"Rapidly increasing digitalization across industry verticals, growing penetration of internet and GPS-enabled mobile devices, and increasing utilization of consumer data by marketers are the primary factors fostering growth in demand for location-based advertising," becoming a $62.35 billion global industry (Grand View Research 2020). Location-based marketing (LBM) is the strategy that matches opted-in, privacy-compliant location data received from smartphones to POIs such as restaurants, grocery stores, and shopping malls. Marketers then use this data to create location-based audiences and analytics, reaching their desired audiences to serve them more relevant advertising and content (Handly 2019).

The three main components of location-based marketing are geofencing, geotargeting, and geoconquesting (Handly 2019).

- **Geofencing** allows the marketing company to assign boundaries for a geographic area in which customers of a certain type are expected to visit. Once the customer is within the geofenced area, as measured by their cellphone, they will receive consumer marketing messages that are keyed to the expected type of customer for the area. An example would be for a customer who enters a geofenced area for auto dealerships. While in the area, the customer will receive marketing messages related to the automotive industry—for example, messages for a car brand, car accessories, local travel, vehicular services, or car insurance.

- **Geotargeting** refers to marketing based on geodemographic characteristics of an area, a topic discussed earlier. For instance, consumers in a geographic area in the UK with the geodemographic profile shown in figure 4.6 could be geotargeted by advertising for moderately priced financial management software. Consumers in a zone that has the geodemographics of older, retired people who own their homes could be geotargeted for newspapers, hearing aids, walkers, or in-home health-care services and home repair services.

- **Geoconquesting** refers to efforts, using spatial technology, to pry away a competitor's customers. A business could target customers who can be identified geographically as visiting or nearby a competing firm's store, and then attract those customers to the business's location instead. For instance, a fast-food retailer puts a geofence around its nearby competitors, and once the customers enter the geofence, it sends them special offers for food at reduced pricing to try to snare them away.

Benefits of location-based marketing

A company benefits from location-based marketing by (1) the increased ability to market to customers in or near their stores, (2) the ability to decide on the best geographies for its products or services and to target market those geographies, and (3) the ability to market to competitors' customers with offers to draw them away to become a company's own customers. At the same time, customers may benefit by receiving mobile advertising for products that are likely to be of interest and by being alerted to shopping or service opportunities near their locations throughout the day.

Location-based, on-demand marketing is defined as the use of locational knowledge for marketing efforts. It can involve the internet, mobile devices, and social media, as well as enterprise analytics and desktop or server platforms accessing customer CRM and other data.

Location-based marketing has the following goals:

- Input and maintain accurate and up-to-date digital marketing information
- Map and analyze customer data at varied scales and geographical units
- Use location data from business transactions, mobile apps, social media, subscriptions, memberships, loyalty cards, text mining, and web mining to increase marketing success
- Pinpoint new markets, sales territories, and asset locations to stimulate marketing progress and identify what channels are used by which customers to buy through

The approach used in location-based marketing depends on the goal and customer type. Customers can be typified as local or distant, high or low in extent of internet and social media use, and primarily mobile user or not. In its smartphone app, for instance, Burger King targeted mobile users who were within 600 feet of a McDonald's (Kantor 2018a). A Burger King customer located inside this McDonald's radius and having a smartphone with location turned on was notified that they could order a Burger King Whopper for a penny and was directed to the nearest Burger King outlet. This marketing approach has been effective in diverting many customers away from the competitor.

Location-based social media marketing

Social media has become more and more location enriched, for purposes of marketing as well as for data sharing, customer tracking, and varied business analytics. Several types of social media, such as social networking, collaborative projects, blogs and microblogs, content communities, and virtual social worlds, include the use of location.

Locational social media has varied time lags. If it is time sensitive, it can rapidly inform spatially referenced decisions. An example is rapid check-in to a location using the location data platform Foursquare, in which the information is read synchronously by others. If it is not time sensitive, the message has a locational tag and is read asynchronously (Kaplan 2018). By contrast, some messages are neither time sensitive nor location sensitive—for example, reading an article on a mobile device.

Because social media is mostly accessed on smartphones, the smartphone's location becomes a source of information that can be tagged on social media, which allows others to identify the location of the smartphone and, by proxy, the sender. On the positive side, locational tagging can benefit the user with useful information about nearby friends, places, products, and services, or allow them to receive emergency notifications. It can also help in monitoring the locations of children or people with disabilities. With increasing use of smartphones worldwide, the privacy trade-offs are becoming more salient and have led to regulation of location privacy in European Union (EU) countries, and, by contrast, to control of content in China and other countries.

Social media on smartphones serves as a major source of location-based marketing information, such as the location-tagged commentary that Tripadvisor and other travel apps receive. Also, in some cases, smartphone users voluntarily act as location-based sensors on social media, email, and texting (Ricker 2018). An example is volunteered geographic information (VGI), a form of crowdsourcing in which a citizen acts as a sensor by identifying a phenomenon at a location and communicating it, adding that information as a map point. VGI has been used in emergencies, such as hurricanes and wildfires. In terms of the spatial business of marketing, VGI can be a means to build georeferenced datasets when technical means are too expensive or not yet smart enough. It has been used more in government than in business but has the potential to grow in terms of gathering specialized marketing data.

Case example: Heineken

Beginning in 2016, Heineken sought to market its beer brand to 21- to 26-year-old millennial men, who provided real-time suggestions of night spots that were trending in their cities. A person could engage with this service, @WhereNext, through Twitter, Foursquare, or Instagram. The digital platform was a response to Heineken's research showing that its young, male consumers felt they were missing out on nightlife by not being informed. The Twitter-based service sorted and ranked night spots by aggregated georeferenced tweets, Instagram photos, and Foursquare check-ins to provide prioritized suggestions (MMA Global 2019). The campaign expanded public perception of Heineken as being hip with social media and youth.

The service allowed followers to have a stream of night spots in 15 major cities worldwide. The data-gathering work was outsourced to social media users on a voluntary basis, and a complex algorithm was developed by the outsourcer, R/GA London, to support the sophisticated social media service. It was "able to discover new venues, pop-ups, and parties, which may never have been found via traditional sources" (MMA Global 2019). The highest-priority night spots were summarized in map form, as shown in figure 4.9. This application was successful as a campaign highlighting the Heineken brand as contemporary and appealing to millennials. It also went along with a broader "Cities of the World" campaign the company was using at the time.

PART
2
ACHIEVING BUSINESS AND SOCIETAL VALUE

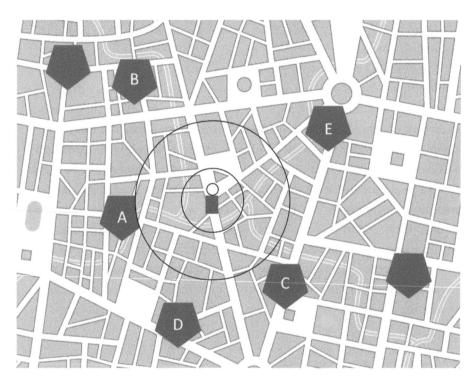

Figure 4.9. A diagram of a city's downtown that illustrates five prioritized @WhereNext night spot locations (*A*, the best, through *E*) relative to a social media user shown in the center, surrounded by distance perimeters. Locations of two more distant night spots are shown as outliers.

A different type of locational social media focuses on social networking—that is, using social media to arrange for meetings of family and friends or for business and marketing meetings. These meeting services include

Foursquare and Meetup LLC, which is now a part of AlleyCorp. Meetup is a website oriented to people arranging group meetings and events.

Foursquare has two offerings: Foursquare City Guide, which helps its customers search and find their way around cities, drawing on ideas from an online community of users, and Foursquare Swarm, an active community in which users can check in to a location and meet with friends or business associates, even maintaining a lifelong log of check-ins if desired.

Mining locational social media provides a remarkable picture of what topics people are interested in. This goes beyond what is possible with geodemographics, which reflects average sentiment of a group rather than an individual. In one example, researchers studied the tweets of London Underground passengers en route to their destinations. This study was possible because the Underground has its own Wi-Fi system, conveying tweets that are geotagged and time stamped (Lai, Cheng, and Lansley 2017; Kantor 2018c). As discussed later in this chapter, the privacy of an individual's personal information is now protected in Europe, although use of aggregated, anonymized information is usually allowable. The goals of the study were (1) to understand the dominant topics of tweets at locations throughout the Underground system, including hourly patterns throughout the day, and (2) to relate these topics to the outdoor advertising appearing near the station exits.

The study showed that popular topics change as an underground passenger moves on a line from the Underground in the center of London to its peripheral arms (figure 4.10). In the central stations, dominant topics are social and business, food and drink, and sports and tourist attractions. Topics in the intermediate areas include movies and shows, whereas at the end of the Underground network's long arms, stretching up to 20 km from the center, topics tend to be toward work and home. Dominant topics also relate to neighborhood sites—for example, the sports topic dominates in the two stations near Wembley Stadium, whereas topics about museums and galleries dominate in the station areas near the Science Museum, Victoria and Albert Museum, Natural History Museum, and the Tate.

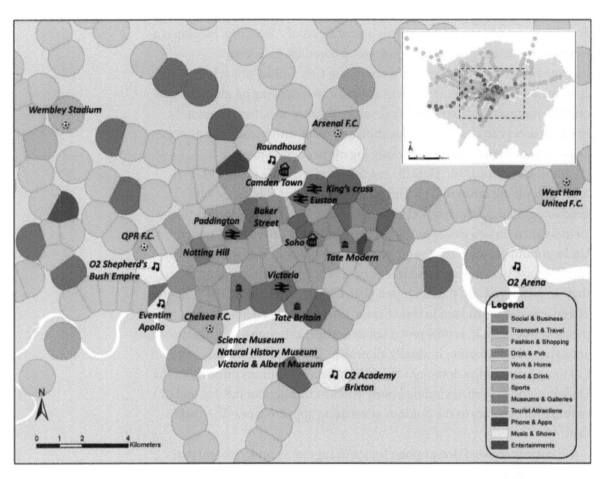

Figure 4.10. A map of downtown London's underground station locations portrays, for the city's areas of egress for subway passengers, the dominant social media topic of passengers. Source: Lai, Cheng, and Lansley 2017.

Hourly patterns of tweets for weekdays reveal a complex pattern of changes in tweet interest from hour to hour and between weekdays and weekends (Lai, Cheng, and Lansley 2017). This space-time social media monitoring approach differs from geodemographics in capturing the ideas of an individual and "could become a critical element in measuring and improving the effectiveness of future out-of-home advertising" (Kantor 2018c). Recent reports indicate that in the US, huge numbers of consumer daily pathways are being monitored and recorded not only by well-known tech giants such as Apple and Google but also by specialized providers that sell the information to other companies, activities that are legal if the consumer consents to their location being turned on (Valentino-DeVries et al. 2018). The ethical aspects of this type of data collection are debatable, as discussed in the next section on location privacy.

Privacy issues related to markets and customers

Although there is rapid growth in location-based marketing, ethical issues are also associated with its use. This section discusses the challenge and the need to maintain location privacy. Prominent among these concerns is customer privacy. The consumer included in a location-based marketing database might have little or no knowledge that their personal information is included and thus lose control of this data and the purposes for which it is used. A subindustry has developed in the US that sells location-based databases of potential customers. Although the subindustry enterprises mostly strive to maintain the personal privacy of the information, a related issue is the challenge of protecting the security of locationally private information. Hackers have broken into databases of private companies containing customer addresses and even into US federal government databases, stealing personal information that they can geolocate to get people's addresses.

In the US, there is no federal legislation to uniformly protect personal privacy information (PPI) with associated geolocation data (Boshell 2019). However, some states, including California, Massachusetts, New York, Hawaii, Maryland, and North Dakota, have put laws into effect that restrict access to PPI for extraction and selling (Green 2020). In California, a business is not permitted to sell a consumer's PPI without giving visible notice and allowing the consumer to opt out. Also, US federal law has specialized restrictions on PPI for certain sectors, such as health care (HIPAA regulations) and data of the US Federal Trade Commission (Boshell 2019).

Although the question of protecting personal information and locational data is being debated in US courtrooms and boardrooms, the European consumer already has greater protection. Under Europe's General Data Protection Regulation (GDPR), passed by the EU Parliament in April 2016 and effective in May 2018, personal information is protected unless the consumer opts in. Privacy incursions without prior assent are subject to large fines.

Social media tagging raises ethical questions because the user might not be aware that it has taken place (Angwin and Valentino-DeVries 2011). The exposure of an individual's location without their consent is a violation of personal privacy. And even if the user is aware of the tagging, social media and technology companies may still share and monetize the data (Valentino-DeVries 2018).

Other ethical concerns are highlighted in a study of the use of the Foursquare app for locating retail outlets in Kansas City, Missouri. The study found that only about a third of Kansas City's 2,668 accommodation and food outlets were available on the app, with only nine Foursquare outlets in Black census tracts compared with 584 in White census tracts (Fekete 2018). The deficits in access represent a digital divide and raise questions of corporate social responsibility.

Nonetheless, social media and GIS are converging, not only for a variety of personal uses but also for business marketing purposes, as social media becomes a larger advertising and marketing channel. Although dynamically changing, location as part of social media is here to stay as a potential source of locational value.

Closing case study: Oxxo

Oxxo is a convenience retail chain in Mexico, with thousands of stores all over the country and increasing market penetration aided by rapid growth, not only in Mexico but also in South America, in Chile, Colombia, and Peru. Oxxo's 18,000 stores and gas stations in Mexico and South America as of 2018 are part of a vast network of stores and gas stations. In 2018, Oxxo served 120 million customers in Mexico, and the company employed approximately 225,000 people in stores, gas stations, and distribution centers. An Oxxo store (figure 4.11) carries an average of 3,200 SKU scannable bar codes for items such as food, beverages, mobile phone cards, and cigarettes (FEMSA 2018). With the acquisition of fast-food restaurant chains such as Gorditas Doña Tota and the introduction of financial and payment services, Oxxo's store-level business has diversified over the years to cater to customer needs for convenient, efficient shopping experiences.

Figure 4.11. Typical storefront of an Oxxo convenience store in Mexico.

Understanding markets and customers

Starting in the early 2000s, Mexicans increasingly shopped at convenience marts on their way to and from work. This trend reflected a rise in two-income households as well as increasing traffic in densely populated urban areas. As consumers became more time-poor, they demanded convenience and flexibility in their shopping experiences and were drawn to bright aisles, longer hours, and varied product selections in convenience marts, compared with mom-and-pop corner stores or street concessions.

Location intelligence has been at the core of Oxxo's expansion and sustained growth. Spatial thinking at Oxxo stems from the need to continue to enhance its value proposition—provide proximity, accessibility, and convenience to its customers. With GIS, Oxxo's location intelligence team conducts demographic and psychographic analyses of its markets to better understand its customers and drive decisions on the type of store to open in its trade areas.

Location differences drive a differentiated retail approach

Store segmentation is an important strategic function of GIS-based location intelligence at Oxxo. For example, Oxxo uses GIS to map population densities, income, traffic patterns and directions, the rate of local car ownership, and shifts in demographics in the new markets (Elliott 2019). This helps executives decide whether small convenience stores for on-the-go purchases, larger outlets similar to grocery stores, or stores that combine both formats are appropriate for a market. Thus, based on location differences between markets, Oxxo executives decide the type of store appropriate for a market.

Location analytics provides Oxxo's real estate and expansion team with location intelligence on sites previously deemed unprofitable—for example, niche stores in smaller spaces at airports, train stations, and other such locations (Sandino, Cavazos, and Lobb 2017). As GIS drives store segmentation depending on market conditions and differences, product placement in stores is optimized and appropriate SKUs are introduced, depending on local consumer preferences, in yet another manifestation of location differences and location context.

In addition to store segmentation and product customization, location differences have informed Oxxo's differentiated retail approach for its store locations. Location strategists at Oxxo realized that, as much as on-the-go customers visit Oxxo's stores to take advantage of one-stop convenience—for example, to purchase a quick drink, grab a prepared meal, or buy a household product—they would value additional services. Accordingly, Oxxo introduced services such as diverse banking by partnering with 10 banking institutions, cash remittances, in-store payment of phone and electric bills, prepaid gift cards for streaming online services, and replenishment of calling cards. By 2016, 70% of daily cash at Oxxo stores came from financial and payment services, with the rest from sales of merchandise (FEMSA 2018). Oxxo has also provided a solution to Mexican consumers who face significant barriers to online shopping by entering a "click and collect" partnership with Amazon that allows customers to securely pick up their Amazon packages at their local Oxxo store (FEMSA 2018).

Location intelligence drives business expansion

The first Oxxo store opened in Monterrey, Mexico, in 1978. By the year 2000, the company had almost 1,500 stores in Mexico, which ballooned to 10,600 stores in 2012, and finally 18,000 stores in Mexico, Peru, Chile, and Colombia by 2018, when it became Mexico's largest retailer. On average, a new Oxxo store opens every six hours, and the company plans to responsibly expand its retail footprint by opening approximately 1,300 new stores per year, with a goal of 30,000 stores by 2025.

Each Oxxo store is part of a geographic and strategic unit called a plaza. In 2020, there were 52 such plazas, each of which has an expansion team of five to six people, led by an expansion manager, responsible for the performance of stores in its trade area. The expansion manager collaborates with hundreds of Oxxo workers on-site because field research is an important component of Oxxo's expansion strategy. On-site workers provide expansion managers valuable guidance about local needs and business conditions. As part of its workforce, Oxxo employs brokers, who collect information on potential sites for stores using mobile data collection apps. This authoritative data is uploaded to form layers in Oxxo's GIS and is ultimately used at the operational level at Oxxo's plazas.

Business expansion at Oxxo is informed by location intelligence, particularly spatial statistical analysis. Oxxo's GIS includes spatial layers of locational data on various demographic and socioeconomic attributes and complementary or competing businesses such as grocery stores. Other layers include hospitals, schools, malls, and other generators of business activity (location linkages) that are part of the trade area (usually 300 meters from an existing or planned store location). Taken together, these layers provide location context and the foundation for forecasting models of sales potential of an existing trade area (figure 4.12), generating sales forecasts, comparing sales potential of potential market opportunities, and assessing the risk of cannibalization. Ultimately, using location analytics, executives at Oxxo can make faster decisions about store openings in new markets.

Location intelligence at Oxxo: The future

Oxxo's sustained growth has been marked by an intimate understanding of the Mexican convenience retail landscape and customers' wants and needs. From the beginning, proximity, accessibility, and customer service have been hallmarks of Oxxo's value proposition. To remain flexible and adapt to local customer needs, Oxxo's department of expansion and infrastructure has prioritized store segmentation, product customization, and an expansion strategy backed by authoritative data and location analytics. Senior leaders of Oxxo are strategic consumers of GIS, driving Oxxo's continued expansion within Mexico as well as growth in Latin America. Oxxo aspires to diffuse GIS adoption and usage more broadly across the enterprise in departments such as supply chain for integrated management of a vast network of suppliers. Although GIS adoption and use at Oxxo is not yet enterprise-wide, Oxxo is positioning GIS to support management of digital transformation and enhance its value proposition to customers as consumer preferences continue to evolve in response to the COVID-19 pandemic and its aftermath.

PART
2
ACHIEVING BUSINESS AND SOCIETAL VALUE

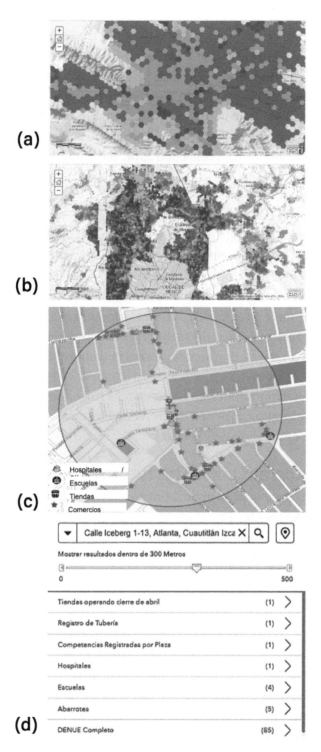

Figure 4.12. A mixture of images portrays Oxxo's location analytics, such as (a) maps of store segmentation, (b) sales potential, (c) a map of data collected by on-site workers, and (d) the location of other generators of business activity, such as hospitals, schools, and malls. Source: Oxxo; Esri 2019c.

CHAPTER 5
Operating the enterprise

Introduction

Operations is an integral part of an organization's value chain, responsible for producing goods or delivering services. The creation of goods or the delivery of services requires support and inputs—for example, labor, capital, and information—from other organizational functions. The inputs are transformed to generate outputs—the product or the service itself. During the transformation process, value is added by different operational activities, such as product and service design, process selection, selection and management of technology, design of work systems, location planning, and facilities design, to name a few.

The need to improve business operations stems from competitive pressures to offer an expanding array of new products and services to customers, shorter product development life cycles, increased demand for customization, increasing customer reliance on e-commerce, and improving the resiliency and transparency of supply chains that are prone to risks posed by climate crises, economic uncertainties, or unsustainable and sometimes unethical business practices.

Considering the centrality of the operations function in the organizational value chain and its interdependence with supply chain management, this chapter provides an in-depth look at the role of location intelligence to inform decision-making relative to operating the enterprise, beginning with operational considerations and then broadening to supply chain considerations.

The five main sections of this chapter explore the role of location intelligence to do the following:
- Provide real-time situational awareness
- Monitor operations KPIs
- Design efficient distribution systems
- Optimize facilities layouts
- Design resilient and transparent supply chains and logistics systems

Real-time situational awareness

Location intelligence is critical for situational awareness—that is, "the perception of the elements in the environment within a volume of time and space, the comprehension of their meaning, and a projection of their status in the near future" (Endsley 1988, 97). In the context of business operations, it is essential to know what is happening when and where. With distributed networks of assets, facilities, and infrastructure, breakdowns can happen anywhere, any time, and in many economic sectors, most of the workforce may be mobile. Organizations in sectors such as transportation, logistics, utilities, and telecommunications need to have real-time knowledge of the locations, condition, risks, and performance of their assets to improve decision-making, particularly in emergencies. Real-time tracking and monitoring of asset location and condition can also improve productivity, prevent breakdowns, ensure safety, and reduce costs.

GIS-powered spatial platforms provide a holistic visual overview of the performance of a system—people, sensors, devices, and other internal assets—which may be affected by external factors such as weather, emergencies, or network and technology disruptions. Using dynamic maps, apps, and dashboards, firms can track movements and changes within a system in real time and ensure that both field personnel and office staff use the same authoritative data. This can help an organization boost data accuracy, reduce errors, adopt automated workflows, and improve efficiency.

Location intelligence can also provide guidance for the dynamic navigation of field assets (people and vehicles), reducing travel time and ensuring that service time windows are honored. In breakdowns or emergencies, location intelligence can reroute drivers and vehicles, ensure safety, and maintain timeliness of operations. Beyond navigation, location intelligence can help trigger predictive maintenance or interventions, such as reducing the temperature of mobile trucks transporting perishable goods or medical supplies.

Technologies such as AR and IoT-based sensors and devices complement location intelligence in providing real-time situational awareness. Using IoT-based sensors mounted on infrastructure and assets, above and below ground, can help generate additional streaming data on KPIs of assets. All this data can be managed, organized, and geoenriched within a GIS for visualization and analysis to provide situational awareness in real time (Radke, Johnson, and Baranyi 2013).

Case example: Sulphur Springs Valley Electric Cooperative

Sulphur Springs Valley Electric Cooperative (SSVEC) is a distribution cooperative providing consumers with electricity, which is measured by more than 52,000 meters over 4,100 miles of energized line in southeastern Arizona. The cooperative's service territory covers parts of Cochise, Graham, Santa Cruz, and Pima Counties. Apart from cities such as Tucson and Sierra Vista, which is a medium-size city with urban and exurban areas, SSVEC's service areas are largely rural and include meters that serve agricultural areas. As a medium-size not-for-profit entity with 175 employees, SSVEC's annual revenues, generated predominantly through sales of electricity, have grown steadily at 2% to 3% per year in recent years. SSVEC's highest annual load in a year is a moderate 250 instantaneous megawatts.

Agricultural meters account for 50% of SSVEC's electricity sales, and another 45% is residential. The balance is commercial, industrial, other-use categories. SSVEC's service area in southern Arizona's high desert (about a mile above sea level) has high soil quality, making the region attractive for agriculture, but it also needs a lot of water. In these agricultural areas, the primary use of electricity is to power irrigation equipment.

In the 1990s, engineers and technicians relied on paper maps to guide field operations. For almost a decade, service technicians used map printouts to navigate to customer locations and find poles, transformers, and meters for routing and emergency maintenance and repairs. The first major GIS initiative in 2003 centered on creating an exhaustive inventory database of field assets to reduce response times during power outages. This was especially critical for field crews deployed to conduct repairs in the middle of the night when it is hard to locate power lines located 1,000 feet off a dirt road in a mountainous area. In 2008, SSVEC's crews started using tablet computers and subsequently mobile devices to access digitized maps when conducting field maintenance and repair.

At present, SSVEC's enterprise GIS equipment, at any given time, has approximately 1,000 open work orders that reflect some change to the asset infrastructure and power systems. Some of these involve installing IoT-enabled sensors on critical assets that stream geotagged systems performance data in real time. The company's operations managers monitor this "health data" of company assets in real time at SSVEC's command center using the Line Patrol Dashboard (figure 5.1). In other cases, manual intervention is needed to monitor the health of assets such as wooden power poles. Once put in the ground, wooden poles must be monitored on a cyclical basis for rotting. This work is outsourced to a third-party contractor, which inspects the locations of SSVEC's power poles.

The dashboard in figure 5.1 is used by the company to plan overhead pole inspections. It shows locations of more than 4,000 poles in a part of SSVEC's service area by pole type, along with the outcomes of inspections (percent passed versus percent failed) conducted over the past month and year. This provides the company a simple comparison. If there is an uptick in failed inspections for a given month compared with the past year, underlying causes can be examined along with their location characteristics (for example, if the poles failing inspection are predominantly in one part of the transmission network). The number of poles that require inspection are shown along with their type (light poles, primary, and secondary). Depending on pole type and location, SSVEC can schedule inspections and assign inspectors with the right skills to the job.

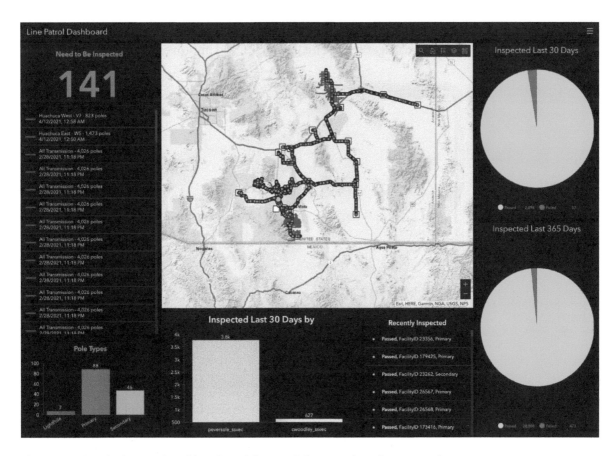

Figure 5.1. SSVEC's Line Patrol Dashboard, providing a real-time map view of outcomes of inspections of critical transmission infrastructure along with facilities awaiting inspection.
Courtesy of SSVEC.

Based on inspections, SSVEC updates the enterprise GIS layer of assets to reflect whether a pole is serviceable or needs to be replaced. If replacement is needed, the enterprise GIS system automatically produces a work order and notifies the engineering team. Outfitted with mobile devices, repair crews and service technicians see repair orders and inspection status, conduct repairs, and update work orders from their respective field locations. Figure 5.2 shows SSVEC's mobile iOS app for field inspections. Back at the company command center, supervisors see the updated status of equipment and work orders in real time and adjust repairs and technician schedules as needed. Among other benefits, this tool helps SSVEC reduce overtime and optimize its deployment of service crews. Relying on spatial intelligence that originates in the field, decision-makers in various units use SSVEC's enterprise GIS to seamlessly automate the predictive maintenance, repair, and customer service decision-making processes. This work reduces system failures, manages service inefficiencies, and improves customer satisfaction.

Figure 5.2. SSVEC's mobile iOS app for field inspections, showing inspection status of a pole along with the option of reporting a failed facility. Source: SSVEC.

Location intelligence for life cycle repairs of electric poles has an important secondary benefit for SSVEC. Because its infrastructure has demonstrable reliability, telecom companies partner with SSVEC and enter joint-use attachment agreements to attach their telecom assets and equipment to SSVEC's poles. These attachment locations are also monitored by SSVEC using its enterprise GIS, which allows additional revenue capture to help offset the cost of maintaining the pole infrastructure.

The next planned phase of location analytics innovation at SSVEC is real-time location-based intelligence from the field using a distributed network of IoT-enabled sensors. Outage management is an innovation that allows SSVEC to take phone calls and out-of-power meter messages as inputs to a predictive analysis of where the outage is happening. An improvement over sporadic phone calls from customers, outage management systems use GIS-maintained network graphs to identify locations where crews are needed. Dispatchers manage the life cycle of an outage from identification, verification, and repair to restoration. When the outage is verified and later restored, SMS, or text, messages are automatically sent to affected customers to communicate the incident status and provide better customer service.

Besides the utilities sector, similar needs arise in other asset-intensive industries such as telecommunications, oil and gas, and transportation and logistics. However, the business need for dynamic monitoring of system performance transcends industry verticals. GIS coupled with other technologies and data such as IoT-based sensors, drones, AR, mixed reality, RFID, and machine learning can provide sophisticated real-time geotagged data and locational insights of considerable business value for operational and tactical decision-making in close to real time.

Monitoring operations KPIs using dashboards

Monitoring the fluctuations of operations KPIs, often in real time, is critical for business continuity. Observing and analyzing the spatial variation of KPIs, such as raw materials availability, supply capacities, demand requirements, inventory levels, stockouts (when an item is out of stock), manufacturing productivity, system efficiency, and operations startup and shutdown times, are central to efficient business operations and supply chains. Diagnosing spatial patterns of customer service needs, including service outages, equipment breakdowns, customer service complaints, quality issues, and on-time deliveries, improves customer satisfaction and consequently customer retention.

Operations managers face the challenge of continually monitoring system performance. In a manufacturing setting, this could entail monitoring operational KPIs such as the following:

- **Productivity and efficiency**—multifactor productivity, process efficiency, capacity utilization, and scrap rates
- **Quality control**—machine downtimes, mean time between maintenance, startup and shutdown times, and breakdowns
- **Material requirements planning (MRP) and inventory management**—supply capacities, demand requirements, inventory levels, and stockouts on a plant-by-plant basis

In a service scenario, some generic yet important KPIs closely tied to operations include the following:

- **Business performance**—numbers and types of work orders, on-time repairs and resolution rates, incomplete work orders and their reasons, extent of delays, and on-time arrivals and deliveries
- **Sales performance**—lead conversion rates; revenue by product, channel, and market; and sales versus targets

PART 2 ACHIEVING BUSINESS AND SOCIETAL VALUE

- **Customer service**—customer loyalty, customer churn, customer complaints, and net promoter score, among others

Like manufacturing KPIs, service KPIs need to be tracked on a location-by-location basis to analyze spatial patterns and trends. To track KPIs and monitor and report performance, businesses are increasingly relying on dashboards. With the rapid adoption of data science in both the public and private sectors, dashboards have become ubiquitous and are ranked as the highest-rated type of business intelligence technology use (Dresner 2019). Increasingly, dashboards incorporate a location component to examine geographic patterns, variations, and trends over space and time.

The previous section included a description of SSVEC's Line Patrol Dashboard. It enables the electric utility to monitor the performance of critical assets and perform predictive maintenance. A node utilization dashboard (figure 5.3) for an internet service provider (ISP) in the greater Tampa, Florida, area has a chart of real-time performance of nodes—that is, devices actively connected to its wireless network. Maps display the provider's market area, including Tampa's international airport, railroad facilities, a US Air Force base, the University of South Florida, and a variety of businesses, tourist hot spots, and residential communities. The maps, charts, and graphs on the dashboard provide operational insights into historical average bandwidth capacity over the previous 12 weeks.

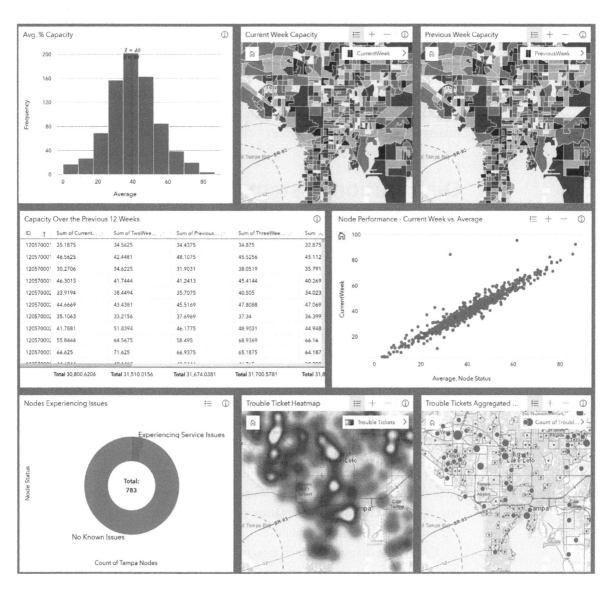

Figure 5.3. Operations dashboard of a broadband service provider showing average bandwidth and average capacity utilization in Tampa, Florida. Source: Esri 2022.

With approximately 800 nodes servicing this major metro market, operations managers need to closely monitor average bandwidth capacity, compare it with demand, and quickly pinpoint any service nodes experiencing issues that might disrupt service. Maps in the top layer of the dashboard provide detailed locational insights on capacity utilization at various units of geographic resolution. By clicking any red dot in the node performance scatterplot, an operations analyst can pinpoint a node experiencing service issues and connect it to a trouble ticket on the bottom set of maps, shown in figure 5.3, so that field crews can be deployed. Also, by monitoring geographic fluctuations in capacity utilization—a key operational planning KPI—managers can decide to split nodes into subnodes for areas experiencing spikes in demand and predict trouble hot spots ahead of time. Among other things, monitoring this KPI can affect resource allocation planning, prevent outages, and ultimately improve customer service.

Distribution system design

The design of an efficient distribution system comprising a network of facilities is a strategic challenge for many businesses. An efficient distribution system allows businesses to meet the needs of their customers—for example, deliver products and services in an e-commerce setting within tight delivery time windows, strategically maintain inventory levels, and manage service-level agreements. An efficient system will also reduce impact to the environment, in transportation and logistics settings. Integral to the design of an efficient distribution system is the strategic location of facilities that are going to serve customers and allocating customers to those facilities.

Facilities location

A critical aspect of designing an efficient distribution system is to make optimal facilities location decisions—for example, locating a manufacturing plant and a set of stores for a retail business to accomplish a desired objective. Such objectives may include maximizing market share, maximizing demand coverage, minimizing transportation or shipping costs, and in some cases, minimizing the number of facilities.

Consider a manufacturer that wants to build a set of warehouses to supply or stock stores in a target market so that distribution costs are minimized. Two sets of decisions are involved: (1) where to locate the warehouses and (2) how to allocate demand originating from stores to the warehouses. This combination of location and allocation arises frequently in supply chain contexts and has been formulated as an optimization problem, traditionally known as the location-allocation problem (Cooper 1963). The general planning problem may be stated as follows:

Locate multiple facilities in a service area and allocate the demand originating from the area to the facilities so that the system service is as efficient as possible (Church and Murray 2009).

In a typical location-allocation scenario, some candidate locations are preselected and prespecified. For example, when designing a distribution system as a location-allocation problem, a set of location-specific criteria such as local rent and taxes, workforce availability, labor costs, and distance from highway can help identify candidate locations from which the optimal ones can be selected based on demand efficiencies.

Figures 5.4 and 5.5 illustrate the application of location-allocation modeling to determine new store locations of a retailer with one existing store in the San Francisco market. In the risk-averse scenario, with business expansion budget restrictions in mind, the retailer wants to open only three additional stores with travel times from 208 demand locations that are not to exceed five minutes.

Because of these constraints, close to half the demand points (115 out of 208) are allocated to the three best locations, as shown in figure 5.4, achieving a maximum market share of 33% as determined by the popular spatial interaction model known as the Huff model (1964). The three new store locations are dispersed, and only one is close to the competitor's locations, as shown in figure 5.4.

Because of the retailer's rather low market share, the company further examines how many stores might be required to achieve market coverage of at least 70%. As shown in figure 5.5, the retailer must open nine additional stores in addition to its existing store to cover at least 70% of the demand. This analysis provides guidance to the retailer's senior leadership, which can now prioritize appropriate parts of the market and enable the retailer's real estate team to focus on additional market context factors such as possible cotenants.

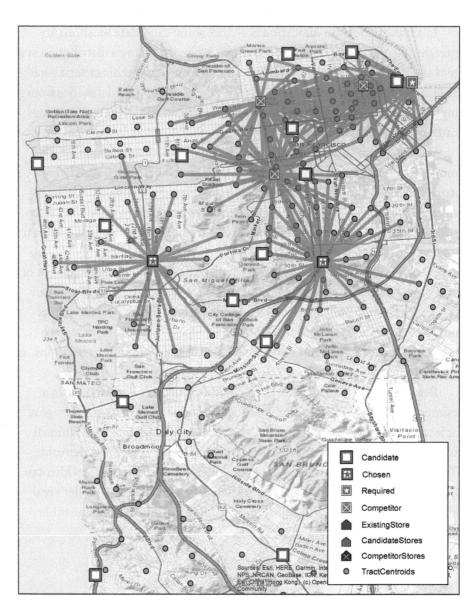

Figure 5.4. Location-allocation model for retail site selection with travel time (not to exceed five minutes) and facility (three additional stores) constraints for San Francisco, California.

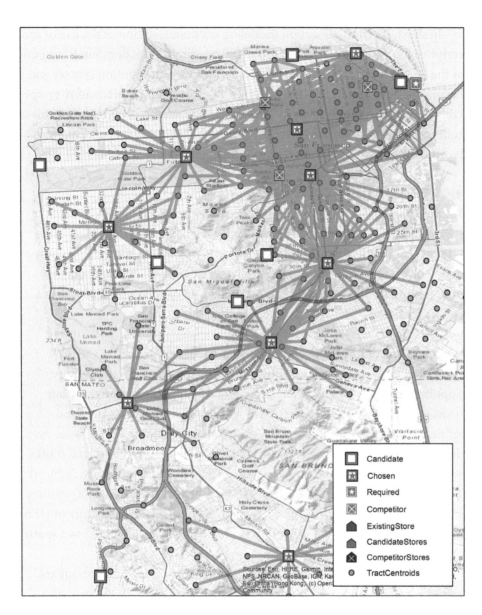

Figure 5.5. Location-allocation model for retail site selection with travel time and facility constraints to cover at least 70% of the demand in San Francisco.

In short, location-allocation modeling is a manifestation of the use of prescriptive location analytics for supply chain optimization, demonstrated here at the demand end of the supply chain. From siting distribution centers and basing the transportation plans of goods on more sophisticated industry-specific modeling of supply chains (Kazemi and Szmerekovsky 2016), optimization models provide prescriptive decision-making guidance and valuable location intelligence to achieve supply chain efficiency.

Routing optimization

Leading package delivery and logistics service providers such as United Parcel Service (UPS) and FedEx have achieved routing optimization using GIS as a competitive advantage for many years. With the sustained growth of e-commerce and explosion of delivery services (meal delivery, grocery delivery, and so forth), there is renewed focus on routing optimization in a variety of sectors.

Routing of delivery vehicles is a natively spatial problem, and routing optimization is at the heart of designing efficient supply chains. ORION (On-Road Integrated Optimization and Navigation), a UPS technology, popularized the notion that "left isn't right," minimizing unnecessary left turns on drivers' routes (Horner 2016). The system was developed and refined over the years to guide UPS drivers making dozens of deliveries over dense, complex traffic networks. In 2016, 55,000 ORION-optimized routes were documented to have saved 10 million gallons of fuel annually, reduced 100,000 metric tons in CO_2 emissions, and saved an estimated $300 million to $400 million in cost avoidance (Horner 2016). The full case study of UPS in chapter 9 sheds light on ORION's strategic role in shaping UPS as a spatial business leader.

Another example is Instacart, whose green-shirted "personal shoppers" are now instantly recognizable at neighborhood grocery stores, especially in the aftermath of the COVID-19 pandemic. As explained in chapter 4, Instacart competes with FreshDirect, Amazon Fresh, Peapod, and services run by big grocery chains to deliver groceries to an ever-broadening base of customers. Instacart deploys sophisticated routing optimization models (Stanley 2017) to route its personal shoppers and streamline their deliveries. For personal shoppers who make multiple trips to the neighborhood grocery store to deliver multiple sequential orders to customers within tight time windows, routing optimization algorithms factor in multiple sequential trips made by the shoppers to deliver groceries to customers using personal vehicles with limited capacity (in some cases, bicycles) within narrowly defined time windows prespecified by customers.

Over the past several decades, tremendous advances have taken place in routing optimization. Many of these advances have been catalyzed by blending location analytics and optimization modeling. Yet, in real-life operations, the quality of a route—often defined by its theoretical length, duration, and cost—can be improved by drivers' tacit knowledge of the complex operational environments in which they serve customers daily (MIT 2021). Still, location analytics can play a central role in improving last-mile routing in such environments, leading to the design of safer, more efficient, and environmentally sustainable deliveries and overall route planning.

Facilities layout

Designing facility layouts is essentially a spatial exercise. Facilities layout involves many of the same issues of proximity, distance, separation, layering, and organizing that are fundamental in GIS-based location analytics. For single facilities, layout may include spatial problems such as placing aisles within a warehouse, situating job shops in a manufacturing plant, organizing cubicles in an office, locating self-service kiosks within a restaurant, or colocating products on shelves in a retail store. In manufacturing, efficient layouts can improve the efficiency and productivity of production lines or assembly lines, reducing costs.

For multifacility networks, such as networks of stores, warehouses, and distribution centers, the layout challenges are more complex. But descriptive mapping of multifacility networks, along with spatial optimization models based on operations research, can produce optimal layouts in retail, transportation, and logistics, as well as in industries such as utilities and telecommunications. For example, in transportation and logistics, location analytics can help design efficient networks that consolidate the number of dispatch facilities and depots, avoid overlapping service territories, and reduce the time spent routing and miles per stop—with the added benefit of narrowing delivery time windows and improving on-time performance. This, in turn, helps minimize costs, enhance customer service, and reduce emissions.

Indoor GIS for facilities layout design and management

Industry forecasts indicate significant growth in the indoor location analytics segment in the next several years. Whether for a company campus with multiple connected buildings, a sprawling multifloor convention center or mall, or a large facility such as an airport, indoor GIS holds great promise.

With indoor GIS, companies can track the movement of people, goods, and assets, improve productivity and throughput of the space, enhance situational awareness in real time, and provide navigation and routing services, saving time, effort, and money. At the macro level, indoor GIS can provide location-based intelligence for building layout planning and space optimization. In large public transit facilities such as airports and in health-care facilities such as hospitals, multipurpose spatial data is used for asset management, including underground utilities, architectural planning, and space optimization, and for tracking the movements of goods and people. At transportation hubs such as airports or rail and bus terminals, facility managers can ensure smoother passenger flow and a stress-reduced travel experience by optimizing the facility layout, consisting of parking, check-in, security, duty-free shopping, and ultimately departure/arrival. Indoor GIS is also critical for emergency managers at airports, convention centers, and hospitals to plan and execute emergency procedures that can track both employee and customer locations in real time to maximize safety and minimize response time in a large-scale emergency.

Case example: Los Angeles International Airport

Consider Los Angeles International Airport (LAX), where geospatial data and indoor GIS are key to understanding and visualizing changes to the built environment (such as passenger terminals), as well as for infrastructure management so that the maintenance and renovation of critical infrastructure, such as runways, can be performed efficiently. At LAX, Indoor Mobile Mapping Systems (IMMS) uses lidar processes together with 360° imagery (shown in figure 5.6) to capture large, complex, and dynamic interior spaces as digital, interactive visual representations of data (LAWA 2019). IMMS facilitates the management of space leased by airlines, freight companies, and concessionaires and ultimately informs the management of tenant lease and rental agreements and related pricing (Stenmark 2016). In addition to facilities management and serving as a wayfinding platform, indoor maps in LAX's IMMS use business rules, localization, and IoT to create a smart airport that enables users to visualize spatial data and create real-time indoor location intelligence.

Figure 5.6. x-Spatial's guidelines to indoor lidar scanning in support of a digital twin shows 360-degree indoor imagery of ghost figures of passengers. Source: ©2019 by x-Spatial.

At LAX, indoor GIS provides up-to-date building floor maps and planning maps, facilitates asset management, and forms the basis of a variety of surveys, including for emergency evacuation and planning, signage, design, "as-builts," and equipment clearance. Indoor GIS also facilitates line-of-sight analysis, which is critical for ensuring security within terminals and other important airport buildings and facilities (LAWA 2019). LAX's indoor GIS can be used to identify the locations of security breaches, hazmat incidents, equipment breakdowns, and maintenance issues and to deploy the nearest personnel. Using location intelligence derived from indoor GIS applications, command centers can be set up, nearby assets such as surveillance cameras can be queried, nonoperating assets can be taken offline, and staff, tenants, and occupants can be evacuated. In short, indoor GIS can be effective for designing incident management strategies and implementing them in real time. LAX's indoor GIS is a hub of authoritative, accurate, and up-to-date data that is used by airport staff as well as first responders and emergency managers to develop familiarity with the buildings and plan and execute emergency procedures.

Combining indoor mapping with existing geospatial data and workflows provides a wealth of vital information to several stakeholders: environmental, operations, security, safety, commercial, engineering, facility management, and human resource management (HRM), as well as external organizations such as police and fire departments. This facilitates coordination, planning, and airport project management and accelerates the speed of decision-making. The value of LAX's indoor GIS is multiplied when the geospatial data collected is mapped, shared, and mined, and the location intelligence thus produced is consumed beyond its initial intended purpose by multiple stakeholders for a wide range of benefits (LAWA 2019).

Overall, indoor GIS adoption for space optimization and facilities layout planning and design is burgeoning in the private sector. Emerging trends such as coworking and the resulting coworking spaces will catalyze further innovation and investment in indoor GIS. In the aftermath of the COVID-19 pandemic, indoor GIS is well positioned to provide guidance in reconfiguring the layouts of workspaces, plants, warehouses, and congregate facilities to ensure workers' health and safety. Indoor mapping to reconfigure facilities for safe use and advanced spatial analysis to identify congregation hot spots, proximity, distancing, and separation are all critical to business continuity in the post-COVID era (Chiappinelli 2020).

Supply chain management and logistics

At the systems level, location intelligence is required for managing and designing robust and resilient supply chain and logistics networks. Modern supply chains are critical for business continuity. Consider this extreme example from March 2011, when a magnitude 9.0 earthquake hit Japan, followed by a tsunami. As the disaster unfolded, a nuclear facility in Japan was compromised, resulting in severe radiation leakage. In the days that followed, an international consulting firm forecast that, because of the disaster, the cumulative production of Japanese automakers would drop by 2.2 million units, compared with 2010, when annual production of Japanese-made passenger cars totaled 8.3 million. Postdisaster, Toyota suspended production in 12 of its assembly plants and estimated a loss of around 140,000 vehicles. Because of *keiretsu*—that is, interlocked supply chains—disruption in parts supplied by tier 2 and tier 3 suppliers affected tier 1 suppliers, in turn disrupting the entire supply chain.

As parts shortages hit and shipping parts from Japan came to a complete halt, production stopped in Toyota's US assembly plants. Honda also had to stop its operations as more than 20% of its tier 1 suppliers were affected by the earthquake. Nissan was the hardest hit and lost 1,300 Infiniti and 1,000 Nissan cars to the tsunami, shutting down operations in five plants for several weeks (Aggarwal and Srivastava 2016). Each day of lost production was reported to cost Nissan $25 million.

In another, more recent example, Wendy's restaurants all over the US experienced beef shortages as employees at congregate facilities such as meat-processing plants contracted and then spread the COVID-19 virus, resulting in communal outbreaks. The price of beef increased significantly, and a federal executive order invoking the Defense Production Act to classify meat plants as essential infrastructure became the subject of robust public discourse (Yaffe-Bellany and Corkery 2020).

Whether for cars or burgers, the objective of a supply chain is to be efficient and cost-effective across the entire network. Hence, supply chain management requires a systems approach. Also, because a supply chain integrates suppliers, manufacturers, warehouses, distribution centers, and stores as part of a network, network planning is essential. Network planning is the process by which a firm structures, optimizes, and manages its supply chain to do the following:

- Find the right balance among inventory, transportation, and manufacturing costs
- Match supply and demand under uncertainty by positioning and managing inventory effectively
- Use resources effectively in uncertain, dynamic environments (Simchi-Levi, Kaminsky, and Simchi-Levi 2004)

Supply chain network planning involves the following:

- Network design—decide the number, optimal locations, and optimal sizes of plants, warehouses, and distribution centers
- Inventory positioning and management—identify stocking points, optimal stocking levels, and facilities to stock
- Resource allocation—determine when and how much to produce, procure, or purchase and where and when to store inventory (Simchi-Levi, Kaminsky, and Simchi-Levi 2004)

Consequently, managing a supply chain involves making site location decisions—a natively spatial problem that has strategic, tactical, and operational implications. Alongside site location are inventory management and resource allocation issues. All three have strong spatial connections to business operations.

Spatial technologies for supply chain management

Managing a supply chain effectively starts with combining internal organizational data with external data from varied sources. Internal enterprise data may originate from CRMs and enterprise resource planning (ERP) systems, bills of materials, business forecasts, schedules, and project management systems. External data may be sourced from various governmental agencies, third parties, business partners, and industry organizations, as well as digital sources such as social media. Use cases may originate in different areas of the enterprise according to business needs such as inventory management, forecasting demand, and generating just-in-time (JIT) production plans. Other needs may include MRP (operational), territory optimization, route planning, warehouse layout and facilities design (tactical), outsourcing, and site selection (strategic).

As these disparate data streams reside in individual silos, their business use needs, whether upstream- or downstream-facing, are equally siloed. However, as an interface, a GIS acts as an integrative platform between the siloed data streams and business use cases, as shown in figure 5.7. GIS enables users across the enterprise with different business needs to collaborate, drawing on descriptive visualization of georeferenced datasets, which provides the foundation for predictions, decisions, and informed actions.

Figure 5.7. GIS as an interface between data silos and supply chain use cases (adapted from Chainlink Research). Source: Esri 2018b.

Digitizing and geomapping a supply chain as part of organizational digital transformation can have several benefits. For a global business, it can provide a reliable operating picture of how the supply network chain performs and where it might be failing. In addition, a digital, fully mapped supply chain can deliver valuable situational awareness powered by real-time alerts and notifications, asset tracking, and monitoring. It can also identify geographic stress points that may be prone to risks. This can help accelerate a company's response time during the normal course of business and enable it to plan, prepare, and respond in an emergency.

Closing case study: Cisco

Consider the case of global networking giant Cisco, which provides networking hardware, software, and telecommunications equipment, among many other high-technology services and products to its customers. A critical issue for Cisco's customers is network downtime, which may be caused by the failure of a hardware product, a part, or related equipment. When such breakdowns occur and data transmissions are disrupted, prompt restoration of networking connectivity for customers is critical. However, the networking equipment or part may not be available in the immediate proximity of a customer. Even if a replacement part was available at a parts supplier within the firm's territory, logistical issues could slow down the actual transportation of the part from the supplier to Cisco's customer. In some cases in which specialized training is needed, such as for hot swapping (replacement or addition of parts or components without shutting down or rebooting a system), another issue may be the lack of availability of a nearby field engineer (FE).

Next, Cisco's global supply chain network is incredibly vast and complex. At any given time, Cisco services networking and telecom at roughly 20 million or more customer sites in 138 countries. When breakdowns happen at any of these sites, parts are sourced from 1,200 warehouses globally, and a delivery driver is assigned to ship the part from the depot to the customer. In addition, out of approximately 3,000 FEs, an individual with the right skills who is within a reasonable service time needs to be deployed.

Making matters more complex, the warehouses are not owned by Cisco but by third parties. Similarly, delivery drivers and FEs are part of Cisco's vast network of partners, adding another layer of complexity to Cisco's operations.

To ensure that customer networks are operational as soon as possible when breakdowns occur, Cisco has deployed location analytics to produce two- and four-hour service-level agreements with its customers, depending on their locations and proximity to parts warehouses and FEs. To do this, Cisco uses GIS to map its entire supply chain, producing descriptive visualizations of facilities and two- and four-hour drive-time polygons (based on local traffic and weather conditions) indicating proximity of customers to parts and FEs. Plotting these locations and intersecting them with drive-time buffers allows Cisco to color-code its customer sites based on whether they are in two- or four-hour service windows for a given warehouse, depending on the type of part ordered.

The process of assigning customer sites to warehouses is automated. As soon as a part is requisitioned, the automated assignment system recommends the appropriate service-level agreement (two versus four hour) to a customer and initiates the delivery of a part from the warehouse to the customer site. In addition, for each warehouse location, the automated system produces real-time reports of parts inventory, oversubscribed parts that run the risk of becoming out of stock, and heavyweight parts that may require special shipment. Armed with this intelligence, Cisco's partners can replenish inventories at specific locations or move parts to other warehouses based on local needs. This location-based holistic approach minimizes the risk of stockouts system-wide. Using location analytics, Cisco also assigns the correct FE to a customer site, minimizing the lead time between the arrival of an FE and a replacement part and providing notifications to a customer when an FE is en route.

This use case primarily highlights the principles of location proximity (between warehouses and FEs and client sites) and location differences (differences in inventory portfolio and quantities at warehouses). It also showcases both the descriptive and prescriptive location analytics steps of the spatial analysis hierarchy.

Using location analytics, Cisco can solve its customers' most pressing problem: timely and accurate resolution of networking issues that disrupt business operations, causing losses, lost revenues, and so forth. Guided by spatial modeling, the company sells the right service contract to each customer and services them in the quickest time possible by deploying appropriate assets and resources. This enhances the customer's postpurchase experience.

In summary, Cisco's GIS provides a common operations platform for its complex and expansive network of customers, parts suppliers, warehouses, and logistics service providers. Using location analytics, the company achieves improved visibility of service territories, eliminates coverage overlaps and service gaps, and optimizes the service part delivery network.

PART 2 ACHIEVING BUSINESS AND SOCIETAL VALUE

CHAPTER 6
Managing business risk and increasing resilience

Introduction

This chapter is an in-depth exploration of the role of location intelligence for risk management and mitigation in business operations. Recent history has made managing risk more salient than ever for global business. In 2020, the COVID-19 pandemic ravaged the world. Nations around the globe took unprecedented measures to contain the spread of the novel coronavirus by closing national borders, stopping international travel, shutting down schools and nonessential businesses, and implementing stay-at-home policies. The economic fallout has been unlike any in contemporary history, and it may take years for communities and businesses to fully recover. Pandemics represent the newest frontier of risk factors affecting businesses, along with economic and geopolitical uncertainties, rapidly changing customer preferences, evolving competitive threats, climate change–induced shifts in weather patterns, and data/IT security breaches.

From business and operational risk to risks posed by market factors and competition to environmental factors, the timely assessment and mitigation of risk is key to sustaining growth and staying ahead of the competition. Strategic risk occurs whenever a business voluntarily accepts some risk to generate superior returns from its strategy. For example, expanding a business into new territories—domestic or international—is an avenue for strategic risk. On the other hand, external risks arise from events outside a company's influence or control, such as climate change, natural disasters, pandemics, economic fluctuations, geopolitical uncertainty, regulatory environments, and cybersecurity breaches.

In confronting external risks such as geopolitical crises and natural disasters, the lack of a visible plan can render CEOs and their organizations vulnerable. Recent surveys have shown that during such times, two out of three CEOs feel concerned about their ability to gather information quickly and communicate accurately with internal and external stakeholders (PricewaterhouseCoopers 2020). As a framework for gathering, managing, and analyzing many types of data on risk, a GIS may be viewed as a unified source of truth. For example, it can combine layers of internal organizational data on customer locations, store closures, supply network disruptions, and compromised infrastructure with public data such as imagery, regulations, restrictions, and mandates from governmental agencies. In addition to organizing data, a GIS can ground-truth data and identify inaccurate data. Dynamic mapping, using real-time location data, can improve situational awareness and help with risk identification and mitigation. This type of information can provide reliable, timely guidance to CEOs and senior leaders needing to mitigate risk by critical decision-making in real time.

Location analytics for risk management

Understanding risks specific to place is key to reliable risk assessment, risk preparedness, mitigation, and crisis response. In the case of a manufacturer, risk management entails understanding spatial exposure to risk posed to facilities along the supply chain. In nonmanufacturing settings—for example, in transportation, utilities, and telecommunications—physical infrastructure and field assets constitute the geographic exposure to risk. Risk management using a GIS offers location-based insights on emergency preparedness. It also helps companies develop business continuity plans and an overall appraisal of business resilience.

A GIS-based risk management process can be synthesized by the five steps of planning, mitigation, preparedness, response, and recovery, as shown in figure 6.1. At each step of the process, location analytics plays an important role, underpinned by the principles of location proximity and relatedness, location differences, location linkages, and location contexts.

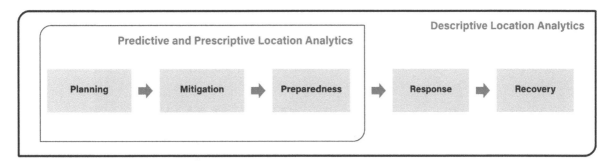

Figure 6.1. The risk management process comprises five steps, each of which uses location analytics.

- **Planning.** In the initial planning step, location analytics can be deployed for descriptive visualization of areas, facility locations, and assets exposed to risk. Geostatistical models can predict areas most likely to be affected by a risk, along with the threat level and how risk might propagate spatially.
- **Mitigation.** Once risk assessment has been completed, protective or preventive actions can be taken in areas exposed to risk. This can be accomplished using spatial analysis in a GIS.
- **Preparedness.** Preparedness involves planning for asset deployment in areas likely to be impacted to minimize response times. Prescriptive optimization models can be used within a GIS to identify optimal locations for assets and resources to be deployed for maximum coverage of affected areas, populations, and facilities.
- **Response.** The response phase occurs after an emergency when business and other operations are disrupted. Response activities might include activation of disaster response plans and implementation of strategies and tactics to deploy location-specific assets to assist, protect, and save employees, customers, properties, and the community affected by an emergency. Layers of geospatial data organized in a GIS can be used to obtain location intelligence that can ensure safe access, navigation to affected people and communities, and timely evacuation. Location-based intelligence can also help local governments and communal organizations as well as federal and state agencies obtain a common operational picture, ensuring coordination of response activities.
- **Recovery.** During the recovery phase, restoration efforts occur in parallel to regular operations and activities. Location intelligence can power the timely and reliable restoration of utilities, telecommunications, and other essential services, rebuilding damaged properties and reducing vulnerabilities stemming from diseases and other threats.

Location intelligence can also provide guidance on areas where it is safe to resume regular business operations and on other areas that require resource-intensive efforts.

Case example: General Motors

The supply chain for General Motors (GM) is a complex network of relationships between tier 1, tier 2, and tier 3 suppliers, globally dispersed. Some 5,500 tier 1 suppliers ship parts directly to GM manufacturing plants. Tier 1 suppliers receive their parts from 23,000 tier 2 suppliers, creating a network of approximately 53,000 tier 2 to tier 1 relationships. There are tens of thousands of tier 3 to tier 2 connections. Clearly, the sheer volume of cars, parts, plants, suppliers, and shipments makes the management of GM's geographically dispersed supply chain a complex task under normal circumstances. In a disruption, such complexity poses enormous challenges for planning, mitigation, and recovery.

GM's supply chain risk management (SCRM) platform consists of a comprehensive database of suppliers, including location, parts supplied, connections, and information on key contacts. All locations are mapped, and with the use of a tracing function, all connections between plants and tier 1 suppliers and between tier 1 and the subtiers are established. This descriptive location intelligence immediately reveals the following:

- Which parts are dual sourced or even triple sourced. This can be vital insight during a crisis.
- The extent of supplier convergence. For example, when one tier 2 supplier provides parts to many tier 1 suppliers, it increases risk exposure if the tier 2 supplier's operations are disrupted.

In its supply chain GIS, GM also incorporates a variety of data feeds, including weather, local and international news, and so forth. This produces 24/7 notifications about current events. In a fire or destructive weather event, the company's supply chain GIS prepares and delivers a report with an overview of the event as well as high-level statistics, such as the number of GM plants and suppliers that may be affected and the part numbers involved. This critical intelligence helps GM's SCRM team answer the following questions to accelerate its mitigation and recovery responses:

- Which GM plants are at risk? Which vehicle lines do they produce?
- Which tier 1, tier 2, and tier 3 suppliers are potentially impacted?
- Which parts are involved?
- Who are the key contacts at affected supplier sites?

For example, when Hurricane Harvey was projected to make landfall in Houston, Texas, in August 2017, the SCRM system identified tier 1 and tier 2 suppliers in the area and their parts. After reviewing the suppliers likely to be affected, the SCRM team had all tier 1 suppliers ship parts to GM plants two to three days ahead of the hurricane's landfall. Similarly, tier 2 suppliers would ship parts to tier 1 suppliers a few days ahead of schedule.

There were two additional benefits to GM's use of GIS. By implementing a reliable yet nimble SCRM process, GM dramatically improved its supplier footprint analysis to better prepare for risks. As a result, the company experienced significant savings in contingent business interruption (CBI) insurance coverage, which protects against losses because of supplier issues (Kazemi 2018).

Improved supply chain visibility also enabled GM to focus on ethical sourcing of raw materials, including minerals such as gold, tin, tantalum, cobalt, and tungsten. The use of conflict minerals for parts or product manufacturing may tarnish the reputation of a company, and GM's GIS system has enabled it to remain vigilant about the origins of the raw materials it requires (Kazemi 2018).

Real estate risk management

In its 2020 annual report, Macy's identified one of its strategic, operational, and competitive risks as the following: "We may not be able to successfully execute our real estate strategy." In the same report, Macy's further added: "We continue to explore opportunities to monetize our real estate portfolio, including sales of stores as well as nonstore real estate such as warehouses, outparcels [building lots separated from commercial development], and parking garages. We also continue to evaluate our real estate portfolio to identify opportunities where the redevelopment value of our real estate exceeds the value of nonstrategic operating locations. This strategy is multipronged and may include transactions, strategic alliances, or other arrangements with mall developers or other unrelated third parties. Due to the cyclical nature of real estate markets, the performance of our real estate strategy is inherently volatile and could have a significant impact on our results of operations or financial condition" (Macy's 2020, 8).

The development of a real estate strategy is key to business success. A location-based real estate strategy can inform business development, help uncover underserved markets, show strategic growth opportunities, model market saturation, and visualize the risk of competitive threats as well as

PART
2
ACHIEVING BUSINESS AND SOCIETAL VALUE

cannibalization. Such a strategy can produce actionable business intelligence that can inform strategic decisions such as site selection; operational decisions such as store design, pricing and promotions, and product selection and placement; and tactical decisions, offsetting manufacturing risk by efficient spatial allocation of scarce resources. Yet, because of ever-changing business environments, shifts in demographics and consumer preferences, socioeconomic changes, geopolitical volatilities, public health crises, and climate change, real estate decision-making in a twenty-first-century business is riddled with uncertainties that often pose risks. Later in this chapter, the vital role of location intelligence to mitigate business risks and build resilience is discussed.

The rise of 3D

Using GIS as a platform, real estate companies deliver location intelligence to their clients by fusing together data from multiple first- and third-party sources. Using powerful visualizations, including 3D, real estate companies help clients make sense of data visually to provide a holistic understanding of markets, customers, spaces, facilities, infrastructure, and their spatial interactions. For example, a property management company can visualize a redevelopment project using 3D views in a GIS (figures 6.2 and 6.3), which integrates layers showing streets, neighborhood green zones, parks, and neighboring property types.

By toggling between the alternative 3D views, the real estate team of the property management company can visually explore the space, conduct before-and-after comparative analyses of places, and zoom in to specific buildings to reveal building data. The perspective can be enhanced further by using location analytics to model transportation access (for example, to underground subway stations and parking garages), access to amenities such as parks and restaurants, and overall quality of life indices, such as noise pollution levels. Advanced forecasting models can also be incorporated within 3D views to provide clients with market potential and relevant KPI estimates based on such factors.

Equipped with such 3D visualizations on phones and tablets, brokers can provide clients with a nuanced, realistic view of market opportunities, advise them about site suitability, and even offer a broad view of profitability. Using advanced 3D information products built within a GIS, the clients of real estate market leaders such as Cushman & Wakefield can enter a space they are appraising and conduct a virtual tour, using a mobile device. Having developed this immersive virtual experience before the COVID-19 outbreak, Cushman & Wakefield considered it indispensable during the pandemic to provide safe, insightful interactions for clients from afar (Lowther and Tarolli 2020).

Figure 6.2. 3D view of a fictive redevelopment project, showing the built environment of a Philadelphia city block. Source: Esri 2016b.

Figure 6.3. 3D view of a fictive redevelopment project, showing proposed additions to the built environment of a Philadelphia city block. Source: Esri 2016b.

Business risk mitigation and building business resilience

Location intelligence can also help businesses analyze risks associated with supply chain interruptions, which disrupt the flow of raw materials essential for business continuity. Many businesses such as grocers establish layered and complex supply chains sourcing raw materials, such as perishable frozen foods, from geographically disparate suppliers. Any food safety event, including instances of food-borne illness such as salmonella or E. coli, may adversely affect the price and availability of raw materials, such as meat and produce. In addition, food-borne illnesses, food tampering, contamination, or mislabeling may occur at any point during the growing, manufacturing, packaging, storing, distribution, or preparation of products. Descriptive mapping with reporting dashboards provides a unified, up-to-date, reliable source of truth, producing actionable business and location intelligence.

Business continuity: The case for dashboards

In a recent industry survey (Dresner 2019), mapping in dashboards was the highest-rated feature of location visualization. Consistent with this trend, organizations have embedded smart mapping capability within COVID-19 business dashboards to monitor facility status (for example, which factories are open or closed, where warehouses are operating), identify business segments (customers, trade areas, markets) most vulnerable to risk, develop contingency plans, manage and care for a distributed, remote workforce, improve supply chain visibility, and craft strategies to safely reopen businesses and facilities where appropriate. Such dashboards also enabled businesses to untangle myriad local, state, and national regulations and guidelines that were frequently at odds with one another. Examples include Walmart's Store Status dashboard and Bass Pro Shops's supply chain risk mitigation and business continuity dashboard (Sankary 2020).

As part of their public health response to the COVID-19 pandemic, governments—national, state, county, and city—implemented stay-at-home orders or curfews in places and recommended social distancing. In addition, nonessential businesses in various sectors were ordered to close. What was defined as nonessential varied from place to place, creating a jumble of local, county, and state regulations for businesses to sift through. Grocery stores, pharmacies, and big-box retail were deemed essential, but operations at Costco, Walmart, and Target were somewhat altered to allow time for sanitization work. In many cases, on-premises pharmacies and departments such as optical shops, photo printing units, tire and auto centers, and gas stations were closed. Under such circumstances, business continuity dashboards were an effective tool in the location intelligence arsenal of businesses.

Case example: Bass Pro Shops

Consider the case of Bass Pro Shops's retail operations, comprising stores in 45 US states and eight Canadian provinces. In Alaska, one of the world's finest sources of wild seafood, fishing is critical for the local economy. At the outset of the pandemic, the fishing gear retailer was among essential businesses in the state. However, under more restrictive local orders in Anchorage, the company's two main stores in the state were deemed nonessential. Because Bass Pro Shops's executives had been using GIS for making real estate decisions, its GIS team constructed a dashboard showing the exact state of store operations for 169 stores in the US. Open, closed, modified, curbside pickup, and ship-only stores were distinctively shown on this internal dashboard, enabling decision-makers to develop business strategies aligned with local restrictions.

For example, in Anchorage, Bass Pro's two stores were designated as ship-only because the retailer was deemed nonessential. A vast majority of Bass Pro's stores could remain open (140 out of 169) but had to implement six-foot social distancing guidelines. This meant that, like many other businesses, store employees and managers had to implement queueing strategies outside the stores to prevent too many people in a store at a time.

As a unified source of truth, the dashboard also showed stores impacted by closures because of employees who had tested positive for COVID-19. Employees at those locations had to be immediately quarantined or switched to remote work. Most importantly, the dashboard enabled senior leaders in different departments to collaborate closely, with access to the same information. It shifted the conversation from closed stores to those locations that remained open (a vast majority). This prevented unnecessary panic and focused decision-makers on amending retail strategies consistent with local health guidelines. Also, as COVID-19 cases spread rapidly, the case count information provided location intelligence on how to allocate one million masks donated by the company's founder to health-care workers on the front lines of the crisis.

Although descriptive in nature, Bass Pro's business continuity dashboard provided valuable location intelligence–based situational awareness and guidance during a volatile period of uncertainty. In addition, using data and

PART
2
ACHIEVING BUSINESS AND SOCIETAL VALUE

location intelligence, the dashboard helped guide the company's philanthropic efforts.

Case example: CSX Corporation

Real-time monitoring of disruptions can aid in rapid recovery. In the aftermath of Hurricane Florence in the Carolinas in September 2018, CSX Corporation, a large railroad company with more than 21,000 miles of lines extending through 23 states, Washington, DC, and two Canadian provinces, needed to identify compromised lines and other infrastructure rapidly and accurately.

With an army of drones, CSX conducted reconnaissance in flooded areas with no electricity and poor cell coverage. The firm was able to identify washouts (figure 6.4) that were displayed in a central GIS-based war room in real time. This information enabled senior leaders to work in concert with field crews who could prioritize the deployment of resources to fix compromised infrastructure and proactively shut down compromised assets to protect workers and communities from harm. This, in turn, allowed operations to begin in a safe and timely manner, ensuring that critical supply chains in North Carolina, severely affected by the hurricane, could be restored expeditiously.

Figure 6.4. CSX culvert washout in North Carolina after Hurricane Florence in September 2018. Source: CSX.

Case example: Mid-South Synergy

Trees are good for the environment. For an electric utility, though, tree cover in forested areas poses a significant business risk. Downed power lines are known to cause forest fires that may ultimately spread to nearby communities, causing untold damage and suffering through loss of property, livelihood, and even life.

Mid-South Synergy's grid provides service to 23,000 customers across six Texas counties—Grimes, Montgomery, Madison, Walker, Brazos, and Waller—located north-northwest of Houston. Part of Mid-South's service area overlaps Sam Houston National Forest. Historically, 30% of Mid-South's power outages are because of fallen trees and branches and vegetation encroachment. Exacerbating the risk, many trees had been killed in its service area by a severe drought. Despite right-of-way maintenance, dead trees outside the company's service area increased the risk of power outages and fires in the national forest. Mitigating this risk to improve the reliability of service and reduce the likelihood of catastrophic forest fires prompted the company to use GIS technology.

Using soil data from the US Geological Survey and tree coverage from the US Forest Service (Esri 2020b), Mid-South located tall pine trees in dry soil types, which posed the greatest hazard to its power lines. Using predictive modeling in ArcGIS software, the company generated the probability of dead trees falling on the utility's electric wires across the service area. The entire service area was subsequently categorized by risk level using a weighted overlay model (figure 6.5), which helped Mid-South's field crews prioritize areas that posed the greatest hazard. Trees in those areas were then removed and encroaching vegetation cleared.

Within the first year, tree-related outages dropped by more than 60% whereas customer complaints about trees dropped by more than 90%. Equipped with predictive location intelligence, the company could proactively schedule the removal of dead trees from parts of its service areas before they posed significant threats to service. This boosted the utility's system reliability, secured its grid, improved customer service, and provided location data and analytics-based guidance for risk mitigation (Esri 2020b).

Innovations in remotely piloted aerial systems now enable utilities such as Mid-South to collect high-resolution imagery—for example, of tree cover—and then use machine learning–based pattern recognition to identify threats to their infrastructure. This automated processing and pattern recognition from imagery accelerates the generation of accurate location intelligence from geospatial big data. Such advances illustrate the promise and potential of predictive modeling of risk in the private sector.

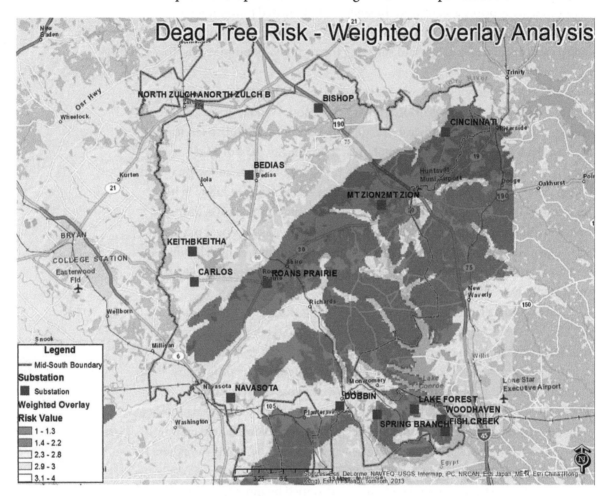

Figure 6.5. Weighted overlay analysis by Mid-South Synergy for showing risk levels posed by dead trees in the Sam Houston National Forest in Texas. Courtesy of Comfort Manyame, Mid-South Synergy.

Business risk management: Predictive big data modeling

GeoAI methods are at the forefront of predictive modeling of business risk. With the prevalence of geospatial big data, the role of predictive analytics for risk management and mitigation is expanding. A large amount of big data is unstructured—for instance, spatial imagery captured by drones or curated from satellite imagery. Allied with powerful visualization, data mining enabled by machine learning and pattern recognition can help uncover patterns and relationships to accelerate decision-making during emergencies such as natural disasters. For example, a major full-service insurer uses thousands of aerial photos of residential properties damaged by forest fires to train machine learning algorithms to detect the extent of property losses. When the Malibu area of Southern California was devastated by the deadly Woolsey Fire in November 2018, GeoAI models applied to before and after imagery of properties damaged by the fire were able to detect with close to 100% accuracy those that were a total loss. This helped the insurer proactively reach out to affected customers, ensure their safety, and expeditiously process their claims.

Closing case study: Travelers Insurance

Travelers Insurance is a leading property and casualty insurer, with more than 30,000 employees and 13,500 independent agents and brokers. It operates in four countries, including the US and Canada, with revenues totaling around $30 billion in 2019 (Travelers Companies 2019). Travelers provides coverage to individuals and businesses; its product portfolio also includes bond and specialty insurance, such as contract and commercial surety. The firm counts Allstate and Nationwide among its main competitors.

Over the years, Travelers's use of GIS and location intelligence across the enterprise for competitive advantage has encompassed many organizational functions, making it a spatially mature firm. Enterprise GIS at Travelers is a platform for collaborative engagement that is guided by three main principles:

- **Pay what you owe.** The business objective is to accurately price risk for a location to underwrite appropriate location-specific insurance policies.
- **Improve customer experience.** The business objective is to provide speedy claims resolution and timely assistance to customers whose lives may have been greatly affected by an emergency.
- **Increase efficiency and productivity.** The business objective is to match resources such as adjusters to the realities on the ground so that claims can be appraised quickly, with shorter processing times.

Pay what you owe

As an insurer, one of Travelers's main business objectives is to accurately price risk for any location. To do so, the company's R&D team examines vast repositories of data that include addresses, property taxes, and weather history. Weather history consists of multiple peril layers, such as hurricane, tornado, hail, and wildfire. Earthquakes are also included. Other factors include weather or climate variability, population density, population growth (in areas with weaker enforcement of building codes), urban expansion, and increase in the average size of a house.

Travelers also examines up to 120 location-specific risk factors, often at the street level. These factors, along with other geographic data, are modeled to predict the risk level for that location. This allows Travelers's R&D team to determine whether existing insurance products are suitable for a market or if new policy products need to be developed. Also, based on risk, the extent of coverage can be determined and then reconciled with regulatory requirements. This drives insurance premiums and deductibles, ensuring optimal polices for customers and better returns for Travelers.

Travelers's use of location intelligence for hyperlocal modeling of risk has several related benefits. In addition to rate making, Travelers can make decisions on reinsurance purchase. Depending on the risk profile of a location or business, Travelers decides whether to purchase insurance for its own insurance policies. Location intelligence also provides inputs to the company's annual financial planning.

Improve customer experience using innovative predictive models

Predictive modeling of risk has been a hallmark of Travelers's focus on improving its customers' experience, often at a traumatic time in their lives. For this reason, Travelers has made significant investments in its technology platforms, talent, and data to integrate geospatial capabilities and location intelligence into all areas of the insurance life cycle. For example, the insurer employs 650 certified drone pilots, who logged more than 53,000 flights in the Lower 48 by early 2020 to build a robust portfolio of high-resolution imagery. Travelers National Catastrophe Command Center teams also aggregate millions of data points from weather services, satellite imagery, and geospatial and location information.

In addition, Travelers partnered with the National Insurance Crime Bureau (NICB) and the Geospatial Insurance Consortium (GIC) to capture "blue and gray sky" (before and after) imagery of events. The imagery is critical during the response and recovery stages of risk management. For instance, after the Kincade Fire that ravaged California's Napa Valley in October 2019, Travelers's claims professionals began to manually review images of the devastation within days to assess the damage at each insured location. By comparing before and after images (figures 6.6 and 6.7), properties that were total losses were identified manually before many of the affected customers could even reenter the area.

Figure 6.6. Neighborhood in Santa Rosa in Sonoma County, California, before the Kincade Fire in 2019. Courtesy of City of Santa Rosa.

Figure 6.7. Same neighborhood in Santa Rosa after the Kincade Fire in 2019. Courtesy of City of Santa Rosa.

Teams of insurance experts, software engineers, and data scientists work in tandem with the enterprise GIS team to automate pattern recognition from imagery for faster and more accurate incident response and recovery. By combining artificial intelligence with location analytics, these teams built the company's innovative Wildfire Loss Detector, a PyTorch-based deep learning model that analyzes tens of thousands of images from damaged and undamaged homes to evaluate the space around a property and determine its likelihood of damage during a wildfire (Travelers Insurance 2022). Using its Wildfire Loss Detection model, the company anticipates advancing payments to its customers before physical inspection for more than 90% of its claims. Overall, AI-based innovations are being used for a variety of purposes at Travelers, including catastrophic modeling.

Increase efficiency and productivity

Location intelligence also plays an important role in deploying assets on the ground in the aftermath of an emergency. With location analytics, the company has now fine-tuned its staffing approach during the recovery phase of an event, depending on location and the type of emergency. This efficient allocation of critical resources (adjusters and claims handlers) helps Travelers handle and pay out claims expeditiously and accurately.

Finally, location intelligence can be key to detecting fraud and reducing costs stemming from fraudulent claims. All fraud happens somewhere; it has a spatial dimension. Many insurance companies use mapping and statistical modeling to detect spatial patterns of claims, especially those that are much higher than average for certain types of repairs. In this way, insurers can isolate high-value claims and trace them to particular service providers, such as auto repair shops, by determining service outlets to which customers have traveled unusually long distances. This is another example of how, through its use of GIS and location intelligence across the enterprise, Travelers is attaining the competitive advantage of a spatially mature firm.

CHAPTER 7
Enhancing corporate social responsibility

Introduction

In making important decisions, organizations must consider how such decisions will affect not only shareholders, management, employees, customers, and the communities in which they operate, but also the overall planet. Finding optimal solutions that are in the best interests of all the varied stakeholders is not always easy, but it is an integral responsibility of business. This chapter examines how location intelligence can guide and shape ways in which a contemporary business can balance its financial goals and competitive pressures with environmental, social, and human objectives.

Corporate social responsibility, or CSR, calls for a company to be socially accountable in ways that go beyond making a profit. The company must take a broader view of its goals, thinking not only of its stockholders but also of the benefits to its employees, customers, community, the environment, and society. As mentioned in chapter 1, the 2019 Business Roundtable's "Statement of Purpose of a Corporation" made a major shift by declaring that a company serves the needs of all its stakeholders (Business Roundtable 2019). The statement includes commitments to development and compensating employees fairly, fostering "diversity and inclusion, dignity and respect," interacting fairly with suppliers, enhancing the communities a business is involved with, supporting sustainable practices, and generating "long-term value" for shareholders.

Environment, society, and governance

Whereas CSR articulates the range of a company's business societal intent, environmental, social, and governance, or ESG, criteria represent the actionable, measurable outcomes of intended practices and the alignment of a company's business strategy, initiatives, investments, and partnerships. The broadest and most widely accepted ESG framework is the UN Sustainable Development Goals, or SDGs, adopted in 2015 with targets in 17 areas set for 2030 (figure 7.1). As noted in the UN (2022) statement:

"On behalf of the peoples we serve, we have adopted a historic decision on a comprehensive, far-reaching, and people-centered set of universal and transformative goals and targets. We commit ourselves to working tirelessly for the full implementation of this agenda by 2030. […] We are committed to achieving sustainable development in its three dimensions—economic, social, and environmental—in a balanced and integrated manner."

Some countries and companies are now taking aggressive steps to advance their ESG agenda, using location analytics and related GIS and data to do so. The successful implementation of UN SDG data hubs by more than 15 countries over the last four years has established a consistent, scalable pattern for reporting and monitoring the progress of the SDGs (Esri 2021b).

Figure 7.1. United Nations Sustainable Development Goals. Source: UN 2022.

The United Nations Sustainable Development Goals website is at https://www.un.org/sustainabledevelopment/. **Note:** The content of this publication has not been approved by the United Nations and does not reflect the views of the United Nations or its officials or member states.

Business implementation of ESG

As noted in chapter 1, a substantial percentage of global businesses report on ESG achievements. Location plays an important role in integrating this information. Using GIS mapping and location analytics, a company can do the following:

- Collect and analyze data about its ESG practices, in a scalable way, and share it across various business platforms.
- Geoenrich such data with location-specific indicators of interest to the firm—for example, indicators of health and wellness or racial and ethnic diversity. Other indicators might include psychographic attributes of customers, such as attitudes toward the environment, social causes, and activism.
- Prepare location-specific GIS maps, reports, and dashboards that inform business strategy and ESG practices, monitor progress toward specific goals, and measure their impact.
- Engage various stakeholders, both within and outside the organization, who are likely to be affected by the firm's ESG actions.
- Gain necessary insights about the demographic and socioeconomic composition of communities in which the company operates. This, in turn, can inform community engagement projects.

Sustainable supply chains

One area of ESG focus is supply chain transparency. Companies need to know what is happening in their supply chain and communicate it both internally and externally to employees, customers, and other stakeholders. The reputational risk and cost of engaging with suppliers who unethically source raw materials or with manufacturing partners who do not hire locally or pay fair wages or who engage in child labor can be immense. To this end, many companies are using mapping and geoenrichment to ensure supply chain traceability and provide full disclosure about internal operations, direct suppliers, indirect suppliers, and origins of raw materials to various stakeholders.

Early adopters of supply chain mapping are companies such as Nike, which maps its manufacturing plants and offers insight about individual factories (Bateman and Bonanni 2019). UK retail giant Marks & Spencer provides interactive mapping of its more than 1,300 factories worldwide in 44 countries employing more than 900,000 people (Bateman and Bonanni 2019). As shown in figure 7.2, Nike (supplier locations shown using the letter *N* in figures 7.2 and 7.3) is part of a global coalition of multinational companies, such as Carrefour (CF), Tesco (TE), Target (T), VF Corporation (VF), Inditex (I), H&M Group (H&M), Gap (G), Puma (P), New Balance (NB), Samsung (S), Lenovo (LN), and many others, that have committed to supply chain transparency and environmental management as part of an interactive platform known as the Green Supply Chain Map. The mapping application links suppliers disclosed by these multinational corporations to publicly available data concerning supplier environmental performance, including real-time monitoring data for air, emissions, and wastewater discharge (IPE 2022).

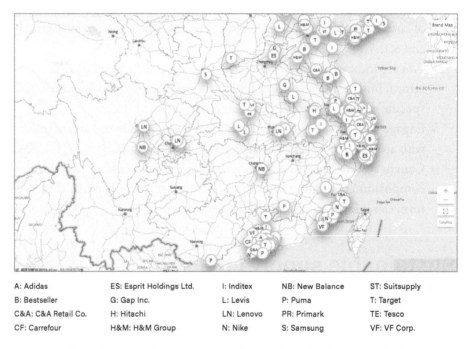

A: Adidas	ES: Esprit Holdings Ltd.	I: Inditex	NB: New Balance	ST: Suitsupply
B: Bestseller	G: Gap Inc.	L: Levis	P: Puma	T: Target
C&A: C&A Retail Co.	H: Hitachi	LN: Lenovo	PR: Primark	TE: Tesco
CF: Carrefour	H&M: H&M Group	N: Nike	S: Samsung	VF: VF Corp.

Figure 7.2. Green Supply Chain Map shows supplier locations of major multinational companies in China in June 2022. Source: IPE 2022.

As part of this initiative, brands have committed to transparency in their upstream supply chains, including tier 2 and tier 3 suppliers where production and manufacturing activities often pose higher impacts to the environment. Such suppliers include, but are not limited to, fabric mills, dyeing and washing mills, wastewater treatment facilities, and hazardous waste treatment facilities. Information regarding suppliers is updated quarterly, and data on their performance is validated and often updated in real time. By committing to supply chain transparency, leading multinational brands such as Nike (figure 7.3) are opening themselves up to public scrutiny. This enhances consumer trust in the brands, forges social trust, ensures compliance with regulations, and boosts collaboration.

Figure 7.3. Select Nike (N) supplier locations in China in June 2022, including Tong Hong Tannery Co. Ltd., also a supplier for Puma (P), Adidas (A), and New Balance (NB). Source: IPE 2022.

VF Corporation, whose brands include Timberland, The North Face, Dickies, and Vans (VFC 2018), has gone one step further in using location analytics to improve product traceability and supply chain transparency. After creating an exhaustive database of tier 1, tier 2, and tier 3 suppliers of materials (such as fabric, leather, yarn, foam, laces, trim, and so forth), traders, textile mills, factories, and distribution centers, VF Corporation has created traceability maps of its brand-name products that communicate to consumers exactly where raw materials for a particular product are sourced; where it was manufactured, assembled, and shipped for distribution; and how components of the product flow between different facilities in the supply chain. For example, Timberland's women's premium waterproof boots can be traced back to 20 facilities across seven countries over four continents.

Traceability maps (VFC 2020) also include information on each facility's workforce diversity, as well as its certifications on (1) sustainable materials use, (2) environmental and chemical management, and (3) health, safety, and social responsibility, along with worker well-being, community development, and environmental sustainability programs. These product-by-product supply chain traceability maps take transparency and disclosure to a high level, inviting all stakeholders, including consumers, to become more informed about where and how the products they buy are being made.

Preserving biodiversity

Companies can play an important role in preserving biodiversity. An example is Natura, the largest manufacturer and marketer of cosmetics, household, and personal care products in South America. As part of its commitment to sustainability, Natura seeks to conserve biodiversity in the Amazon region, where its agroforestry farming and employment strategies aim to build community wealth. Using a spatial approach, Natura has fostered interactions with rural communities and developed sustainable value chains that generate superior returns for the company (Cheng 2021).

Case example: Natura

In the early 2000s, Natura launched its Ekos line of beauty products, consisting of bath products, premium fragrances and cosmetics, hair care, and skin care products, as well as products for infants and children. Raw materials for these products included Brazil nut, passion fruit, andiroba plant–based oils, murumuru butter, cacao (from which cocoa butter is sourced), and other biodiverse elements native to the Amazon rain forest in Brazil. By the 2010s, with burgeoning demand for such products, one of the problems encountered by Natura was how to find potential suppliers in a region plagued by a lack of logistics. To do so, the company needed to compile production and harvest data, including the locations of thousands of participating farms. Retention of suppliers was another challenge. But the company's policy was to maintain open relationships with suppliers and constant interactions with the community (Boehe, Pongeluppe, and Lazzarini 2014).

To achieve its objectives, the company built a geospatial platform. Supply chain data collected from the field was combined with internal business data, analyzed, and then published in the form of interactive web maps and apps. Using the company's geospatial platform, farming cooperatives, consumers, and shareholders could design different views of data, specific to their workflows, and gather location intelligence to make decisions about sourcing, pricing, and distribution. The company's platform also improved traceability and transparency of its investments, production, and supply chain infrastructure. With a greater ability to view the entire supply chain, Natura has maintained its commitments to biodiversity and environmental stewardship while generating sustainable competitive advantages for the company (Esri 2015b). By using a "quadruple bottom line" approach that balances financial, environmental, social, and human objectives, Natura has continued to diversify its product offerings using an expanded array of supplier communities and bio-ingredients while simultaneously protecting the Amazon and committing to the ethical sourcing of biodiverse ingredients (Natura 2020).

Climate resiliency

The world economy could shrink by 10% if the 2050 net-zero emissions and Paris Agreement targets on climate change are not met, according to a recent study (Swiss Re 2021). Around the world, business leaders are enacting strategies and tactics to address climate change. As climate crises disrupt business operations and increasingly pose threats to business continuity, companies can monitor their environmental and carbon footprints over space and time by using geovisualization, dashboarding, and predictive modeling approaches.

Case example: AT&T

AT&T serves as an example of a corporation taking an active role in understanding the impacts of climate change, helping businesses mitigate those impacts, and taking action to mitigate global warming. Through its climate resiliency initiative, the company, in collaboration with Argonne National Laboratories, is building a climate change analysis tool. "Using data analysis, predictive modeling, and visualization, this tool enables AT&T to react to climate change by making the adaptations necessary to help increase safety, service, and connectivity for its employees, customers, and communities," according to the company's *Road to Climate Resiliency Report* (AT&T 2019). An example of this initiative is assessing the potential impact of climate-induced flooding on AT&T's infrastructure, such as fiber lines and cell sites that are at risk of flooding because of hurricanes, and taking appropriate mitigation actions. Readers are encouraged to refer to a visualization of flooding data overlaid on AT&T's fiber and cell sites in the company's report (AT&T 2019, 15).

AT&T plans to make the tool widely available to other businesses and the public, citing a recent survey which found that most US businesses (59%) view climate change as a priority, yet less than a third (29%) have assessed the risks of climate change to their business (AT&T 2019).

COVID-19 pandemic dashboard

Dashboards provide visual displays of critical business information arranged on a single screen to provide a consolidated, unified view of a business or phenomenon (Sharda, Delen, and Turban 2018). The COVID-19 pandemic has accelerated the need for businesses, organizations, and communities to visualize fast-moving and rapidly changing business patterns and trends, often in real time. Because of the rapidly increasing volume of data from disparate sources, the demand for scalable, efficient, locationally sophisticated visual analytics is at an all-time high. The importance of accurately depicting on-ground realities and "telling the story" to different stakeholders, from senior leaders to frontline employees, has never been higher. This unprecedented demand for data visualization and predictive modeling of business risks in real time has catalyzed the use of sophisticated dashboards, with mapping, for COVID-19 and other government and business applications.

The COVID-19 dashboard by Johns Hopkins University (JHU) (figure 7.4) received worldwide attention during the pandemic because it seamlessly combined data from dozens of sources to provide spatial and temporal depictions of critical COVID-19 trends in real time. Viewed up to a trillion times or more, the dashboard fuses COVID-19 data from hundreds of sources such as the World Health Organization (WHO), European Center for Disease Prevention and Control (ECDC), US Centers for Disease Control and Prevention (CDC), and various country, state, municipal, and local governments and health departments (Johns Hopkins University 2020).

To identify new cases, JHU researchers have monitored various Twitter feeds, online news services, and direct communications sent to the dashboard. COVID-19 cases, incident rates, fatality rates, and other metrics of interest to governments, health authorities, businesses, news organizations, and the public were reported at various geographic resolutions. Initially, for some countries, such as the US, Australia, and Canada, data was reported at the city level, and at the country level for others. At present, US COVID-19 data is reported on the dashboard at the county level. Data was updated multiple times a day to keep the dashboard and its visualization up-to-date and meet expectations as an authoritative source of COVID-19 data at a time when the spread of the disease became rampant in many parts of the world (Dong, Du, and Gardner 2020).

Figure 7.4. Johns Hopkins University's COVID-19 dashboard showing cumulative cases worldwide in December 2020. Source: Johns Hopkins University 2020.

The JHU dashboard has also informed modeling efforts by experts in governments, public- and private-sector agencies, and academia to generate accurate spatiotemporal forecasts of transmission and spread of the disease. These models have informed the formulation of public health policy worldwide to prevent further escalation and spread of the virus. For all these reasons, JHU's COVID-19 dashboard is an illustration of the power of dashboards for data description, fusion, and visualization to inform numerous stakeholders.

Predictive modeling of the pandemic

Although Johns Hopkins's dashboard provided an update on indicators of the pandemic's outbreak, predictive analysis was needed for targeting resources. Such a model was developed and implemented by Direct Relief (2020b). Direct Relief (2020a) is a nonprofit humanitarian aid organization operating in the US and more than 80 nations worldwide, providing critical relief to the most vulnerable populations. The company's mission is to "improve the health and lives of people affected by poverty or emergencies—without regard to politics, religion, or ability to pay." The range of relief events includes catastrophic floods, storms, fires, and earthquakes, and pandemic diseases such as COVID-19, Ebola, and Zika virus, as well as persistent infections such as human immunodeficiency viruses (HIV), malaria, and tuberculosis that threaten millions annually (Schroeder 2017).

To achieve its mission, Direct Relief needs precise geographic information and accurate spatial models to predict the needs for humanitarian assistance when normal information channels are disrupted or destroyed. Such information helps the organization identify specific needs on the ground in an impacted area, coordinate its response with dozens of other organizations, and then deliver targeted relief, such as supplies, equipment, and personnel, in a timely manner.

During the COVID-19 pandemic, providing protective gear and critical-care medications all over the world to as many health-care workers as possible and as quickly as feasible was a crucial part of Direct Relief's operations. Timely shipping of personal protective equipment (PPE)—millions of N95 and surgical masks, gloves, face shields, and tens of thousands of protective suits—in coordination with public health authorities, nonprofits, and businesses posed an immense logistical and supply chain challenge.

To address the challenge and meet critical needs at the point of care in the US, Direct Relief needed to identify hot spots of COVID-19 infections and hospitalizations. To do this, Direct Relief used Facebook-provided data, data from other third parties, and AI to predict, visualize, and analyze the spread of COVID-19 in US counties (Smith 2020). Specifically, Direct Relief employed a neural network–based AI model developed by the Facebook AI Research (FAIR) team. This FAIR model combines reliable first- and third-party data on a wide variety of important factors, such as confirmed cases, prevalence of COVID-like symptoms from self-reported surveys, human movement trends and changes across different categories of places, doctor visits, COVID testing, and local weather patterns to forecast the spread of COVID-19 in the US (Le et al. 2020).

Using spatial cluster and outlier analysis based on the outcomes of the FAIR model, Direct Relief identified emerging, receding, and persistent hot spots, cold spots, and outliers of COVID-19 spread. For instance, figure 7.5 illustrates outcomes of cluster and outlier analysis to predict that Los Angeles, San Bernardino, and Riverside Counties in California would become hot spots of COVID-19 spread between December 20, 2020, and January 9, 2021, whereas Maricopa County, Arizona; Miami-Dade County, Florida; and Cook County, Illinois, were predicted to be outliers (counties with high prevalence of COVID-19 surrounded by other low-prevalence counties).

Figure 7.5. Predicted COVID-19 case spread from December 20, 2020, to January 9, 2021 (based on the FAIR model), in US counties. Source: Direct Relief 2020b.

In addition to the FAIR model, Direct Relief analyzed human mobility patterns to predict surges and regional acceleration of COVID-19 in rural northern Ohio and western Pennsylvania and in states such as Wisconsin. The organization predicted accurately that hospitalization rates were likely to lag periods of elevated mobility by about 12 days (figure 7.6), whereas mortality rates would lag by another 10 days (Smith 2020).

Figure 7.6. Change in human mobility in US counties during the COVID-19 pandemic from March 2020 to March 2021. Source: Gao et al. 2020.

Armed with such predictive spatiotemporal insights into disease spread, Direct Relief overlaid its shipment facilities on its dashboard of COVID-19 spread to identify their proximity to hot spots. This, in turn, enabled the organization to position critical-care resources and supplies, track deliveries, and prioritize its financial support to health-care facilities responding to the pandemic. Such predictive location intelligence can also inform and accurately time the responses of public health officials, help them develop policies, and provide recommendations to the public to slow the spread of the virus. Overall, using location modeling and intelligence, the company can fulfill its mission of serving the most vulnerable populations during times of crisis.

Diversity, equity, and inclusion

Issues of racial inequities and injustice have been more salient in societal and business discourse in recent years, coming to the forefront in 2020. As corporations have navigated social and racial unrest, their role in addressing socioeconomic inequities has increasingly come under the microscope. There has never been a more important time for businesses to understand the importance of location and local geographies in addressing these deep-seated challenges in diversity, equity, and inclusion (DEI).

Location intelligence can inform a company's efforts to engage in racial justice efforts in their immediate communities by providing a geographically nuanced, data-enriched view of community conditions (for example, access to affordable housing, health care, education, transportation, banking and financial services, and parks and open spaces) and identifying gaps that stem from causes such as racial inequities, discrimination, and lack of access to power and resources.

Spatial statistical modeling can yield powerful location-specific insights about correlations between community conditions and barriers to equality. For example, race- and ethnicity-based discrepancies in reliable broadband access and usage spawn economic, educational, housing, and health inequalities. Insight into such inequities can inform a company's decisions to prioritize its racial justice efforts, customize location-specific resources in alignment with community conditions, identify partners in the community, provide a platform for collaboration, monitor the progress of initiatives, and communicate their impacts using tools enriched by location insights and intelligence.

In another example, the "Business Case for Racial Equity" study estimated that $135 billion could be gained per year by reducing health disparities (Turner 2018). Healthier workers have fewer sick days, are more productive on the job, and have lower medical-care costs. The study estimates that disparities in health in the US today represent $93 billion in excess medical-care costs and $42 billion in untapped productivity. This is in addition to the human tragedy of 3.5 million lost life years annually associated with these premature deaths (Turner 2018). Companies such as ProMedica, Kaiser Permanente, Cigna, and UnitedHealth Group report having created geographically focused shared-value approaches that address racial health inequality in a manner that improves health and reduces costs (De Souza and Iyer 2019). The COVID-19 pandemic, which has had a disproportionate impact on underserved communities, has made the challenge greater (United Health Foundation 2021).

Location intelligence can also provide companies with a valuable window for creating a diverse, more equitable workplace. Location-infused dashboards can provide insights into the workforce diversity of an organization operating in multiple locations. This can be benchmarked against industry standards to identify gaps based on demographic, socioeconomic, and diversity metrics, such as duration of tenure and prior experience. Based on these gaps, organizations can target specific employees for transfer from one location to another and tailor attractive compensation packages based on locational analysis of factors such as the cost of living.

For example, San Diego, California, has undertaken an inclusive economy initiative. The goal is to contribute toward the regional goal of 20,000 skilled workers (degree or credential holders) in San Diego County by 2030, and to achieve it through a more "inclusive economy." Part of the initiative is the use of location analytics to address regional talent shortages and access to education and jobs (figure 7.7).

PART 2 ACHIEVING BUSINESS AND SOCIETAL VALUE

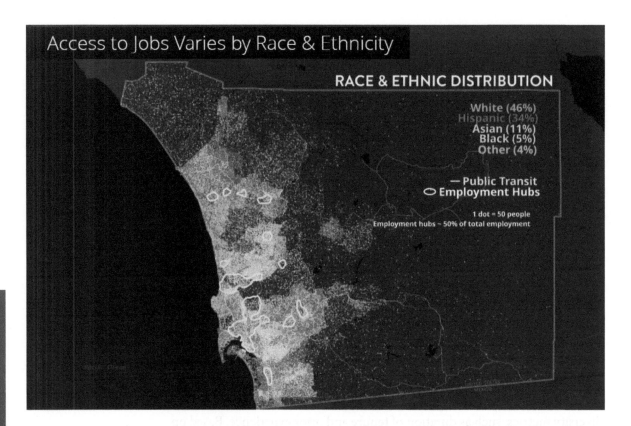

Figure 7.7. Disparities in access for jobs by race and ethnicity within the context of an inclusive economy in San Diego County, California. Source: Gao et al. 2020.

Location intelligence can also shape human resources (HR) recruitment strategies by providing insights into the diversity of graduates in communities surrounding an organization. Companies can direct resources accordingly to participate in job fairs and launch geotargeted advertising of open positions to create a diverse pool of prospective applicants. Armed with location intelligence on the composition of students in institutions that serve underrepresented populations, including historically Black colleges and universities (HBCUs), tribal colleges and universities (TCUs), and women's colleges, organizations can build a pipeline of new job candidates.

Community development

Finally, spatial analysis of industry clusters can produce location intelligence on regional concentrations of employers and employees for a particular industry. Regions consisting of diverse communities can also be geotargeted for recruitment of employees who are likely to contribute to creating a more diverse and equitable workplace. One example is the creation of Opportunity Zones as part of the 2017 US Tax Cuts and Jobs Act (TCJA). A total of 8,764 Opportunity Zones have been designated in the US (figure 7.8), many of which have experienced a lack of investment for decades.

The Opportunity Zones initiative is a tax policy incentive to spur private and public investment in America's underserved communities. The aim of the program is to encourage private investment in communities of need. The Council of Economic Advisers, or CEA (2020), estimated that, by the end of 2019, Qualified Opportunity Funds had raised $75 billion in private capital. Although some of this capital may have been raised without the incentive, the CEA estimates that $52 billion—or 70%—of the $75 billion is new investment. These activities are tracked by multiple sources, including an ArcGIS StoryMaps story (figure 7.9) by the Economic Innovation Group (2021).

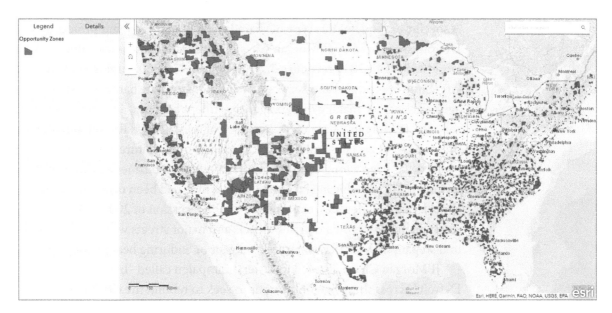

Figure 7.8. More than 8,700 census tracts designated as Opportunity Zones in the US.
Source: HUD.

Figure 7.9. ArcGIS StoryMaps story for the Opportunity Zones Activity Portal, showcasing economic activities and development in Opportunity Zones in the US. Source: Economic Innovation Group 2021.

Case example: JPMorgan Chase

A specific example of this type of shared value is an investment project in Detroit, sponsored by JPMorgan Chase. JPMorgan Chase is a leading bank worldwide, with 2019 revenues of $110 billion, 257,000 employees, and a large suite of products and services, including corporate banking, risk management, market-making, brokerage, investment banking, and retail financial services. JPMorgan Chase was a signatory of the Business Roundtable statements on CSR and has embedded CSR as part of its culture. One of its CSR projects has been a long-term program to help small businesses thrive in the city of Detroit, Michigan (Heimer 2017), which had been on a downward spiral for several decades, exacerbated by the recession of 2007–2009. As a result, many downtown neighborhoods and major streets were deserted and in disrepair, with small businesses bankrupt or enduring heavy losses.

JPMorgan Chase decided to foster a campaign called "Invested in Detroit" across these neighborhoods to seek to rebuild the city and its economy (Heimer 2017). It created a program of credit for small businesses combined with bank-initiated training of affected managers and employees and a highly skilled analytics team rotated to Detroit from the bank's array of prosperous divisions and offices. The bank invested $150 million in the project, partnering with local redevelopment enterprises to identify businesses with potential that were not able to meet loan criteria.

The bank discovered it could help these businesses most effectively by using Community Development Financial Institutions (CDFI) loans, which are keyed to low-income areas to help disadvantaged small enterprises and nonprofits. JPMorgan Chase's analytical team assisted in locationally analyzing a plethora of data points by neighborhood and pinpointing micro districts of 10 to 15 blocks each for the initial credit and job-training push. The bank started with loans to three initial micro districts and planned to scale up to a dozen more while rolling out this CSR approach to depressed areas of other American cities. JPMorgan Chase is also realizing eventual financial benefit because in Detroit it holds $20 billion in deposits. Hence, the Invested in Detroit project can stimulate long-term business growth and conversion of many new and renewed businesses into bankable entities, adding to JPMorgan Chase's market share of deposits and loans (Heimer 2017).

Corporate initiatives based on shared value, such as JPMorgan Chase's Invested in Detroit, allow businesses to contribute to the greater good. This can ultimately enhance their reputation and standing as ethical, responsible, and trustworthy enterprises, which in turn can help retain customers, improve employee morale, lower turnover, and instill a purpose-driven corporate culture.

Closing case study: Nespresso

Nespresso is an operating unit of Nestlé, headquartered in Lausanne, Switzerland. Nespresso produces coffee pods in aluminum-coated packets, which can be used in Nespresso espresso machines or equivalents. Raw, high-quality coffee from developing nations, mainly in Africa and Latin America, is shipped to three factories in Switzerland, where the coffee is ground, encapsulated in aluminum pods, and sold worldwide. The Nespresso (2022) single-serve system was patented in 1976 and today is sold in more than 81 nations.

Nespresso is committed to the UN 2030 goals, tracking its performance on 10 of the 17 goals through various initiatives (Chiappinelli 2018). In 2003, Nespresso formed the AAA Sustainable Quality Program with the assistance of the Rainforest Alliance. The AAA program guides and equips farmers with the technical knowledge and financial resources necessary to pursue sustainable practices. Nespresso then pays the farmers a premium market price for coffee that meets the AAA program quality standards (Rainforest Alliance 2021).

The AAA program started with 500 farmers in 2003 and now reaches more than 122,000 farmers in 15 countries, representing a total annual investment of more than US$43 million per year (Nespresso 2021b). The company sources 93% of its coffee through that program, and 95% of its global coffee purchases for 2019 met the Fairtrade Minimum Price (Nespresso 2021b). The AAA program is part of Nespresso's "Positive Cup Framework," which focuses on long-term sustainable coffee supplies, analytics to support farmers, transparent communication to customers, and responsible practices in communities. These priorities are supported by the AAA platform, which includes the Farm Advanced Relationship Management System (FARMS) (De Pietro 2019). At the farm level, the geospatial platform can be used for a variety of analyses, such as biodiversity protection. At the global level, it can track the achievement of AAA sustainable goals.

This long-term multidecade commitment to sustainability has led to the lauding of Nespresso for its commitment to sustainability and enhancing local suppliers and communities. M. Porter and M. Kramer (2011) recognized this when they introduced the concept of shared value in 2011. In the article, they called out Nespresso for its community-building impact, noting: "Embedded in the Nestlé example is a far broader insight, which is the advantage of buying from capable local suppliers. […] Buying local includes not only local companies but also local units of national or international companies. When firms buy locally, their suppliers can get stronger, increase their profits, hire more people, and pay better wages—all of which will benefit other businesses in the community. Shared value is created" (Porter and Kramer 2011, 10).

Nespresso, as well as the other examples in this chapter, confirms the interrelatedness of businesses and the communities they operate in and the mutual business and societal gains that can be possible. Geospatial platforms enable location analytics that can reveal these patterns, trends, and opportunities.

CHAPTER 8
Business management and leadership

Introduction

This chapter examines the human and behavioral side of spatial business. Mounting great geospatial efforts and design is not likely to succeed without the human factors of management and leadership. In this context, leadership involves skilled management, championing spatial initiatives, continuing training and education of employees, and understanding the human elements that strengthen locational transformation of the organization. It encompasses corporate social responsibility, or CSR, for which a company considers, in addition to its profits, its full effect on society, including environmental, social, and economic impacts. Another important management concern is the ethical question of location privacy.

Consider an Asian cruise shipping firm that is seeking to develop location intelligence because its senior vice president of marketing is interested in how location information can be applied competitively, leading to more profits. The director of global marketing, who is beginning to learn about the spatial aspect and is also enthusiastic, is working with an analytics expert who has been given the job of pushing forward a powerful spatial marketing and customer system to offices company-wide. The problems are that senior managers have been unaware of the importance of location not only to track cruise ships' positions but also to understand customer demographics, locations of intermediary travel businesses, and spatial patterns of brand strength versus the competition, whereas middle managers have missed opportunities to create location value.

Among the firm's challenges are how to evaluate and tweak a starting enterprise GIS built by an outsourcer, how to train 25 middle managers and skilled business analysts in seven major business units, how to motivate managers who are trained to move forward in their units with creative use of the new system, and how to gauge progress and measure location value. A looming challenge is how to break down organizational walls and widen the location analytics initiative to other units such as navigation and supply chain. Also, because building long-term customers is crucial, the leaders and managers of the firm must protect the location privacy of their records.

All the issues in this chapter are captured in this example: spatial maturity, workforce development, middle and senior management, digital and spatial transformation, ethics and privacy, and the pulls and tugs of executive championing of location analytics versus competing internal initiatives.

Spatial maturity stages

Figure 8.1 shows an organization's stages of spatial maturity, based on a stage model for analytics in general proposed by T. Davenport and J. Harris (2017). Davenport and Harris also describe a progression through analytics stages, which may be adapted to apply to location intelligence and analytics.

In stage 1, location data is limited and often lacks quality controls. There are limited workforce skills in location analytics and few if any metrics measuring spatial value and productivity. The trigger that moves an organization to stage 2 is often effort by the original supervisor or low-level sponsor to broaden the support base and communicate with senior leaders. Because GIS and location intelligence are relatively new to some business leaders, an important step in the process is to engage them, educate them if necessary, and bring them along in the journey.

In stage 2, sponsorship of spatial initiatives comes from a local departmental or divisional manager (Davenport and Harris 2017; University of Redlands 2018). The stage is typified by testing spatial applications locally and assessing net benefits. The initiative may then be taken up by other departments and their sponsors.

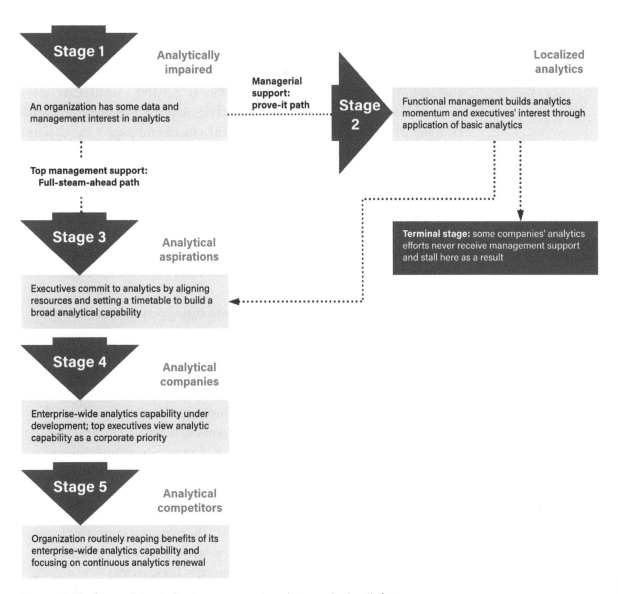

Figure 8.1. The five spatial maturity stages represent moving organizationally from analytically impaired to localized analytics, analytical aspirations, analytical companies, and analytical competitors. Source: Davenport and Harris 2017.

Whether location analytics stays in this stage long term or advances to stage 3 depends on whether initial support is gained from senior management for a company-wide effort. An example is a leading international commercial real estate firm, in which a highly skilled technical manager succeeded in gaining traction for a spatial intelligence initiative in US business units but had mixed success in persuading overseas units to start local projects, in some cases encountering resistance to a new technology. In this instance, spatial maturity was temporarily stalled at the local stage overseas.

PART

3

TOWARD SPATIAL EXCELLENCE

Stage 3 involves sponsorship by a senior executive and the formation of antecedent structures to launch an enterprise spatial system. Usually, a location analytics project is improved to the point of garnering visible attention company-wide. Another crucial development is "defining a set of achievable performance metrics and putting the processes in place to monitor progress" (Davenport and Harris 2017). At the end of a successful stage 3, the C-suite will begin to recognize the importance of GIS, and sufficient capabilities will have been put in place to implement the program enterprise-wide.

In stage 4, the senior executive team decides that location analytics will be implemented across the company. A centralized and highly skilled GIS team is assembled, bringing in talented location intelligence employees who may have been working in business units, and the team's relationship to the corporate IT group is resolved. A centralized company-wide spatial database is also established.

When an enterprise GIS is installed with strong performance and benefits, the C-suite begins to see it as a competitive force. Stage 5 begins with this recognition from senior management, which then adds resources to position the system competitively. At UPS, for example, top management realized that the ORION enterprise routing system was world class and could create significant cost savings and efficiencies. Once a spatial system enables a firm to gain on competitors, the challenge becomes to maintain that lead with further improvements, such as novel analytics and strategic applications, upgrading infrastructure, and embedding useful applications of emerging technologies.

This progression across stages is helped by facilitators (Davenport and Harris 2017; University of Redlands 2018). The two most important facilitators are a perception of the value of location-based insights for business and the availability of world-class spatial technology. These factors were present in a practical sense for the Walgreens case in chapter 2 and will be seen in this chapter's BP case study. The next two factors are C-suite support and clear business strategy. In the case of UPS, covered in chapter 9, location analytics languished as a project for many years with little recognition from the C-suite, until a regional test finally excited top leaders, resulting in rapid progress in the stages of maturity. The last factor aiding spatial maturity, articulation of ROI in GIS, has less influence and would likely increase in importance in later stages, in which strategic decisions involve larger investments. This is seen in results from a survey of 200 businesses (University of Redlands 2018), in which respondents were asked to indicate the factors that differentiated stages of spatial maturity (table 8.1). Rather than ROI, the most important factors facilitating maturity were cited as availability of best-in-class location intelligence technology and value of location-based insights to the business and customers.

Success in progressing through the stages of maturity benefits from efforts by the GIS team to engage leaders and managers outside the location analytics area, collaborating with them in the progression. Among other things, this collaboration ensures a sustainable support base within the organization for location analytics.

Table 8.1. Perceived net facilitating factors of differentiation of spatial maturity

Facilitator or Inhibitor of Differentiation of Spatial Maturity	Net Percentage Facilitating (Facilitator Minus Inhibitor)
Value of location-based business and customer insights	45%
Availability of best-in-class GIS and location intelligence technology	45%
C-suite sponsorship and support	30%
Clear and coherent business strategy	29%
Clear articulation of ROI of GIS and location intelligence initiatives	17%

Source: University of Redlands 2018.

Management pathways

The location analytics team is rarely located in the C-suite, which underscores the importance of strong technical managers. Such managers can be crucial to obtaining and retaining a sponsor or champion, branching out to other middle managers, leading in improving the quality of data, and spearheading technology and software improvements. In addition, a manager in the location analytics department has responsibilities for planning, day-to-day management of personnel, hiring, and coordinating with the IT department, which tends to be considerably larger than the GIS group. As appreciation for location analytics improves, a direct communication tie-in will need to be made with senior management (Tomlinson 2013).

Steps recommended for effective location analytics management (Somers 1998; Tomlinson 2013) include the following:

- **Devising an effective approach for developing and implementing projects in a firm.** The common system development steps for a spatial project include planning, analysis (including requirements specification), design and build, implementation, and maintenance. However, GIS management needs to be flexible toward scope of project, speed required, human resource capacity to complete the project, and extent of control imposed on the project team. One recommended step for location analytics projects is to hold a technology seminar early on—a meeting of major stakeholders that focuses on training for the project, awareness of its goals and challenges, and gaining understanding and consensus on the development and oversight roles involved (Tomlinson 2013).

- **Long-range planning and vision.** Location analytics teams need to develop and gain consensus on a plan that envisions a desired long-term outcome of location analytics in the organization (Tomlinson 2013; Somers 1998). The plan can serve as a unified series of steps leading to important goals. It should be subject to modification as the planning period unfolds, and it needs to be aligned with plans for IT and for the business.

- **Coordinating team members with users.** As is standard in technology projects, location analytics projects need to have users involved in designing and building systems as well as evaluating systems that are in active use (Pick 2008; Tomlinson 2013). Location analytics is a resource that has multiple potential users, and its outputs should be shared as much as proprietary or security constraints allow. Users can discover beneficial applications that were not planned for.

- **Communicating with stakeholders.** Location analytics managers need to communicate with multiple stakeholders, including technical team members, users, vendors, the IT manager or CIO, and often senior management. Communications must be proactive, timely, and appropriate to the level and interests of the other party or parties (Somers 1998).

To sum up, as stated by Roger Tomlinson (2013), a "GIS manager must not only have a firm grasp of GIS technology and capabilities, but also be a meticulous organizer, a strong leader, and an effective communicator."

Case example: CoServ Electric

As an example, consider the role of GIS middle management at CoServ Electric, a Texas utility cooperative. CoServ is an electric and natural gas distribution company founded in 1937, serving more than 250,000 electric meters in six counties north of Dallas (CoServ 2020). The firm also offers solar renewable energy. The company started in a region of rural farmland, in which a group of residents formed the nonprofit cooperative to provide energy. Today, to the north and northeast of Dallas, former farmland has increasingly been converted into corporate headquarters and other facilities, but CoServ's western area still functions, for now, as a rural cooperative.

CoServ originally started its location analytics unit to upgrade its small orange map books of its electrical systems, which were manually copied for use in the field. Today, CoServ deploys an enterprise system, web mapping for business units, and full access to the system by field personnel on their mobile devices. It also provides corporate-level enterprise support to business-unit GIS teams in electric utilities, gas utilities, and engineering.

The GIS manager of more than a decade has developed the workforce, set project goals, established working relationships with the business divisions, collaborated on a workable structure for an integrated IT/GIS department, established strong relationships with vendors and outsourcers, and developed visibility for GIS across the company and within senior leadership.

The IT/GIS group works together well with the understanding that the IT department oversees configuring systems, servers, databases, and networks, but that the GIS team populates the databases with data, installs the GIS software and portal, and runs the administrative accounts. The GIS middle manager has also worked out a productive relationship with the spatial teams in engineering, electric, and gas. Engineering, for example, has specialized utility design and operations software, for which the GIS department serves only as a consultant if needed. Likewise, gas and electric GIS groups use supervisory control and data acquisition (SCADA) software to monitor transmission and pipeline flows, which central GIS installs and supports as needed.

The largest and most challenging project has been developing enterprise location intelligence. The GIS manager and team realized it would take many months of effort, not only technical but also coordinating end users, scoping out the steps of the project, going through iterations of testing, changing time-worn processes, and training users. The system succeeded with electric utilities and is well along the way with gas. The web map portal built on top of the enterprise base has been popular with end users because they can customize spatial applications within hours or days rather than waiting weeks.

Overall, the CoServ story exemplifies many of the key responsibilities of location analytics management: developing an approach that works in a firm, long-range planning, coordinating the GIS team with users, and effective communication.

PART

3

TOWARD SPATIAL EXCELLENCE

Applying management principles to spatial transformation

Digital transformation is the process of applying digital technology to change a business creatively and fundamentally, including its existing culture, organization, and business processes (Tabrizi et al. 2019). As GIS and location intelligence are becoming increasingly digital, organizations are concurrently undergoing spatial transformation, defined as the part of digital transformation that involves locational processes and cross-organizational and cultural changes. If a business is reimagined to have its geospatial information and processes in digital form, based on such features as web maps, portals, cloud computing, broadband internet, 3D or 4D visualization both internal and external facing, and if this changes the way business is conducted, spatial transformation is under way. As part of spatial transformation, people also change in their job roles, skills, productivity, and decision-making.

A business that is spatially transformed is usually in the fourth or fifth maturity stage so that spatial applications have permeated the organization and may already be a competitive force. For example, the BP case at the end of the chapter exemplifies location transformation in the fourth maturity stage.

A practical view of spatial transformation posits a series of steps (McGrath and McManus 2020; Harvard Business Review Analytic Services 2020):

- **Define and communicate the underlying business objectives.**
- **Define the spatial operation experience** (McGrath and McManus 2020)—that is, indicate which locational elements or tools will be digitized beyond their current state. An example would be changing from a disjointed set of maps showing each step in a supply chain to an integrated digital display of the entire supply chain from raw material to customer.
- **Invest in personnel to support and maintain the spatial operating experience.** Although technically trained people are required, there is equal need for investing in people with soft skills, who are creative, adaptable, and flexible (Frankiewicz and Chamorro-Premuzic 2020).
- **Focus on specific location-based problems and use metrics.** For instance, in the state of Connecticut, truck routing displays were transformed from 2D to 3D to solve the problem of trucks being too large for safe passage on routes with bridges, overpasses, and tunnels. 3D mapping enabled precise measurement of the maximum allowable dimensions for truck transit.

- **Emphasize data needs.** It is essential to maintain focus on keeping extensive, high-quality data on which to base the spatial transformation.
- **Look for platforms along with ecosystem implications.** Encourage the user to arrive at or create solutions that can reside on top of a stable platform. An ecosystem implication refers to the interfacing of a robust enterprise spatial platform with the platforms of other collaborating businesses or organizations. For example, the *Arizona Republic* newspaper derived competitive advantage by applying a GIS system to select geographic areas suitable to a particular advertiser and collaborating with advertiser systems that supported decisions on which goods and services to advertise (Pick 2008).
- **Drive spatial transformation from the top.** Spatial transformation changes the business profoundly, to the extent that senior management becomes the driver (Frankiewicz and Chamorro-Premuzic 2020).

Many companies seek digital transformation but fewer succeed. In a 2020 poll of 700 executives, 95% indicated that digital transformation had grown in importance over the past two years and 70% pointed to digital transformation as significant, yet only 20% evaluated their own firm's digital transformation efforts as effective (Harvard Business Review Analytic Services 2020). These findings point to the difficulty of succeeding in digital transformation but also to the competitive opportunity for the firm that succeeds. The same study emphasized that cultural change may be a barrier to overcome. In the instance of spatial transformation, culture that is set on using legacy approaches to GIS can be transformed by top management setting clear business goals, communicating those goals, and using indicators to check performance in reaching them (Harvard Business Review Analytic Services 2020).

Leadership and championing

Leadership is crucial in spatial business. A leader provides vision to an organization, communicates that vision to the people they oversee, motivates and inspires them to work toward the vision, and enables this effort among the relevant people in the organization. The leader or champion of GIS and location intelligence in a business has an even greater challenge because spatial thinking and GIS are frequently unfamiliar concepts, and it requires persistence and patience to educate personnel and stakeholders about what GIS is and why it is important for business. This added challenge is evident in some cases, such as the long delay at UPS for spatial thinking to be recognized by upper management, or by the continual challenge and only mixed success at one of the leading global commercial real estate companies in educating and persuading business units outside the US about GIS and its significance.

Recommended qualities of spatial leadership include the following:

- **Act as a role model.** The leader must set an example with their behavior and beliefs, on which others in the organization or unit can model their behavior.
- **Inspire a shared vision of the business** (Kouzes and Posner 2017).
- **Encourage and counsel others to act.** The leader depends on others to do most of the work and must support their efforts. Ideally, the leader builds trust in subordinates and teams and continues to stay engaged with the work as it is carried out, sometimes over considerable time.
- **Be a friend and guide.** The effective leader must reach out to establish friendship with subordinates and stakeholders. The leader should offer guidance and genuinely be concerned about the people who are carrying the projects forward (Kouzes and Posner 2017).

Specific approaches recommended for leaders establishing geospatial and location intelligence in business include setting priorities, which lead in turn to strategies (Kantor 2018b; University of Redlands 2018). This can be seen in figure 8.2, which defines how to achieve location intelligence in business by setting priorities, leading to strategies, and then turning strategies into implementation (University of Redlands 2018).

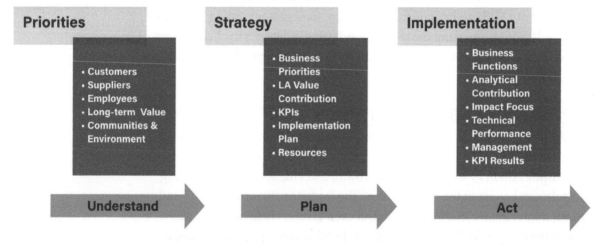

Figure 8.2. The three major steps in achieving location strategy: (1) establishing priorities, (2) determining strategy, and (3) implementing the strategy. Source: University of Redlands 2018.

As an example of setting priorities that lead to strategy, the location analytics leader may set as a top priority the development and implementation of location analytics with big data to provide for improved logistics throughout North America. Further priority areas that the spatial leader might address include the following (Kantor 2018b):

- Analysis of the locational aspects of supply chains
- Understanding how location analytics can be combined with social media sentiment analysis to reveal changes in attitudes across geographies
- Advancing depth of knowledge of the customer through locational tagging of customer ordering patterns in time and space using mobile apps

Other dimensions of spatial leadership include CSR and awareness of the privacy and ethical implications of location intelligence.

Examples of ethical spatial leadership occurred in the 2020 COVID-19 pandemic, during which leaders of several software vendor companies put profit motives aside and provided free spatial software and services to help nonprofit organizations, academia, research institutions, businesses, and governments monitor the geographic spread of the virus, optimize the delivery of needed supplies, and track down the contacts of infectious individuals through georeferenced social media apps while preserving the privacy of those individuals.

Privacy and ethics in spatial business

Notwithstanding the tide of expanding benefits, efficiencies, and innovation from spatial business applications, location intelligence also presents companies and their spatial leaders with ethical dilemmas. Location has its own set of ethical issues. Often a decision must be made that must balance the risks between location value at one end of the scale and harm at the other, which can be unintended or intentional harm to customers, employees, or the public.

One of the main ethical concerns for spatial business is location privacy, defined as control over the locations of people and their associated personal information and over the primary and secondary uses of this information. This ethical issue has grown to widespread prominence through the proliferation of methods to determine the location of people and assets and the increasing accuracy of these methods.

The escalating use of cell phones worldwide means that the locations of billions of people can be tracked over long periods without their knowledge.

PART
3
TOWARD SPATIAL EXCELLENCE

At the same time, satellite imagery of the planet is available from dozens of providers at varying scales, resolutions, spectral wavelengths, and frequencies of collection. Imagery can be scanned rapidly by machine learning to identify features and, at very high resolution, to recognize vehicles, people who are outdoors, and other identifiers. People's locations can also be collected from fixed video cameras and wearables.

A location-tracking industry has sprung up that is unregulated in the US and sells detailed tracking information about people and assets to other companies and organizations. The ethical issues of location privacy are relevant to purveyors of georeferenced data but also to executive decision-makers in the location-tracking industry and to companies that purchase and use the location information.

An example of the ethical issues for personal privacy can be seen in a database from a location information firm that was provided anonymously to a research team at the *New York Times* (Thompson and Warzel 2019). The database, with 50 billion location pings from cell phones of more than 12 million people in the US, reveals the ordinary daily-life mobility patterns of individuals—but also unusual patterns, including visits to drug rehabilitation facilities, medical offices, or more potentially worrisome places. The individuals have consented to reveal their location by clicking Yes to the legal notices that pop up with many apps. Some software apps include little pieces of code called software development kits (SDKs) that provide normal location information for the app but also can be collected by location information firms (Thompson and Warzel 2019).

Given the growing threat of intentional or unintentional misuses of personal data and many other situations in which location information and analytics have the potential for harm, what can individuals do to protect themselves? What can the company and its leaders do to protect workers and customers and ensure that spatial business adheres to ethical standards?

Measures that can help reduce this threat include government regulation and the privacy policies of businesses, as well as tools for anonymizing information and data obfuscation (Duckham 2013). Companies can set high standards that reject misuse of personal information, including not allowing purchase of unconstrained location files, and can require GIS, IT, and business managers to weigh the ethical balance in any decision that presents the potential for locational harm. In addition, regulation needs to come from federal and state legislation, which so far in the US has not sufficiently regulated private-sector data controls beyond some industries such as health care and banking. The US Constitution supports some aspects of locational privacy rights through the Fourth Amendment, although more legal tests are needed to clarify these rights (Litt and Brill 2018). In Europe, the General Data Protection Act of the European Union has constrained use of personal information without permission but does not include substantive regulation of location privacy. On the individual level, anonymizing and obfuscating data can be effective, up to a point, but is often difficult for the individual to control, especially with large spatial datasets.

Developing a spatial business workforce

This chapter now turns to a critical management and leadership concern, which is to understand the competencies of the geospatial workforce, how they lead to career pathways, and the need for improved university education that combines competencies in business and geography.

Because skilled team members and managers at different levels are crucial to supporting business use of location analytics across the spectrum of stages, spatial workforce development is essential. This topic has received attention from varied stakeholders, including universities, governments, professional groups, and businesses. Several key questions arise, among them: What mix of geospatial knowledge and skills is needed for the challenges of working in industry? How can universities best prepare future workers in spatial business? What is the market in the US for geospatial knowledge and skills in business?

In terms of knowledge and skills needed, a general reference point is the Geospatial Technology Competency Model (GTCM), shown in figure 8.3, which was developed through a collaboration between the US Department of Labor Employment and Training Administration and the GeoTech Center (DiBiase et al. 2010; GeoTech Center 2020).

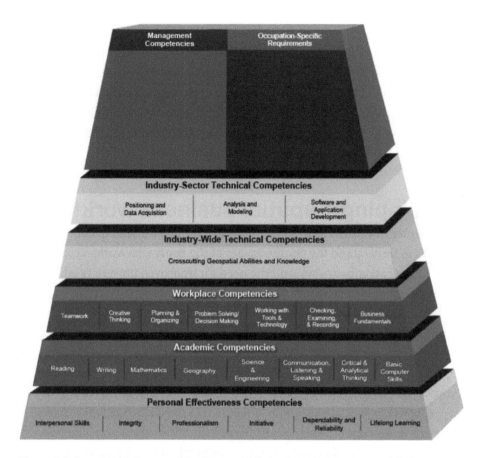

Figure 8.3. A pyramidal diagram of the Geospatial Technology Competency Model of spatial business competencies includes personal effectiveness at the base; academic, workplace, and industry competencies in the middle; and management competencies and specific occupational requirements at the top. Source: The Competency Model Clearinghouse, a website sponsored by the US Department of Labor, Employment, and Training Administration, used under the CC by 4.0 license, https://creativecommons.org/licenses/by/4.0/.

In this model, multidisciplinary academic competencies and workforce competencies form a foundation for industry competencies. The GTCM includes broad human competencies, such as interpersonal skills, combined with knowledge of geography, science, engineering, math, computing, critical thinking, and communications. The workplace competencies include business fundamentals, problem solving, planning and organizing, and teamwork. The upper half of the pyramid emphasizes management competencies, such as organizing, formulating strategy, leading, controlling, making decisions, and communicating, as well as technical competencies and occupation-specific requirements.

The level of knowledge and skills depends on the overall responsibilities of the position. Table 8.2 outlines these spatial business GTCM-related competencies at the entry level (for example, analyst), midlevel (for example, manager), and senior level (for example, director). It also serves as a model pathway for a spatial business career. To that end, a sample of existing position titles is provided across a range of industry sectors.

Table 8.2. Spatial business competencies

Spatial Business Competencies	Spatial Business Career Pathways		
	Entry: Analyst	**Mid: Manager**	**Senior: Director**
Academic	Required undergraduate degree, preferably with business and GIS elements. Certificates can substitute for business and GIS elements.	Preferred advanced degree (at master's level) with business and GIS elements. Certificates can substitute for location analytics in degree.	Required advanced degree (at master's level) with business and GIS elements. Certificates can substitute for location analytics in degree.
Workplace	Preferred 1-3 years of experience in workplace environment involving GIS.	Required 3-5 years of experience in workplace environment involving GIS.	Required 5-10 years of experience in workplace environment involving GIS.
Industry-wide Sector	Industry sector experience preferred but not required.	Ability to manage technical and business aspects of selected industry.	Ability to lead location analytics enterprise to achieve business goals and strategies.
Management	Management experience not required.	Required 1-3 years supervisory experience.	Required 3-5 years management experience.
Sample Current Job Titles	Senior GIS Analyst (Silicon Valley wireless services start-up). Business Systems (GIS) Analyst (regional utility company). Geospatial Data Analyst (national security company).	Senior Product Manager, Location Intelligence (global business data consulting firm). Geospatial Strategy and Analytics Manager (regional e-commerce company). Manager of GIS Analytics and Insights (large regional grocery company).	Executive Director, Enterprise Location Intelligence (global pharmacy company). Director Geospatial Data Science (global life insurance company). Associate Director, Geospatial Services (national nonprofit).

Universities play an important role in preparing a spatial business workforce at each level of knowledge, skills, and responsibilities noted in table 8.2. What is needed for this model to work well in practice is coordination between academic preparation, workplace training, and mentoring from experienced geospatial professionals. Ideally, there would be a spectrum of programs that integrate business, geography, GIS, and location analytics into a unified curriculum, with practicums of students networking with industry people in communities of practice.

To date, however, university programs that integrate critical areas of business and geography or GIS are relatively rare (Marble 2006; DiBiase et al. 2010; Tate and Jarvis 2017). Geography departments have long been

PART
3
TOWARD SPATIAL EXCELLENCE

viewed as the most important source of geospatial workers, and with good reason, because the original base disciplines of GIS in the 1960s and 1970s were geography and cartography (Solem 2017). However, the discipline of geography is becoming more multidisciplinary (Tate and Jarvis 2017). Correspondingly, although business schools have increased the business analytics components of the curriculum, many have lagged in integrating location analytics into their curriculum (Sarkar et al. 2022).

Although more integration will undoubtably occur as the need for this knowledge and skill continues to grow, professional certificates can also serve as a useful complement to traditional academic training. For business degrees, this can be a certificate in location analytics. For GIS degrees, this can be a certificate in a business area such as marketing or supply chain management. Another suggestion for broadening geospatial education is to encourage education that complements standard GIS technical courses with holistic courses on ethics, citizenship, social relations, and human welfare (Solem 2017). This approach can provide broader societal viewpoints than can be addressed through location analytics alone.

Overall, the value of academic and professional training in spatial business is high. Although the US federal government does not have separate job categories for geospatial managers, analysts, or specialists, US Bureau of Labor Statistics (2020) data for related categories such as cartographers, geoscientists, statisticians, and software developers shows high rates of growth, pointing to demand-driven job markets for spatially educated people entering the workforce in the 2020s.

Communities of practice

Several studies of geospatial education in geography have called for broadening this education considerably beyond traditional academic topics by introducing communities of practice and more holistic ways of thinking (Tate and Jarvis 2017; Solem 2017). Communities of practice are proposed as a bridge between academia and industry. As shown in figure 8.4, the GIS community of practice includes current and newly graduated GIS students along with two types of experienced professionals, those with a graduate degree in GIS and those without a formal degree (Tate and Jarvis 2017). The community, which can interact virtually, is regarded as complementing formal courses. It provides an informal way of bridging the gap between students and the active business workforce, with information exchange going both ways: the business practitioners confront real projects without disciplinary boundaries, and recent and current students bring insights on technologies, platforms, and concepts that increase lifelong learning and awareness for both students and business professionals.

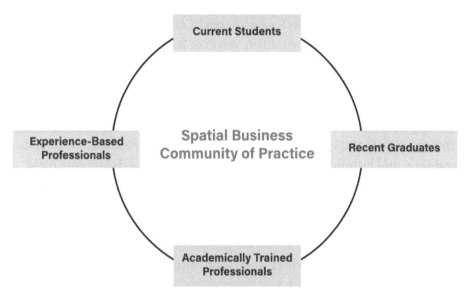

Figure 8.4. The GIS community of practice consists of, and brings together, current students, recent student alumni, business GIS professionals with GIS degrees, and other GIS professionals who have been schooled on the job. Source: modified from Tate and Jarvis 2017.

An example of job preparation and transition to industry is the career progression of Beth Rogers, who went from an undergraduate education in biology to a master of science (MS) in geoscience and then to a first business job as an intermediate software developer at Fruit of the Loom, a major underwear and clothing company that is part of Berkshire Hathaway (Kantor 2020). She joined the firm's analytics group, which has access to a vast database of company clothing data. Although the environment and problems were very different from her graduate school study of the geography of fish, she applied her spatial background to develop algorithms that saved shipping costs in supply chains and relocated products to alternative distribution centers. On the job, Beth received mentoring from the CIO and others and was so successful that she was advanced to senior manager of data science (Kantor 2020). This story illustrates how a solid and broad science education can be converted, with mentoring, into an intensive and rapid-moving sequence of spatial business positions.

PART
3
TOWARD SPATIAL EXCELLENCE

Closing case study: BP

BP, formerly British Petroleum, is the world's seventh-largest petroleum company, with revenues of US$227 billion and 65,900 employees. In the mid-2010s, a decision was made by senior BP management to overcome mounting IT glitches with its legacy system by initiating company-wide digital transformation (Jacobs 2019; Venables 2019). The company made a major transition from maturity stage 3 to stage 4 by rolling out an enterprise architecture, which the geospatial lead and team named One Map.

The One Map enterprise platform replaced the company's existing decentralized silos with an integrated system that includes big data across the enterprise; IoT; access for any authorized BP employee; inclusion of all static, real-time, and historical data; and storage in regional clouds for more rapid response. The platform includes systems of record for field assets, as well as spatial analysis and location analytics tools (Boulmay 2020). Infrastructure is regional, consisting of installations in multiple countries, each of which has enterprise servers, portals, and full geospatial software. With this modern platform, any user anywhere worldwide, with permission, can access the complete set of BP map layers and information. Monthly, there are more than 2,100 active spatial portal users and more than 4 million map service requests. For backbone applications, automation of widely repeated workflows is emphasized, which simplifies use and maintenance (Boulmay 2018).

BP's small geospatial team was originally given the job a decade earlier of supporting four siloed US BP business units spread over four states. BP made the decision to leave critical specialist systems inherited from the silo period in place, but now they are also linked to the enterprise backbone, which supports a common enterprise-wide centralized database that contains more than 40,000 datasets (Boulmay 2019). This system allows robust storage of data accessible across the company's matrix of regions, portable devices, and functional teams. For example, the managers of a BP natural gas field in Indonesia can access BP enterprise data on their mobile devices. Through collaborative conversations and organizational networking, the GIS manager learned that specialized business units preferred to develop their own dashboards and visualizations, which put those analytics applications in the hands of the specialists who understood pipeline design or raw material supply chain routing. Specialist analytics were handed over to special teams known as citizen developers (PESA 2020).

The geospatial lead exemplified spatial leadership in other ways as well. He rolled out continual training and emphasized marketing and justification of GIS at maturity stages along the way. He also realized that, after building standardized software, infrastructure, and data, he needed to lead by shifting attention to the data services being used by the most user departments and emphasizing the most used applications. For example, he led in supporting the mapping and spatial analysis required for the COVID-19 pandemic. The standardized central data could be analyzed in new ways and quickly, allowing valuable reports to be produced within days.

The lessons from this case are reflected in the stages of spatial maturity, as shown earlier in figure 8.1. All along, it was important to educate internal "customers"—that is, managers of peer groups—and, later, higher-level executives, in the value of location intelligence. The geospatial platform was carefully chosen as best in class. As it grew and matured, the spatial unit had a consistent strategy of providing a platform while letting the users develop applications. The C-suite became supportive and directly involved as part of the location-intelligence enterprise rollout. Specific lessons at BP are summarized in table 8.3.

PART
3
TOWARD SPATIAL EXCELLENCE

Table 8.3. Digital transformation at BP—10 lessons learned

	Lesson	Description
Lesson 1	Embrace the enterprise platform.	Decide which part of the organization should take ownership of geospatial capabilities. Do not try to do everything.
Lesson 2	Find the right home.	For BP, the original home was in the subsurface business under the Upstream segment of the firm.
Lesson 3	Set your data free.	Make data across the entire organization as freely available as possible, subject to security and privacy constraints.
Lesson 4	Let business users extend the platform.	Provide tools that are as user friendly as possible, delegating to business users the extension and upgrading of applications in their areas.
Lesson 5	Tailor user support to the new paradigm.	Foster collaboration between the location analytics team, IT, and the business units, which leads to support.
Lesson 6	Automate.	If technically feasible, automate a workflow early if it is likely to be repetitive.
Lesson 7	Mind your marketing.	Market concertedly the locational transformation internally and externally.
Lesson 8	Measure success.	Evaluate the locational transformation at steps along the way. Later review of the steps can provide invaluable feedback and lead to necessary tweaks and improvements.
Lesson 9	Build and maintain teamwork and appreciation for the players.	Give attention to support and appreciation of team members.
Lesson 10	Communicate clearly and widely, and repeat the message as needed.	Keep a focus on communicating activities and accomplishments.

Source: Modified from Boulmay 2018.

As the system rolled out, the small GIS team shifted from reporting to a small-scale business unit to reporting to corporate IT, and later to the leaders in core business divisions served in a major way by the system because they had the deep business knowledge of value and workflows (Boulmay 2018). Subsequently, senior management came to understand that geospatial transformation was a key part of the corporation's digital transformation, which increased their interest and support. In the latest reorganization of the company with the arrival of a new CEO in early 2020, the geospatial team joined a new high-level group, innovation and engineering, which is a locus for the people leading BP's corporate digital transformation, a key goal of the CEO.

CHAPTER 9
Strategies and competitiveness

Introduction

Geospatial strategy begins with justification of the importance of location intelligence and analytics weighed against multiple other uses of organizational resources. Decision-makers need to ask how strategizing will pay off and how, where, and why location value can be realized. Then, if strategic planning is to occur, what are the formal steps? How can policy be turned into action, and how can it be kept current?

For information systems, a well-known success factor is to align IT strategy with business strategy (Peppard and Ward 2016) so that parts of IT strategy complement and strengthen the corresponding parts of the business strategy. For instance, if the business strategy seeks to offer decision-making to an organization's workers on the ground, the IT strategy seeks to provide decision software on a cloud-based delivery platform that connects the mobile devices of the workforce worldwide. The importance of alignment likewise applies to location analytics strategy (Lewin 2021).

Geospatial strategic planning has external and internal elements. The external element focuses on how location analytics can strengthen the firm's competitive position or modify forces affecting competition, such as customer relationships or new products. Internal planning emphasizes improving the firm's own GIS infrastructure and processes. The internal element focuses on alignment with business needs, technological capacity, and human resource requirements to achieve desired location and business benefits.

Several themes have arisen in the book that provide strategic themes for organizations to consider, including the following:

1. Identify and enhance the location value chain
2. Enable spatial maturity pathway
3. Match analytic approach to the business needs
4. Build a spatial business architecture
5. Use market and customer location intelligence to drive business growth
6. Measure, manage, and monitor the operation
7. Mitigate the risk and drive toward resiliency
8. Enhance corporate social responsibility
9. Develop a spatial strategy and capacity
10. Provide spatial leadership for sustainable advantage

This chapter considers these themes within the context of strategic planning, and the next chapter elaborates on their implications for practice.

Geospatial strategic planning

Strategic planning is standard practice for midsize and larger organizations, whether they are a business, university, or governmental unit, and strategic plans are often required by senior management or the board overseeing the organization (Hitt, Ireland, and Hoskisson 2016; Hitt 2017). Likewise, IT planning has become commonplace in medium to large organizations (Peppard and Ward 2016). Formal location analytics planning is growing and shares many concepts with IT planning but has some unique features (Pick 2008; Lodge 2016), which are examined in this chapter. Also, many organizations develop an informal geospatial strategy, even if it is not performed as a formal plan.

Steps to developing a geospatial strategy

A geospatial strategy can be developed as follows:

1. *Initiate the plan with self-assessment and identify the business issue or opportunity that location analytics is intended to address.*

    Getting started on a geospatial strategy is challenging, especially if it takes resources away from short-term projects and ongoing operations. For that reason, the strategic effort should start with the highest-level senior manager or executive who is responsible for the overall outcomes of the strategy. The self-assessment needs to consider the capacities of the firm's human resources, IT infrastructure, finance, and management, and how they compare with the demands of the location analytics strategy (Peppard and Ward 2016; Piccoli and Pigni 2022).

2. *Identify the current spatial business architecture components of the company.*

    These include people, infrastructure, data, applications, users, business unit emphases on location intelligence, and governance. This step gives an overall picture of the present state of GIS throughout the enterprise and the current capabilities.

3. *Determine what the value-added benefits of the geospatial strategy are to the corporation.*

    Evaluate the value-added benefits of a new or enhanced location intelligence capacity and indicate how they help the firm's business objectives. Tangible benefits are measurable, such as the benefit of faster delivery times, greater value-added productivity, and the quantifiable increase in customer satisfaction. Intangible benefits include such nonmonetized advantages as high-quality executive decision-making, improvement in company brand image, and improved readiness to cope with supply chain interruption.

    Costs must also be appraised, including hard costs such as personnel, spatial software, data, virtual infrastructure, servers, and facilities, as well as the soft costs of insurance, security, and consulting. The net location value is the difference of GIS value benefits minus costs.

    In considering value, look across the relevant business functions and consider social, community, and environmental dimensions that may be appropriate. Such an approach reflects the CSR aspect of the geospatial strategy.

4. *Assess markets that new or substitute products and services can be released into.*

    Michael E. Porter's five-forces model of competitive forces (Porter 2008) can be applied to assess the competitiveness of spatially enabled products being released into a market. As explained later in the chapter, new and substitute products and services can alter the existing dynamics of competition. Other competitive forces that can alter the market are changes in relationships of a firm with buyers and suppliers. The geospatial strategy needs to assess the competitive impacts of spatially enabled innovations.

5. *Determine the vision and mission of location analytics as a component of the company.*

The geospatial vision is a picture of what the company's location intelligence will be in the future. It will serve as a guide for the organization to reach its desired role for location analytics, including how location intelligence will operate. It will reflect a full realization of value to a variety of customers. This vision will complement the firm's business vision.

The geospatial mission is a statement of the key long-term broad purpose of location analytics in the organization. For instance, the mission might be to achieve world leadership in applying location intelligence to evaluate insurance risks. Or the mission might be to have the most accurate geospatial prediction for siting new car dealerships in Brazil. The mission is often brief so that it is understandable and can have wide adoption throughout an organization. It serves to unite the firm's stakeholders around a primary goal.

A leadership team should include those with technical expertise and those with business expertise to ensure that the vision and mission capture the business strategy and the role of GIS in achieving the business strategy. This team should be included in the vibrant back-and-forth of discussion, argument, and eventually consensus on mission and vision. As seen in the review of spatial maturity stages in chapter 8, gaining a voice in upper management decisions is a key factor for success in attaining stages 4 and 5. Geospatial strategy progression flounders without the inclusion of business and technical expertise in formulating vision and mission. For example, in a global commercial real estate company, the leader of its geospatial initiative was excluded from corporate strategy setting, and GIS became a hard sell around the company, falling short of its potential.

6. *Define the scope of infrastructure to achieve strategic objectives.*

What technical steps need to be accomplished? These might include building software applications, outsourcing to a cloud platform, providing intensive spatial training for new managerial users, prototyping innovation in emerging spatial technologies, or strengthening the physical geospatial infrastructure (Lodge 2016). Scope can be examined in terms of departments and regions or internal and external stakeholders.

7. *Assess risks.*

The strategy being proposed should consider risks of financial losses, lower-quality outcomes, underperforming personnel, poor management decision-making, reputational damage, and adverse events in the external environment (Peppard and Ward 2016).

Other risks include the following:
- Information for operational efficiency or management decisions is missing.
- Investment in strategic development of GIS is out of alignment with IT and business strategies.
- GIS infrastructure and related IT infrastructure are insufficient to support the GIS improvements called for in the strategic plan.
- Location value is underestimated because intangible value is not recognized.
- Strategic spatial applications and solutions are implemented with short life cycles, so the benefits are reduced by the need for constant redesign.
- Management priorities change in unexpected ways, requiring major revision of the GIS strategy.

If carefully conceived, a geospatial strategy can serve as a touchstone over several years. Smaller activities and projects can be measured against the plan in approving them for funding. This approach has been shown to steadily move an organization toward achieving its strategic goals. However, the external environment and markets may change more rapidly than the pace of the strategic plan. An example is the COVID-19 pandemic, which impacted many firms in their spatial deployments, depending on industry. Consider, for instance, the map-intensive sharing economy for on-demand ride-sharing. In ride-sharing, the GIS benefits of locational intelligence in Uber and Lyft cars were overshadowed by a sharply reduced customer base. On the other hand, the pharmaceutical industry benefited by urgent need to apply predictive location analytics to optimize vaccine supply chains.

Building a robust and complete geospatial strategic plan that is updated regularly serves as a reference point for all the location value contributions that a company should strive for, yet the extent of strategic planning tends to vary by the spatial maturity stage of the firm (Peppard and Ward 2016).

When a geospatial strategy is undertaken as an effort within a nascent department (stage 2 in the spatial decision model), the spatial strategic focus can be limited to finding the immediate opportunities, obtaining sufficient technology, and determining the value-add of the endeavor.

As spatial maturity progresses to stage 3, the focus of planning typically shifts to incorporating strategic goals. At stage 4 of the enterprise platform, most of the recommended strategy planning steps are in effect. Because spatial awareness is now firmly implanted throughout the organization, coordination of location strategy with the company's business strategies might now be initiated by members of the senior executive team. Finally, in maturity stage 5, the spatial strategy has matured to include research on competitors, risk analysis, and the appraisal of innovative spatial technologies.

BP, the closing case study in chapter 8, is an example of making the shift to more comprehensive strategic planning. BP jumped, in a transformative single year, from planning on a multidepartmental performance basis to enterprise-wide planning keyed to strengthened connections to senior management. Maturation of spatial strategic planning paralleled the jump to a firm-wide enterprise locational approach for competitive advantage.

Case example: United Parcel Service

United Parcel Service, or UPS, is the world's largest package and delivery company, with 481,000 employees, performing more than 2.3 billion route optimizations annually and serving more than 2,000 facilities in 220 countries and territories (Westberg 2015; Perez 2017; CFRA 2021). Its revenue in 2020 was US$84.6 billion (CFRA 2021). It represents a case of long-term geospatial investments that have strengthened the core of the corporation, but not without some setbacks.

In 1991, the firm introduced the first delivery information acquisition device (DIAD). At the time, the DIAD was an innovative mobile device for the UPS driver that provided updated delivery information and allowed drivers to electronically capture information throughout their route. Today, the latest DIAD includes these features, plus scanning of bar codes, tallying of cash on delivery, a programmed personalized map route that can be modified during the day with corresponding route stops and time card information, and many other features.

UPS's ORION delivery system is one of the world's most sophisticated and powerful locational optimization systems (Westberg 2015; Chiappinelli 2017). It minimizes the driver's daily route based on advanced optimization models, data from planning systems, and customized map data (Westberg 2015). By optimizing throughout the day, the UPS delivery truck might take surprising and unexpected paths. For example, for the next delivery, the truck might drive past four delivery points without stopping, on the way to a more distant fifth point. Although this seems puzzling, the counterintuitive reason is that it would optimally save travel time, gasoline, and money to proceed directly to the fifth point and return later to the missed points. This approach was a giant step forward from UPS's previous routing routines, which did not optimize beyond the next delivery point.

The GIS strategic planning had a slow start. Jack Levis, formerly UPS's senior director of process management, started at the firm in 1975 and took over a project in 2002 to provide spatial optimization for UPS delivery routing. He and his small team produced extraordinary innovation in mapping optimization for the UPS fleet but lacked a strategic plan and management support to operationalize the mapping software until 2012. In that year, senior UPS management finally gave him the go-ahead to prototype it for one region. The results were startling, showing high ROI and driver satisfaction. The ORION software quickly became a UPS-wide strategic initiative and remains at the core of UPS's integrated data infrastructure, now with additional regulatory and service components (Perez 2017). The contemporary ORION includes dashboards for control in the local delivery office. In figure 9.1, UPS workers are viewing a map to plan daily ORION deliveries on a monitor, also visible on a handheld DIAD.

The lesson of the decade-long, low-profile ORION testing and the subsequent decade-plus of strategic use highlights several points. First is that, in retrospect, the development period was too long, considering the subsequent competitive strength of ORION. During the 10 years of R&D, this project was not included in the strategic business plan or IT plan of the company. Because of this misalignment, the R&D innovation was somewhat siloed until its practical importance was suddenly realized (Levis 2017). After 2012, ORION turned out to be the force of direct competition, a secret weapon developed internally; the system currently generates more than $400 million in annual cost savings and avoidance (Gray 2017).

Figure 9.1. Two UPS logistics and delivery employees view a map using the company's ORION delivery system, with one employee holding a DIAD mobile device that can access ORION on the fly in deliveries.

UPS now places strategic emphasis on improving ORION further, developing a real-time and dynamic updated version with even more complete global coverage. This real-time version has a much shorter development cycle of two to three years (Gray 2017). For the future, CIO Juan Perez (2017) foresees the "dispatch [of] a fleet of autonomous package cars each morning that are guided by a real-time version of ORION." Another service under R&D is Network Planning Tools (NPT), which builds on ORION with a mixture of AI, advanced analytics, and optimization, a set of tools that can yield better efficiencies (Perez 2017). ORION and its successors are now part of UPS's strategic business plan—aligned, prioritized by senior management, and highly competitive.

Location analytics strategy in small business

Location analytics strategy development for a small business follows the seven steps outlined earlier in this chapter but has some distinguishing features that arise from the limited resources available and a different competitive landscape. Specific considerations include the following:

- Self-assessment of spatial capabilities may be more challenging if a small firm's senior management is less aware of location intelligence. Management may encourage greater proportionate use of outside spatial consultants.
- Alignment of location analytics goals with corporate strategy is essential. For example, a small blinds and draperies firm adopted web-based single-user business mapping software to compete effectively with a more numerous and varied range of competitors over a large geographic market. In this case, the GIS strategic goal to understand the expanded geographic patterns of competition was aligned to the business strategy.
- In identifying its internal location intelligence components, the small business can more quickly survey its people, resources, software, data, and so forth. Typically, in a small firm, resources are scarce, and hence, it may have to adjust its strategy to make the most effective use of internal and external talent.
- Calculating the net benefits of location intelligence may be regarded as too difficult and time consuming for a small staff.
- In the context of Porter's five-forces model, the small company may face asymmetric competitive forces from large, incumbent firms.
- In a small firm, establishing the GIS vision and mission may be diluted in the "haste to get to market" (Gans, Scott, and Stern 2018).
- Assessing risk might be more difficult for the small business because such firms are often innovating into unfamiliar markets and environments. For instance, the small blinds and draperies firm felt it lacked its own capability to determine its GIS risk, so it turned to the US Small Business Administration, which in turn referred the company to a nearby university to help determine risk. On the plus side, innovation may benefit from the small firm's flexibility.

In summary, the same seven steps for formulating GIS strategy apply also to small enterprises, but with the caveats of less geospatial internal workforce capability, time pressure from leadership to move rapidly to implement, and heightened competitive forces from much larger players.

PART 3 TOWARD SPATIAL EXCELLENCE

Consequently, locational intelligence strategy may be cast aside in the rush to get their product out.

Case example: RapidSOS

RapidSOS is a small, growing private firm founded a decade ago, which developed and offers an innovative approach to enhance the readiness of response to 911 distress calls. This approach involves sourcing and organizing location intelligence and other enriched digital information to accompany the distress calls sent to 911 emergency centers, which are relayed to first responders. The business and societal importance of providing fuller and more accurate information to expedite emergency response has been accentuated in the COVID-19 pandemic, which at its peak contended with an overload of critical 911 calls.

The enriched information that RapidSOS sends along with the call to emergency communications centers (ECCs) includes the accurate location of the caller, information on the caller's real-time health, vehicle crash indicators, the caller's personal profile, and building security features at or near the emergency location (RapidSOS 2021). The enriched location information can also be passed directly to government emergency dispatch centers, known as public safety answering points (PSAPs) (figure 9.2). A first responder who is dispatched from an ECC or PSAP with the enriched information is quicker to arrive at the emergency, more prepared, and more knowledgeable in addressing the situation. For example, in a boating accident in Florida, a man fell overboard and was tangled in lines in freezing water in mortal danger. He reached for his cell phone in a waterproof pouch and called 911. The RapidSOS-enhanced information informed a helicopter of his exact point location, with considerable background information on him, which led to his rescue and resuscitation (RapidSOS 2021).

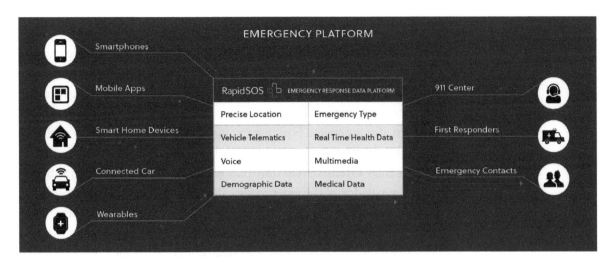

Figure 9.2. The RapidSOS emergency management system consists of sensors that register an emergency and feed information into the firm's 911 Clearinghouse of data, which is then processed and sent to government 911 emergency centers, first responders, and emergency contacts. Source: RapidSOS, in FinSMEs 2018.

Location intelligence is the cornerstone of RapidSOS's business model. The model is based on smartphones, which can determine location in multiple ways, including GPS, triangulation with multiple cell towers, Wi-Fi connections, and signatures of neighboring signals. This yields accurate location identification of callers' mobile phones, including indoor location and, in some circumstances, even emerging ways to identify 3D location. The latter has the potential to locate the emergency caller by floor and room in a multistory building. Analytics are also crucial to the RapidSOS model in data-mining large amounts of big data on health, social media, and business during an emergency and extracting what is relevant for that situation.

Although the US federal government seeks to augment 911 calls with more contemporary enhancements, it is doing so gradually. The NextGen 911 initiative, supported by the National Telecommunications and Information Administration (NTIA) and National Highway Traffic Safety Administration (NHTSA), is on a slow track to work with states to make more contemporary information available to first responders (NTIA 2021). However, this program would not match the extent of data provision that RapidSOS is seeking, and it does not include providing portals to ECCs and PSAPs.

The spatial strategies of RapidSOS evolved from phase 1 of developing geospatial strategy, which centered on innovation, to phase 2, in which the firm pivoted its spatial strategy to go to market while formalizing collaboration with Esri, GeoComm, and several other spatially oriented businesses

PART

3

TOWARD SPATIAL EXCELLENCE

(RapidSOS 2020; GeoComm 2021). In phase 1 of its geospatial strategy, RapidSOS developed its emergency support platform, which has geospatial data at its foundation. The heightened accuracy enables precise locating of a caller in 2D or 3D dimensions. That translates into first responders getting to victims crucial minutes earlier.

The firm also innovated building strong, long-term relationships with leading real-time digital data providers such as Uber, Apple, and Google so it could use their extensive real-time data to provide first responders with enhanced knowledge of the emergency caller/victim, the emergency site's built infrastructure, and a socioeconomic profile of the geographic area around the incident. RapidSOS additionally sought out ties with hundreds of PSAPs and ECCs, explaining what the firm could offer to each of them.

In phase 2, to get fast acceptance by PSAPs, the firm offered its portal product to PSAPs for free. RapidSOS astutely realized that, because a PSAP would be wary of the risk of holding its own extensive digital information, a free offer of RapidSOS's geospatially enabled portal could overcome that concern.

In the rush to market with the free portal product, how could RapidSOS generate revenues and assure profit in the long term? The answer is that RapidSOS mainly relies on payments from its data vendors, including Uber, Apple, and others, which benefit in turn by having their data in use in the 911 space. In addition, RapidSOS garners revenue from companies that pay to add their apps to its platform installed in the emergency communications and dispatch centers—an example of an ecosystem approach.

RapidSOS's capabilities are evolving to offer analytic modeling of the likelihood of different types of emergency problems at the caller's location. For instance, an emergency call arrives at an emergency call center at 8:05 a.m. from a smartphone caller at an exact location near a small Wyoming city, but the caller is incoherent and unable to reveal what the emergency is. Using the enriched location data, RapidSOS can use predictive analytics to generate the most likely emergency problem to be a heart attack, with 45% certainty. On the other hand, RapidSOS must overcome concerns about data privacy and meet the challenge of providing consistently accurate data to more than 20,000 emergency dispatch locations nationwide. Data violations can occur when the victim's personal information is used to inform first responders, constituting a trade-off between emergency relief to the victim and the victim's privacy.

This case supports the steps for forging a GIS strategic plan by a small, start-up enterprise while also demonstrating the challenges of achieving success. Of the GIS strategic planning steps outlined earlier in the chapter, RapidSOS included the vision and mission for GIS, the intended GIS solution, and covering most other steps in its GIS plan. What the start-up did not include in its strategy was determining the net benefits for the firm and assessing risks. Phase 1 involved a disruptive strategy (Gans, Scott, and Stern 2018), which is a typical option for start-ups. Because of innovation and upsetting of value chains, the emphasis was on rapid market growth without sufficient time or capability to assess risks and determine net benefits. Phase 2 focused on collaboration with major players (Gans, Scott, and Stern 2018). This allowed more clarity on net benefits. Risk was reduced by the cooperative tripartite agreement with GeoComm and Esri. Throughout phases 1 and 2, location intelligence remained at the heart of corporate strategy and was integrated from the start with corporate strategic planning. As the company matures, the firm will also need to strategically raise the quality of its data and serve many thousands of emergency centers with consistently high reliability. Also, as emphasized in chapter 7, the firm will ideally need to include CSR in its strategic plan, assuring a standard of data privacy as well as equity and inclusion in providing services across cities and municipalities nationally.

For location intelligence business start-ups, two essential strategic decisions are encountered: (1) whether to compete or collaborate, and (2) whether to be defensive, protecting products and technological advances, or to focus on rapid growth, development, and experimentation or risk taking in the marketplace (Gans, Scott, and Stern 2018). In both decisions, RapidSOS chose the latter option.

Geospatial alignment and value added

The geospatial strategy needs to correspond to the company's mission and vision. This has been well documented in studies of information systems (Peppard and Ward 2016; Piccoli and Pigni 2022), as well as specifically for GIS (Pick 2008; Carnow 2019; Lewin 2021). A business that has achieved consonance between its geospatial strategy and the strategic direction and mission of the firm is in alignment, which improves performance in the long term. Because the GIS leader is increasingly being invited in as part of the firm's strategic planning process, strategic spatial alignment is becoming the norm. The more active the GIS manager can be in the planning effort, the better. The manager may need to assert the importance of GIS to senior management by pointing to its role in addressing and mitigating pain points for the business, while indicating that an aligned GIS strategy can contribute

PART

3

TOWARD SPATIAL EXCELLENCE

to mission and result in tangible benefits for the company (Dangermond 2019).

Sustaining the alignment of geospatial strategy and business strategy over time requires continuing effort and adjustment because both technology and the external environment are changing rapidly. Maintaining this alignment is often referred to as coevolution (Peppard and Ward 2016). An example of coevolution, shown in the Walgreens case study in chapter 2, is the shift from an earlier strategy that emphasized US regional management decision-making using GIS to an international strategy that encompasses the expansion of Walgreens through the acquisition of the Alliance Boots pharmacy firm into a global company with an enlarged GIS strategy that seeks to provide spatial value to the Boots division.

Business value can be increased by prioritizing the initiatives in a geospatial strategic plan. In assessing priorities, the following considerations apply: determine (a) the most important of the strategic initiatives based on the expected value of benefits, (b) the enterprise's capacity to undertake an initiative, based on its current resources, and (c) the likelihood of an initiative's succeeding, based on benefits and risks (Peppard and Ward 2016). In assessing benefits and management risks for GIS, it is useful to categorize the certainty of benefits compared with the risk of the challenges (Carnow 2019), as shown in figure 9.3.

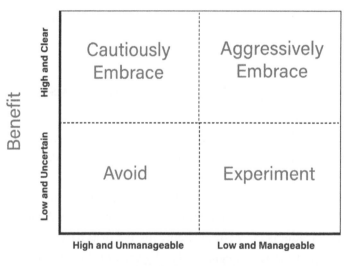

Figure 9.3. A two-by-two table shows high and low geospatial risks and challenges cross-categorized with low and high benefits, leading to four risk approaches: avoid, cautiously embrace, experiment, and aggressively embrace. Source: Esri 2019b.

Using this matrix, the highest priority should go to initiatives with high benefit and low, manageable risk. These might be considered the obvious choice as the easiest to pick. A very risky initiative with high benefit should be regarded cautiously, whereas one with low benefit and low risk should be considered an experiment for testing. A high-risk, low-benefit initiative should be avoided. Prioritization is evident In the UPS case in this chapter, in which the ORION system initiative was viewed as experimental for years before being raised to the level at which senior management aggressively backed it.

Competitiveness

Location analytics can expand competitiveness in a firm, leading to lower costs of goods and services to differentiation of products and services to entry into specialized market niches (Porter 2008). For UPS, the proprietary ORION software optimized daily routing of trucks, leading to significantly lower average cost of deliveries at scale. In another example, a small firm, "GIS Consulting Inc." (anonymous name), was able to establish a strong niche in high-end location analytics software for sophisticated federal government agencies that deploy the applications in real-time, spatially dynamic environments. For instance, it designed a standardized spatial surveillance system for government vehicles and personnel that provided support for a US presidential inauguration.

According to Porter's five-forces model (2008), direct competition is the primary force a firm must confront (figure 9.4). Four additional forces can disrupt and impact the competitive arena: new market entrants, substitute products, firm-buyer relationships, and firm-supplier relationships 2008). GIS and location analytics can influence all four of these forces, offering strategic advantage as follows:

- A new and successful market entrant can divert economic benefits from a company and its direct competitors—for instance, autonomous self-navigating vacuum cleaners, which use spatial algorithms with input from locational sensors to provide hands-free cleaning, have disrupted the competitive vacuum market.
- Substitute location-based products or services can usurp the benefits of an existing product or service by providing competitive market benefits. In the sharing economy, Uber or Lyft services substitute for traditional taxi service by outfitting their cars with interactive mapping that displays customer and vehicle locations with pickup and transport routes in real time, attracting riders.

- Location analytics can have a positive influence on the firm-customer relationship in various industries and markets. For instance, at a large midwestern insurance company, the speed of response to impacted customers after a destructive event is improved through a GIS model that dispatches a team immediately to a large disaster site by spatially modeling it, according to the amount and type of loss by location. This rapidity of response, in turn, boosts customer satisfaction and loyalty.
- The last competitive force, the firm-supplier relationship, depends on the positioning of the supplier in the market—that is, whether the supplier or the firm holds costing clout over the market. An example is the supply of coffee plants from hundreds of farmers in the Nespresso case study in chapter 7. The geography of the suppliers is crucial to costing; a large supplier in an optimal coffee-growing area may have costing clout, enabling it to urge Nespresso to charge more. The geography of Nespresso's growers can be studied by location intelligence, leading to decisions that achieve more costing evenness among suppliers, reducing pricing power. In other contexts, government regulation can be a somewhat unpredictable variable that affects supply.

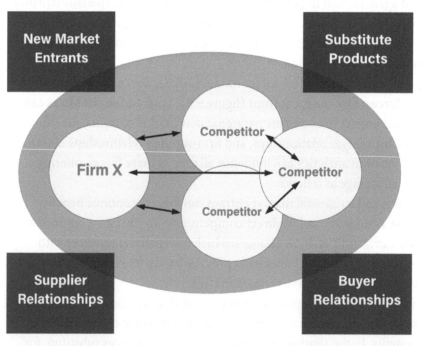

Figure 9.4. Porter's five-forces model, useful for formulating geospatial strategy, has five competitive forces, with direct competition as the central force, impacted by a competing firm's forces of its supplier relationships and buyer relationships and by new market entrants and substitute products. Source: Porter 2008.

Collaboration

Geospatial strategies should include an exploration of the potential benefits of collaboration. In contrast with competitiveness, collaboration involves mutual benefit to partner firms, so each partner gains in market position, value, strength of products and services, profits, and brand recognition. Geospatial collaboration ranges from informal sharing of ideas by individuals to large-scale pooling of technological knowledge by firms to formal collaboration on product development, marketing research, joint ventures, and co-branding.

Collaboration has been spurred to higher levels by digital technology (Kiron 2017), which can facilitate informal behavioral communication networks. An early study of GIS and networks of collaboration (Harvey 2001), based on 212 interviews of GIS employees, found that collaboration of GIS employees at firms in Switzerland tended to involve multiple interpersonal networks that are frequently formed and dissolved. Collaboration remains stable if the perspectives of group members remain consistent over time. The groups included private-firm employees with a focus on collaboration with data providers at the level of cantons, governmental entities comparable to US states (Harvey 2001). The cantons benefited the firms by providing a variety of spatial data, including demographic and cadastral information.

A more recent example is RapidSOS, discussed earlier in this chapter, a growing smaller company that collaborates with big-tech companies for data provision, with local public emergency services to enhance real-time information flow to emergency workers, and with several large GIS firms on development of services.

Ecosystems constitute another form of collaboration that has been hastened by rapid digital transformation sweeping through industry sectors. An ecosystem is an orchestrated network of collaboration that extends across many industry sectors (Jacobides 2019). Companies in the ecosystem have many common standards and share services, software, and platforms. An example is the iPhone, which developed into an ecosystem with other companies to share apps in its Apple Store. In this case, the platform is shared collaboratively, even though the app firms may compete in other business areas. In the case of RapidSOS, that firm's portal is strategically set up so that it can serve as an ecosystem to other firms in the emergency response sector. The post-COVID-19 business world is likely to veer even more strongly toward digitization, which will stimulate strategies that encompass geospatial ecosystems. A geospatial corporate hub might attract a sufficient number and variety of interactive participants to be considered an ecosystem.

Sustainable advantage

Companies are increasingly being held accountable for their impact beyond the bottom line. The triple bottom line adds accountability for social and environmental net benefit. Some companies' business and GIS strategies go beyond the goal of added monetary location value to formalize the social and environmental goals.

In the case of Nespresso, chapter 7 describes how deeply CSR is ingrained into its strategy and practices. Figure 9.5 illustrates the extent to which Nespresso embodies that broad strategy for sustainable advantage. In its priorities under the Positive Cup Framework, Nespresso focuses on long-term sustainable coffee supplies, analytics to support farmers, transparent communication to customers, and responsible practices within communities. These priorities are executed through two dashboards: FARMS, to analyze and manage farm activities, and the AAA Sustainability dashboard, to manage and track sustainable practices and KPIs. Finally, in terms of implementation, the focus is on increased efficiencies in coffee production, progress toward achieving 100% of supplies from AAA-compliant farms, and progress in achieving 11 (of the 17) UN 2030 goals. Part of the sustainability strategy includes GIS and location analytics to apply mapping to farm coffee more sustainably.

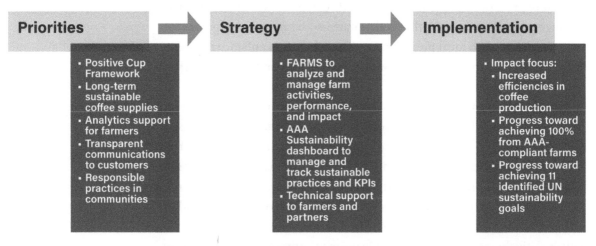

Figure 9.5. The Nespresso case study from chapter 7 is illustrated with respect to its strategic components of setting priorities, determining strategy, and implementing the strategy.

Closing case study: KFC

This case introduces locational strategies in the context of KFC, formerly known as Kentucky Fried Chicken, a global fast-food company that has a distributed, franchised organizational structure. This structure contrasts with UPS's more centralized management structure. The challenge for strategy shifts from centrally optimizing a routing and logistics system to supporting a variety of spatial needs across numerous franchises with varied degrees of autonomy.

KFC is a global brand that represents more than half the unit business of Yum! Brands, a firm that also includes Taco Bell, for about one-third of Yum! units, and Pizza Hut, which accounts for a sixth. Yum! is basically the franchisor but now operates only about 2% of its franchises. KFC has hundreds of franchise owners worldwide, except in China, where it was spun off as a separate company. Franchise owners own from one to more than 800 franchises. They are often independent in their thinking and strategies, although constrained by the terms of the franchise agreements. The thrust of the past decade has been for KFC to eliminate its ownership of franchises, so Yum!'s revenue shrank to $5.9 billion in 2018 but the company's profitability has increased.

Until 2016, KFC did not have in-house GIS, although Yum! Brands had GIS globally. KFC was siloed from Taco Bell and Pizza Hut, and when the corporate manager of GIS was hired in 2016, he was told, "We're not going to run you from the top; you're going to run yourself" (Joseph 2019). The GIS manager has a staff of two, a GIS analyst and business analyst. The GIS group interacts with a much larger IT group, which has vast responsibility in supporting the technology needs of more than 4,000 franchisee restaurants as well as supporting corporate functions.

The focus of the GIS group is to provide competitive spatial tools to the thousands of franchises worldwide. This includes customized applications, data, and training. Although the GIS group has access to franchisee data, it is careful not to share the data among franchisees because they sometimes compete.

The GIS group has key technology partners in Esri, Maptitude, and Intalytics, now a part of Kalibrate, which produces its branded SiteIntel platform. The SiteIntel platform provides location-based data visualization, forecasting, and reporting for real estate and marketing, based on a wide variety of up-to-date data sources. The GIS group adopted SiteIntel and has customized its platform in different versions for internal uses versus external uses that are franchisee facing. This software indicates, at a large scale—that

PART
3
TOWARD SPATIAL EXCELLENCE

is, mapping in great detail—where all the KFCs are located, where all the competitors are, the location of important generators of customers, transportation routes, traffic volumes, and demographics. The spatial tool has functionality to add and superimpose map layers, run reports, and perform spatial analysis. Additionally, the GIS analyst on the team receives numerous general requests for spatial analysis, location analytics, and professional mapping.

The GIS manager classifies KFC's spatial maturity as about a third complete, so there is plenty of opportunity to elevate the GIS to a higher maturity level. Several of the key GIS accomplishments to date are building the GIS capabilities into important parts of the franchisee's marketing plan and then loading the visualization of promising locations for new KFC restaurants. These can be viewed by internal KFC staff, but also, through SiteIntel, by franchisees seeking growth areas. The potential locations on a map for high growth are termed *market calls*, and the software enables them to be prioritized. Recently, KFC has acquired massive mobile-device data for overlaying customer sentiment from social media on top.

The Intalytics models also provide analytical tools based on the competitive details in the immediate neighborhood of a proposed or existing KFC location, including locations of competitors in nearby blocks, signage, traffic flows, vegetation blocking view lines, and other detailed neighborhood features. For larger geographies, trade area analysis is using demographics and geosegmentation. Sometimes, Intalytics sends a team of surveyors to a restaurant to ask questions, understand its location, and perceive where the restaurant is heading. This can be useful in helping a franchisee avoid choosing an underperforming location or treading on another franchise's territory and customers. This is an area in which social media spatial big data may be helpful in the future.

So far, KFC's spatial strategy has been tactical and practical, which would correspond to a moderate spatial maturity level. The KFC strategic planning team can observe other Yum! brands to find out what works spatially for their restaurants in the US or overseas. The strategy is to focus on the development of GIS applications rather than outcomes because KFC, at the corporate level, has reduced power over the spatial decision-making, especially in overseas franchises. Part of the spatial strategy is instilling franchisees with knowledge of their markets and locational opportunities. Ultimately, the spatial strategy is partitioned and focused on the franchisees' priorities.

In sum, GIS within KFC has been restricted to being a support entity within a franchisor, concentrating its spatial group to support the hundreds of separately owned franchises and 4,000-plus franchisee restaurants. The small GIS team has aligned its spatial strategy with the corporate business strategy and IT, and it has reached out to collaborate with other internal units as well as with franchisees worldwide. With GIS planning maturity at a moderate stage, there is still room to provide enterprise-wide, competitive location analytics to the corporation in the future.

PART
3
TOWARD SPATIAL EXCELLENCE

CHAPTER 10
Spatial business themes and implications for practice

Introduction

This book has provided a wide-ranging examination of spatial business with the aim of providing a contemporary foundation for understanding the business and locational knowledge base for integrating location analytics into the functions and goals of business. As noted at the outset, our approach was first to consider the "Fundamentals of Spatial Business" (part 1), then focus on "Achieving Business and Societal Value" (part 2), and finally consider managing and leading "Toward Spatial Excellence" (part 3). This concluding chapter summarizes key themes in each phase and outlines a set of 10 implications for practice that are derived from these themes (figure 10.1).

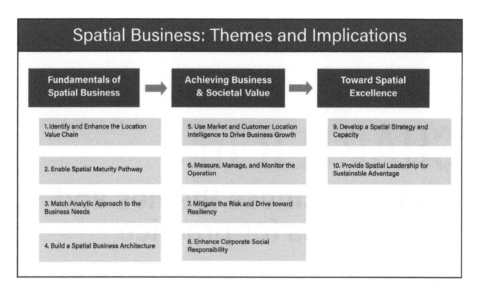

Figure 10.1. Spatial business themes and implications, showing 10 themes and implications for practice associated with the three sections of this book.

Fundamentals of spatial business: Themes and implications

The first phase includes four themes.

1. Identify and enhance the location value chain

The book has emphasized the location value chain as an important conceptual lens for examining location analytics across a business enterprise. Growing the value chain can elevate an organization from a spatial novice, in which GIS initiatives are localized to a particular function, to spatially mature, in which GIS deployment, driven by business needs and strategy, spans enterprise-wide across multiple functions.

Location value underpins the location value chain. Not every function in a business is rooted in location. Although this list is not exhaustive, common functions found in a location value chain include the following:

- R&D
- Business development and sales
- Supply chain management
- Logistics
- Real estate strategy
- Marketing

- Operations
- Risk management
- Community
- Environment

Organizations can use location analytics to heighten the value contribution of individual business units or combinations of business units. This, in turn, enhances the customer experience, creates opportunities for business expansion and competitive separation, and generates benefits for employees and the wider community.

Implications for practice

- **Use the spatial decision cycle to engage business managers and cultivate internal champions.** The book outlines a spatial decision cycle that provides a rubric to enable spatial thinking by considering key business goals, locational elements of that goal, location analytics that can be used to contribute to that goal, and the data needed to produce valid and meaningful results. With a firmly identified location value added that can be achieved, business managers can work with both technical experts and senior management to execute analytic processes that can contribute to gains in key parts of the business value chain.

- **Identify business functions with the greatest tangible value from location intelligence.** Location analytics can help achieve important strategic goals such as customer growth, effective operational management, and risk mitigation. This may occur within the context of a given function (such as marketing) but ideally would evolve through connections to related value chain domains (such as R&D and supply chain), providing an avenue to achieve strategies and metrics not viable by other means.

- **Whether the company is developing a service approach, developing joint marketing strategies, or expanding supplier diversity, there is no replacement for joint visibility and measured action planning.** For example, in revenue generation, location analytics can be used to identify and market to high-performing locations. In regulatory compliance, location analytics can demonstrate compliance. In operations and risk management, examples such as CSX (chapter 6) and Walgreens (chapter 2) demonstrate the value of location analytics to important business goals, especially filling an immediate need and a strategic opportunity.

Consider the benefits of shared value in which data and insights from one function may be valuable to another. The Shopping Center Group, or TSCG (chapter 1), a leading national retail-only service provider, has four main service lines: tenant representations, project leasing, retail property sales, and property management of those retail properties. Location analytics is considered core to each one and a key contributor to TSCG's 30% growth and its emergence as a commercial retail and information company.

2. Enable spatial maturity pathway

Among contemporary companies, spatial maturity ranges from novice to enterprise-wide, competitive status. The book outlines the concept of spatial business maturity, drawing on the analytics maturity model proposed by T. Davenport and J. Harris (2017). Factors that distinguish mature location analytics competitors include the following:

- Value of location-based business and customer insights
- Sponsorship and support of location analytics initiatives from senior leadership
- Clear and coherent business strategy
- Clear articulation of ROI of GIS and location analytics initiatives
- Availability of best-in-class GIS and location intelligence technology

The spatial maturity model can offer a pathway for organizations that may currently have location analytics siloed within a specific function or department but aspire to deploy location intelligence as a competitive force and driver of spatial transformation.

Implications for practice

- **Provide opportunities for location value to gain broad acceptance.** As shown in the John Deere case study in chapter 3, opportunities will come from all levels of the company as benefits are realized. At John Deere, location intelligence is poised to catalyze innovation in every part of the company's value chain, impacting farmers, dealers, and consumers while transforming the company into a technocentric agribusiness. With location intelligence, a company can be confident that profitability is maximized, current resources are optimized, risk is mitigated or avoided, and market share is captured.
- **Move toward deeper analytic uses.** Maps and interactive business analytics dashboards and applications provide immense value to understanding market potential, status, plans, and their interrelationship. Location analytics adds significant value by quantifying and

enriching data—calculating, measuring, and assigning—using real-world constraints and context with real-time feedback. Companies such as Travelers Insurance (2021), examined in chapter 6, employ a full range of location analytics to assist a range of business-critical functions. These analyses include predicting the location of natural disasters (for underwriting purposes), analyzing damage locations (for claims purposes), and identifying high-priority locational impacts (for disaster response). These tools have been used with remarkable success for recent hurricanes on the East Coast and wildfires on the West Coast (Martonik 2019).

3. Match analytic approach to the business needs

By using analytics to make better decisions, organizations generate value that manifests in tangible and intangible business benefits. These include cost savings, revenue growth through an increased share of wallet, uncovering business opportunities and untapped markets, an increase in productivity, process improvements resulting in improved asset efficiency, enhanced brand recognition, an increase in customer satisfaction, and benefits to the environment and society. A critical element in achieving this success is to match the right analytic approach to the business goal or need being addressed.

Although there is no right place to begin, the methods of location analytics often parallel the spatial maturity of an organization. The descriptive approach and visualization may gain initial attention and develop links on the location value chain, whereas the prescriptive and predictive approaches will garner the greatest executive visibility because they result in more direct findings to support future growth, competitive advantage, and collaborative potential for the company.

Hot spot mapping, route optimization, demand coverage, cannibalization assessment, and relocation strategies are examples of spatial modeling approaches. They support a company's ability to best understand its position and orient its products or services to its customers while optimizing resources. In cases such as these, location analytics provides awareness, spurs enhancement of an existing process or the creation of a new process, and then evolves to support strategic plan development. In digitally mature organizations such as John Deere, digital technologies are not just an add-on to existing processes and practices; rather, they prompt such organizations to rethink how they do business. Of these technologies, business analytics—the paradigm of fact- and data-driven decision-making—has been rated by business leaders as the main driver of digital transformation in their organizations, surpassing AI, IoT, mobile, social media, robotic process automation, manufacturing robots, and VR (Kane et al. 2017).

Implications for practice

- **Engage audiences through descriptive visualization.** Smart maps and visualizations have always provided keen descriptive insights that help decision-makers understand what has happened (in the past) or what is happening (in the present) in their stores, sales territories, and service areas, out in the field, or at a supplier location thousands of miles away. Today, powerful dashboards elevate the descriptive power of location analytics and broaden its reach. Dashboards composed of smart maps can be used in any part of the location value chain to provide situational intelligence in real time and facilitate reporting, which is crucial for decision-makers. Depending on business needs, dashboards may be internal or external facing.

- **Consider long-term business decisions.** The predictive power of location analytics is becoming increasingly important as businesses navigate an uncertain world. The cost of business disruption can be tremendous, as was evident during the COVID-19 pandemic. Prescriptive analytics is tied directly to support of decision-making, whether for strategic planning or within an established system. It reconciles a broad array of factors and criteria that may sometimes conflict. This provides a foundation for decisions and actions that enable process-, department-, or enterprise-wide optimization, ensuring business success, improving resiliency, and enhancing competitiveness in the short and long term.

- **Work toward location intelligence.** Businesses ultimately seek the insight of location to help achieve their mission and adjust to unanticipated circumstances. Through location analysis and data visualization, companies can gain insight into the business, social, economic, infrastructural, and climate forces that impact them today and in the future. Achieving location intelligence helps them define their circumstances and set measurable strategic and tactical courses for the future.

4. Build a spatial business architecture

The spatial business architecture outlined in the book and introduced in chapter 2 provides a framework for building a technical foundation for conducting effective location analytics. The architecture begins with the business's goals and needs and includes business users who are responsible for addressing these business goals, using location analytics to do so. The architecture continues with a series of location analytics tools, which depend on various forms of location data. Underlying all these functions are the various platforms that host spatial business processes, such as the cloud, the enterprise, or mobile services. The final component is the net consequence in terms of location intelligence that can be used to provide insights, inform decisions, and influence business performance relative to identified business goals and needs.

The style and extensiveness of the spatial business architecture developed by business can range from a relatively "light" style, with online or desktop use of internal customer data, to a broader enterprise platform with diverse applications, datasets, and user stakeholders. A mature digital business requires a mature data strategy to set up the proper architecture, flow, and governance of data. Without one, masses of jumbled data streams—a "data hairball"—can complicate product development and fail to deliver the intended insights. The development of mature data strategies is designed to quickly cut through the data clutter, align data streams with business initiatives and priorities, and dictate the proper use of the data.

Today, location data is ubiquitous. With the increasing use of smartphones, geotagged sensors, and other IoT devices, and the rapid diffusion of remotely piloted aerial systems such as drones, the availability of location data is at an all-time high. Mobile geolocation data has spawned an entire industry of providers of this data. Also prevalent is geodemographic segmentation data, which helps companies draw generalized conclusions about customers and markets.

As companies become voracious consumers of mobile location data, the ethical use of such data remains an urgent consideration (Thompson and Warzel 2019). However, with ethical standards of data aggregation in place, a heightened awareness of implicit bias, and proper internal governance policies, companies can continue to derive valuable intelligence using location analytics.

Implications for practice

- **Gain competitive advantage through location-savvy information products**. For location-forward companies such as Travelers, which are spatially mature, managing, using, and planning for new location data gives them a competitive advantage. Travelers has built its systems and algorithms with location value at the forefront. Because of this, the company can quickly take advantage of new data in the market and continue to provide premium services to its customers.

PART 3 TOWARD SPATIAL EXCELLENCE

- **Use well-crafted location analytics to strengthen partnerships.** As location analytics becomes embedded in an organization, the resulting business benefits can grow to impact numerous goals and stakeholders. Building trust through insightful and high-quality data products yields new customers, new revenue streams, and closer partnerships internally and externally. Trust builds relationships with customers and creates a competitive advantage, as seen in the Travelers (chapter 6), Natura (chapter 7), and Nespresso (chapter 7) cases. Likewise, trust builds relationships with suppliers and partners by providing a tangible and measurable way to improve collaboration.

- **Develop spatial data as part of the location analytics strategy.** Many companies are considering how their data can be used to create a new revenue stream or make services available for outside use. With C-suite participation and support of a chief data officer, central data organizations achieve the switch from data for business unit reporting to a more strategic level of use. For third-party data, the imagery sector is enriching spatial business by providing basemaps, point clouds, space-time imagery, AI-enhanced map imagery, and raster analytics and modeling (Dangermond 2021). Satellites, planes, and drones typically have digital image collectors, including radar collectors, lidar, multispectral collectors, digital cameras, and GPS. Various modes of collection should be considered for appropriateness for certain business applications because each mode has pluses and minuses (Sarlitto 2020). Social media with location features has become commonplace for individual social users, and analytics teams in businesses are increasingly employing the power of location-based social media to better serve their customers.

- **GeoAI can support decisions at scale.** GeoAI models are likely to play a central role in producing location intelligence at scale to predict demand spikes, identify high-margin prospects, anticipate disruptions in the supply chain, and accelerate logistics delivery services (Raad 2017). Already, in the insurance industry, deep learning–based models are expediting decision-making in damage assessment, claims processing, and fraud detection.

Achieving business and societal value: Themes and implications

The second phase includes four themes.

5. Use market and customer location intelligence to drive business growth

Location intelligence is used competitively in global, local, and hyperlocal markets. Rich geographic information increases competitiveness, fosters new products and services, and provides new ways to strengthen ties with suppliers and buyers. Business expansion, marketing, sales, and service all have location value as a core element in decision-making for short- and long-term growth opportunity assessment.

Marketing is strengthened by location intelligence through the ability to target, measure, and communicate. The location of customers, company stores, storage facilities, competitor facilities, and transportation routing all contribute to the total picture, as do geodemographic and social media metrics. Depending on the nature of the analysis, location intelligence can be made available at different unit scales, such as county, zip code, city, census tract, and individual. For instance, marketing data from major social media vendors is used by RapidSOS (chapter 9) to improve the accuracy and timeliness of the emergency response of its local and regional government clients.

New operations growth, new service revenue growth, and business expansion are all uniquely benefited by location thinking, because models can predict market share, overall sales, revenues, and profit potential of trade areas. This, in turn, drives service and optimization. The ability to measure and target spatially allows companies to see their results in the form of satisfied customers, higher market penetration, a higher net promoter score, trusted service relationships with suppliers, and improved company engagement at each venue and online.

Implications for practice

- **Understand and predict customer behavior.** For business development and sales, companies are increasingly combining proprietary customer data (for example, website, mobile, and CRM) with data from social media feeds and household virtual assistants to generate insights about a customer's mindset and create a holistic 360-degree persona. This can be used to forecast sales, manage inventory levels, and prescribe location-specific target marketing campaigns along with

PART
3
TOWARD SPATIAL EXCELLENCE

individualized engagement and retention strategies that minimize the risk of attrition (Davenport 2018). Increasingly, CRM systems are beginning to include spatial data access and visualization as omnichannel engagement becomes widespread. This fuels GeoAI models used to provide rich, dynamic insights into customer behavior.

- **Bridge digital and physical interactions to meet customers where they are.** CRM data in combination with new data from third parties, such as anonymized human movement data, can be coupled with more traditional sociodemographics and consumer spending data to inform decision-support prescriptive modeling and ongoing monitoring. As shown in the KFC case study in chapter 9, location intelligence furnishes the firm and its franchisees with rich and varied social media and demographic information at the micro level for decision-making on competitive locations of retail units. Such information is used by most retailers and QSRs to support real estate investments and lease agreements and to set up and evaluate KPIs associated with each unit in its trade area classification or cluster. Stronger correlations can be drawn to improve the connection between digital and physical interaction to achieve higher customer conversion metrics, improve the experience for the customer, and find savings in optimized product assortments.

- **Apply across business functions to win priority markets.** In marketing, companies habitually measure their opportunity and study their priority markets to engage the best go-to-market course of action. A location-based approach draws the connection to the 7 *P*s of marketing through sales, investment, and planning. This is illustrated in the FreshDirect case study in chapter 4, in which the output of activities from one function flows into the next, from marketing through sourcing, distribution, and delivery, bringing functions together for better planning and nimble response. In this case, as a beneficial by-product, FreshDirect was able to optimally invest in trucks, some with refrigeration, because the company knew it would help them maintain safety standards within their planned delivery windows.

- **Use service area analytics to gain a competitive advantage.** As businesses increasingly focus on the customer experience, service areas play an equally critical role, improving customer satisfaction as well as cost and operations efficiencies. In the case of CIDIU's environmental services (chapter 3), the ability to measure, monitor, and target drives the business initiatives. By integrating IoT, GIS, and optimization modeling and using location-aware sensors, CIDIU S.p.A. was able to eliminate the third shift for its entire service area. In addition, the number of vehicles used during a test period decreased by 33%, reducing waste collection operational costs and augmenting the company's competitiveness (Fadda et al. 2018). A third benefit is showcased in the Cisco case study in chapter 5, in which premium service areas were developed and services were sold without incurring additional operating expense, resulting in significantly higher profit.

- **Analyze locations for achieving long-term market growth.** For long-term growth, the ability to evaluate underpenetrated and underserved areas helps a business weigh its future investments through partnerships or acquisitions. Location analytics helps set up the desired outcome through detailed evaluation of multiple variables, including risk, country development stage, competitive reach, transportation, utility resourcing, compliance, and climate variables. Such analysis may lead to initial sales testing or operations research to assess greenfield growth, potential acquisitions, and sales potential, even 10–20 years ahead of planned investment. With location intelligence, businesses can reorient supply chains for significant savings or conduct granular or hypersegmented analyses of business development opportunities, as discussed in the Oxxo case study in chapter 4.

6. Measure, manage, and monitor the operation

Facility and process monitoring, historically the center of value in an organization, extends from situational awareness to facilities, supply chain, and logistics. Quality, consistency, cost, and continuous improvement needs are high in these functions, and depending on the industry, so are capital investment and sustainability efforts. Increasing profitability with optimal resourcing has location value chain linkages in service delivery, business growth planning, vendor selection, asset management, distribution, and sustainable development.

In manufacturing, for example, production cannot happen without safe buildings, well-functioning machines, reliable services to make them run, and transportation to get products to market. Hundreds of millions of dollars in capital investment are spent on new plants and the tools to make products. Factory automation is continuously advancing, and there is an ongoing interest in making products to order. These two needs alone illustrate the need for location-based asset management and distribution network planning. Additionally, building automation, energy optimization, and predictive maintenance are areas of focus for companies maintaining physical space, offices, or leasable space. Spatial data about facilities and assets serves as a solid foundation for each of these focus areas and provides the framework to see them all in an integrated manner. At a minimum, this helps an organization boost data accuracy, reduce errors, adopt automated workflows, and improve efficiency.

With improved facility and process monitoring, a company will see higher product yields, decreased expenses, and satisfied customers through more timely delivery of quality products. Companies will have an enhanced ability to respond nimbly to significant pressures and disruptions such as the COVID-19 pandemic, as well as open doors to new revenue streams. The combination of facility, supply chain, and asset data in various permutations with a location-driven approach will more quickly alleviate pressures such as those experienced by Toyota in the aftermath of the Fukushima nuclear incident in Japan in 2011, discussed in chapter 5.

Implications for practice

- **Use real-time tracking to achieve operational benefits.** Transcending industry verticals, the real-time tracking and monitoring of asset location and condition can improve productivity, prevent breakdowns, ensure safety, and reduce costs. This book provides examples of GIS coupled with other technologies and data such as IoT-based sensors, drones, AR, RFID, and machine learning to provide sophisticated, real-time geotagged data and locational insights of considerable business value for operational and tactical decision-making in near-real time. This is exemplified by the Tampa broadband service dashboard that monitors critical dimensions of broadband service delivery (chapter 5). Location intelligence can also guide the dynamic navigation of field assets (people and vehicles), reducing travel time and ensuring that service time windows are met. In breakdowns or emergencies, location intelligence can reroute drivers and vehicles, ensure safety, and maintain the timeliness of operations.
- **Consider indoor analytics for improved profitability.** Although outdoor and mobile assets are more commonly monitored, indoor spatial relationships are increasingly being developed, measured, and tracked, as shown with LAX in chapter 5. Manufacturers, retailers, real estate companies, and public facilities can all benefit from this cross-industry function. In manufacturing, for example, efficient layouts can increase the productivity of production lines. In retail, customer experience is paramount, so companies are improving their layouts to

avoid congestion, aligning basket analysis with product placement, and engaging their loyal customers with a premier experience, as shown in chapter 3. This helps businesses design the layout of facilities to increase shopper traffic and increase average transaction values and profitability (Hwangbo et al. 2017).

- **Use location analytics to enhance supply chain visibility.** Facilities themselves are also a critical node in the supply chain; the network of facilities for a company is a balance of cost, risk, and regulation. Digitizing and mapping a supply chain as part of organizational digital transformation can have several benefits. For a global business, it can provide a reliable operating picture of how the supply network chain performs and where it might be failing. In addition, a digital, fully mapped supply chain can deliver valuable situational awareness powered by real-time alerts and notifications, asset tracking, and monitoring. It can also identify geographic stress points that may be prone to risks. This can help accelerate a company's response time during the normal course of business and enable it to plan, prepare, and respond in an emergency.

- **Consider new technologies to provide holistic views of operations.** Real-time tracking and monitoring of asset location and condition can improve productivity, maintain uptime, ensure safety, and reduce costs. In addition to IoT, GIS technology is also being coupled with the concept of creating a digital twin (chapter 2)—a virtual replica or electronic counterpart of physical assets, processes, or systems (Tao et al. 2019). GIS mapping provides a holistic overview of system performance—people, assets, sensors, devices, and other services—during normal operations but also during disruptions. It allows for the disruption to trigger notifications, maintenance, or necessary interventions to assure a product's safety and prevent costly damage, loss, and disruptions to customers.

- **Use the platform to integrate disparate operational data.** The book details how managing a supply chain effectively requires combining internal organizational data with external data from varied sources. If these disparate data streams reside in individual silos, their business user needs, whether upstream or downstream facing, are equally siloed. However, as an interface, a geospatial platform acts as an integrative platform between the siloed data streams and use cases. The platform enables users with different business needs across the enterprise to collaborate, drawing on descriptive visualization of georeferenced datasets, which provides the foundation for predictions, decisions, and informed actions across the network.

7. Mitigate the risk and drive toward resiliency

Imagine a company's assets, such as a utility company's power lines or transformers, igniting a fire because of poorly managed maintenance. As shown in chapter 6, the Texas-based Mid-South Synergy had to estimate the risk posed by dead trees collapsing on its power lines and potentially sparking wildfires. Perhaps the asset starts a wildfire that ignites thousands of homes or a factory. The fines, product shortages, or bad publicity may financially damage or even bankrupt a company. Or perhaps an uncharacteristic freeze or hurricane halts power distribution, stops an entire material supply chain, and creates housing challenges for company associates, servicers, and customers alike. Also, imagine a washout from severe weather that renders a railroad track unusable, as occurred in the case of CSX Corporation (chapter 6). Although such events cannot be accurately predicted in advance, scenario planning, action planning, and ongoing monitoring provide a more proactive environment for risk response. Every aspect of a company can be affected by risk yet there is no one function that holds ultimate responsibility.

In confronting external risks such as geopolitical crises and natural disasters, the lack of a visible plan can render CEOs and their organizations vulnerable. Recent surveys have shown that during such times, two out of three CEOs feel concerned about their ability to gather information quickly and communicate accurately with internal and external stakeholders (PricewaterhouseCoopers 2020). This need was apparent during the COVID-19 pandemic, when every company wanted to know how its operations were going to be affected and which regions would be most disrupted. Hurricanes and uncharacteristically bad weather make such needs urgent as well.

Risk means different things to different companies and different people. Travelers Insurance, Bass Pro Shops, Mid-South Synergy, and CSX (all in chapter 6) manage their risk and resiliency in different ways, with location at the core. Travelers has a competitive advantage by pricing more accurately and processing claims more quickly for improved customer service. Bass Pro Shops's dashboard of store and associate status provided much needed visibility under the changing conditions of the spread of COVID-19. Both MidSouth and CSX are asset-based companies that need to monitor the status of their assets to provide service to their customers.

Implications for practice

- **Reduce business risk and improve resiliency.** Risk and resiliency preparations (chapter 6) are concerned with physical disruption, brand image, competitive advantage, and impact on communities and the environment. Using location analytics, companies have a new way to measure and initiate action ahead of time, gaining the advantage of being proactive instead of reactive. With improved visibility, businesses can adjust to events and have decreased operational downtime, safe teams, measured climate action, and increased customer service, as well as partner and stakeholder engagement.

- **Use the platform to achieve greater supply chain visibility.** Beyond human-made or natural disaster disruption, compliance and sustainability issues are also key to supply chain management. The need to understand a supplier's or plant's location in the context of labor practices, water, and energy resources is critical to sustainability. Companies are typically aware of the primary address for their tier 1 suppliers but have little insight into the network of facilities supporting them and their suppliers farther downstream. Gathering data to improve location understanding allows companies to set baseline metrics and initiate plans to improve and maintain standards across their supply chain in line with their commitment to sustainable practices and ethical standards.

8. Enhance corporate social responsibility

In 2019, leaders of almost 200 major corporations in the US redefined the purpose of a corporation and signed a statement to promote an economy that works for all, affirming that businesses play an essential role in improving social conditions, locally and globally (Business Roundtable 2019). This expansive role of business to address social, racial, economic, health, and educational inequities has been intensified worldwide by the COVID-19 pandemic.

As corporate leaders navigate their businesses through increasingly uncertain business and geopolitical environments in the post-COVID world and are pressured to achieve growth, they are also at the forefront of shaping their organizations' role in confronting and addressing these inequities. At the same time, they confront an equally urgent challenge in the climate and sustainability crises. In each of these areas—whether it is building a racially diverse and equitable workforce, committing to supply chain transparency, engaging in sustainable business practices and environmental stewardship, or going above and beyond regulatory requirements to be true agents of change—location analytics and intelligence can play a role. Managers and leaders of twenty-first-century businesses are organizing in areas such as racial justice, CSR, sustainability, and shared value, all of which have locational components.

Implications for practice

- **Measure progress on sustainability goals.** Historically, there were few ways to measure business impact on society until the digital era. With the ability to digitally model a business in space and time and bring together extensive global datasets, it is now possible to examine the current state as a baseline and begin to measure changes, set goals, and monitor progress for the environment, community, and human rights to build even greater global resilience. Nike, Nespresso, and VF Corporation, all in chapter 7, are leading the way in delving into their supply chains and disclosing their product origins and impact on local communities.

- **Inform end consumer about supply chain performance.** The reputational risk and cost of engaging with suppliers who unethically source raw materials or manufacturing partners who do not hire locally or pay fair wages or who engage in child labor can be immense. More and more companies are providing interactive mapping to showcase their global supply chains to engage with a variety of stakeholders. USA-based Nike and VF Corporation were both early adopters in making their brands visible and offering insights about individual factories (Bateman and Bonanni 2019). VF Corporation took this a step further and created traceability maps of its brand-name products that communicate to consumers exactly where raw materials for a particular product were sourced; where it was manufactured, assembled, and shipped for distribution; and how product components flow between different facilities in the supply chain.

- **Deliver insights that balance stakeholder needs.** The Natura case study showcases how a popular line of beauty products launched in the early 2000s with ingredients native to the Amazon rain forest in Brazil maintained its commitments to biodiversity and environmental stewardship while generating sustainable competitive advantages for the company (Esri 2015b). After solving the initial difficulties of sourcing logistics in the rain forest, building strong supplier relationships (Boehe, Pongeluppe, and Lazzarini 2014), and building out the supply chain network, the company's geospatial platform now gathers location intelligence to make decisions about sourcing, pricing, and distribution that address the needs of all stakeholders: farming cooperatives, consumers, and shareholders. By using a quadruple bottom-line approach that balances financial, environmental, social, and human objectives, Natura (2000) has continued to diversify its product offerings using an expanded array of supplier communities and bio-ingredients while simultaneously protecting the Amazon and committing to the ethical sourcing of biodiverse ingredients.

- **Build climate-resilient infrastructures.** Companies are increasingly addressing climate resilience. For instance, AT&T (chapter 7) is addressing consumers' safety and security by actively researching at-risk zones and adjusting its fiber and cell networks to improve coverage. Through its Climate Resiliency initiative, the company is building a climate change analysis tool. Using data analysis, predictive modeling, and visualization, this tool enables AT&T (2019) to react to climate change by making the adaptations needed to increase safety, service, and connectivity for its employees, customers, and communities.

- **Guide community investment.** In the case of JPMorgan Chase (chapter 7), one of its exemplary CSR projects has been a long-term program to help small businesses thrive in the city of Detroit, Michigan, which had been economically declining for many decades. JPMorgan Chase decided to foster a campaign named Invested in Detroit across the affected neighborhoods to seek to rebuild the city and its economy. The company, a signatory of the Business Roundtable (2019) statements on CSR, has embedded CSR as part of its culture. It discovered it could help these businesses most effectively by using loans keyed to low-income areas to help disadvantaged small enterprises and nonprofits. Having succeeded with loans to three initial microdistricts, the bank intends to scale up to a dozen more while rolling out this CSR approach to depressed areas of other American cities. JPMorgan Chase is also realizing eventual financial benefit because it holds $20 billion in deposits in Detroit. Hence, the Invested in Detroit project can stimulate long-term business growth and conversion of many new and renewed businesses into bankable entities, adding to JPMorgan Chase's market share of deposits and loans (Heimer 2017).

- **Create dashboards that support global collaboration.** The COVID-19 pandemic has generated widespread use of dashboards, similar to the one published by Johns Hopkins University (chapter 7), in which industry, government, and health leaders use location intelligence to collaborate in providing visibility and metrics of spread and hospitalizations, developing accurate spatiotemporal forecasts of disease transmission, and identifying specific needs on the ground. The dashboard also enables coordination of targeted relief efforts across the globe to provide supplies, equipment, and personnel. Direct Relief and the Facebook AI Research, or FAIR, team collaborated to forecast the spread of COVID-19 in the US, combining reliable first- and third-party data on a range of factors, such as confirmed cases, the prevalence of COVID-like symptoms from self-reported surveys, human movement trends, doctor visits, COVID testing, and local weather patterns (Le et al. 2020).

Toward spatial excellence: Themes and implications

The third phase includes two themes.

9. Develop a spatial strategy and capacity

A coherent spatial strategy and the capacity to execute this strategy are both essential for location analytics to make a significant impact in a business. The strategy brings together business goals and needs with the capacity of location analytics to contribute to those goals and needs. Typical elements of a spatial strategy include the following:

- Determine the vision and mission of location analytics as a component of the company.
- Identify the business issues, opportunities, and needs that location analytics is intended to address.
- Analyze the locational dimensions of current and potential company business lines and operations.
- Align the locational strategy with the business strategy.
- Estimate tangible and intangible benefits expected from the spatial strategy, including costs and risks associated with pursuing these benefits.
- Identify the current spatial business architecture components and determining elements needed to achieve the strategic objectives.
- Develop an operational plan to implement the spatial strategy and KPIs to be measured and tracked.

A leadership team for spatial strategy should include both those with technical expertise and those with business expertise to ensure that the vision and mission capture the business strategy and the role of location analytics in achieving this strategy.

Implications for practice

- **Engage senior management in strategy development.** Location data and location analytics increase the agility of the business, challenge the status quo, connect the dots across the enterprise, drive profitable growth, and increase competitiveness. Spatial transformation changes the business profoundly, to the extent that senior management becomes the driver (Frankiewicz and Chamorro-Premuzic 2020). It also offers an opportunity for varied leadership. The spatial strategy should be closely aligned with the digital transformation office, the project management office, and the offices of the chief sales officer (CSO), chief information officer (CIO), chief marketing officer (CMO), and chief operating officer (COO). These are the offices in which the cross-functional needs will ultimately come together and that will fund the programs and product teams aligned to drive planning and operational work.

- **Gear strategy to benchmarks of spatial maturity.** Realizing the level of digital, analytic, and spatial maturity of a company will help establish a frame of reference for ongoing development and benchmarking to lead with vision, as seen in the cases of BP (chapter 8), Walgreens, and Nespresso. With only 20% of organizations deeming their digital transformation successful (Harvard Business Review Analytic Services 2020), considerations of readiness, resourcing, and talent are paramount.

- **Use strategy to educate stakeholders to a systems-thinking approach.** Devising a spatial strategy provides an opportunity to view the company across the location value chain—that is, as a system. This can provide the framework to consider new business opportunities and cross-company collaborations. It helps break down organizational walls and widens the range of impact while also providing greater awareness of potential risks across functions.

10. Provide spatial leadership for sustainable advantage

The transition from a strategic plan to a successful and impactful strategy is where the action begins. Senior leadership can provide the vision and critical support for integrating location analytics into business planning and operations, including the firm's overall business and IT strategies. In the case of UPS (chapter 9), although there was an extended period for the testing and retesting of truck routing and delivery algorithms, when company senior leadership saw the clear benefit of location analytics, it lent support, funding, and encouragement to middle management to extend location analytics across the company. Soon, geospatial thinking was added to the corporate vision. In the case of Nespresso, a critical mass of location value developed across its sustainability value chain. The Nespresso geospatial platforms supported its stakeholders in various capacities, resulting in award-winning achievements. Nespresso uses the tools in daily operations, spatial analysis, risk analysis, communication, and the development of new partnerships to grow its AAA Sustainable Quality Program for coffee.

Implications for practice

- **Provide leadership in executing the strategic plan.** Ideally, this would be a collaborative leadership with representation from relevant business and technical teams. This would enable working relationships, improved connections to strategy, and potentially new revenue-generating opportunities. In assessing priorities, leadership needs to determine the most important of the strategic initiatives, the enterprise's capacity to undertake an initiative, and whether an initiative can succeed, based on benefits and risks (Peppard and Ward 2016).
- **Contribute to sustainable advantage.** Location intelligence plays a key role in supporting and advancing sustainability initiatives by providing location-specific data on communities and workforce and by producing data and information products for different stakeholders. Companies can measure their impact on communities and the environment, giving them a competitive advantage in the eyes of stakeholders now and in the future. With such visibility, companies can more confidently confirm their global partners' and suppliers' actions toward sustainable use of resources, more equitable treatment of labor, and better stewardship of communities and the physical environment. Companies that invest in location intelligence are well positioned to develop and successfully execute ESG plans and commitments.

Concluding thoughts

Location information has never been more important to businesses. Spatially mature businesses deploy location intelligence to fully realize the power of location data to better understand and serve their customers and responsibly grow the business for the benefit of the enterprise and its employees, as well as to manage risk for the sake of all stakeholders. The location value chain model provides aspiring organizations with a pathway for spatial transformation. The use of location analytics in such organizations is driven by well-defined business needs and usually produces high impact and value. However, without well-defined business needs and a spatial strategy, GIS and location analytics may end up as just another piece of an organization's analytics and technology stack.

In closing, we reiterate the important role of management and leadership in contemporary spatial businesses. Several of the case studies in this book have shown that a key facilitator of spatial maturity is sponsorship and support by the senior leadership of business projects involving location intelligence. From a management standpoint, this book emphasizes collaboration, risk tolerance, overcoming resistance, and a consistent, value-driven focus on business and societal gains. With advances in technology, location intelligence and analytics use cases will continue to evolve. However, we hope that the principles of leadership, management, spatial strategy, and decision-making highlighted in this book will not only endure but also provide inspiration for businesses to compete and lead with location analytics.

PART

3

TOWARD SPATIAL EXCELLENCE

Abbreviations

3PL	third-party logistics
AI	artificial intelligence
AR	augmented reality
AWS	Amazon Web Services
B2B	business to business
B2C	business to consumer
BI	business intelligence
BOPIS	buy online, pickup in store
BP	formerly British Petroleum
CAGR	compound annual growth rate
CBI	contingent business interruption
CDC	Centers for Disease Control and Prevention
CDFI	Community Development Financial Institutions
CDP	customer data platform
CEA	Council of Economic Advisers
CIO	chief information officer
CMO	chief marketing officer
COO	chief operating officer
COVID-19	coronavirus disease
CRM	customer relationship management
CSO	chief sales officer
CSR	corporate social responsibility
DaaS	data as a service
DEI	diversity, equity, and inclusion
DIAD	delivery information acquisition device
DOC	Department of Commerce
DOL	Department of Labor
ECC	emergency communications center
ECDC	European Center for Disease Prevention and Control
EPA	Environmental Protection Agency

ERP	enterprise resource planning
ESG	environmental, social, and governance
EU	European Union
FAIR	Facebook AI Research
FARMS	Farm Advanced Relationship Management System
FE	field engineer
GDPR	General Data Protection Regulation
GeoAI	geospatial artificial intelligence
GIC	Geospatial Insurance Consortium
GIS	geographic information system
GM	General Motors
GNSS	Global Navigation Satellite Systems
GTCM	Geospatial Technology Competency Model
HBCU	historically Black colleges and universities
HIPAA	Health Insurance Portability and Accountability Act
HIV	human immunodeficiency viruses
HR	human resources
HRM	human resource management
ICT	information and communications technology
IDC	International Data Corporation
IMMS	Indoor Mobile Mapping Systems
IoT	Internet of Things
IPE	Institute of Public and Environmental Affairs
ISP	internet service provider
IT	information technology
JHU	Johns Hopkins University
JIT	just-in-time (manufacturing strategy)
KFC	formerly Kentucky Fried Chicken
KPI	key performance indicator
LAX	Los Angeles International Airport
LBS	location-based service
LBM	location-based marketing
LQ	location quotient
MOC	microeconomics of competition
MRP	material requirements planning
MS	master of science
MSP	Minneapolis–St. Paul International Airport
NHTSA	National Highway Traffic Safety Administration
NICB	National Insurance Crime Bureau

NPT	Network Planning Tools
NTIA	National Telecommunications and Information Administration
ORION	On-Road Integrated Optimization and Navigation
POI	point of interest
PPE	personal protective equipment
PPI	personal privacy information
PSAP	public safety answering point
QSR	quick-service restaurant
R&D	research and development
RFID	radio-frequency identification
ROI	return on investment
RPM	revolutions per minute
RTLS	real-time location systems
SaaS	software as a service
SCADA	supervisory control and data acquisition
SCRM	supply chain risk management
SDG	sustainable development goal
SDK	software development kit
SSVEC	Sulphur Springs Valley Electric Cooperative
TCJA	Tax Cuts and Jobs Act
TCU	tribal colleges and universities
TSCG	The Shopping Center Group
UN	United Nations
UPS	United Parcel Service
VGI	volunteered geographic information
VR	virtual reality
WHO	World Health Organization
WSI	warehouse spatial intelligence

References

Aggarwal, S., and M. Srivastava. 2016. "Nissan: Recovering Supply Chain Operations." Harvard case study. Harvard Business Publishing.

Anderson, J. C., J. A. Narus, and W. Van Rossum. 2006. "Customer Value Propositions in Business Markets." *Harvard Business Review* 84 (3): 90–149.

Angwin, J., and J. Valentino-Devries. 2011. "Apple, Google Collect User Data." *Wall Street Journal*, April 22, 2011. www.wsj.com.

Applebaum, W. 1966. "Methods for Determining Store Trade Areas, Market Penetration, and Potential Sales." *Journal of Marketing Research* 3 (2): 127–41.

AT&T. 2019. *Road to Climate Resiliency: The AT&T Story*. https://about.att.com/content/dam/csr/PDFs/RoadToClimateResiliency.pdf.

Bateman, A., and L. Bonanni. 2019. "What Supply Chain Transparency Really Means." *Harvard Business Review*, August 20, 2019. https://hbr.org/2019/08/what-supply-chain-transparency-really-means.

Boehe, D. M., L. S. Pongeluppe, and S. G. Lazzarini. 2014. "Natura and the Development of a Sustainable Supply Chain in the Amazon Region." In *Multinationals in Latin America*, ed. L. Liberman, S. Garcilazo, and E. Stal. The AIB-LAT Book Series. London: Palgrave Macmillan. https://doi.org/10.1057/9781137024107_13.

Boshell, P. M. 2019. *The Power of Place: Geolocation Tracking and Privacy*, March 25, 2019. American Bar Association, Chicago. https://www.americanbar.org/groups/business_law/publications/blt/2019/04/geolocation/.

Boulmay, B. 2018. "BP Shares Eight Lessons on Digital Transformation." *WhereNext* (Esri), November 12, 2018. https://www.esri.com/about/newsroom/publications/wherenext/bp-on-digital-transformation/.

Boulmay, B. 2019. "Enterprising Geospatial: Acceleration, Integration, Innovation." Presentation. Australian Esri User Conference—OZRI 2019, Brisbane, Australia, November 20, 2019.

Boulmay, B. 2020. "One Map for All." *Position*, February/March, 32-34. www.spatialsource.com.au.

Boyle, M., and C. Giammona. 2018. "Walmart and Amazon Clash with FreshDirect in New York Food Fight." *Bloomberg*, December 11, 2018. https://www.bloomberg.com.

Business Roundtable. 2019. "Business Roundtable Redefines the Purpose of a Corporation to Promote 'An Economy That Serves All Americans.'" August 19, 2019. https://www.businessroundtable.org/business-roundtable-redefines-the-purpose-of-a-corporation-to-promote-an-economy-that-serves-all-americans.

CACI Ltd. 2019. *Acorn User Guide.* Arlington, VA: CACI International. https://www.caci. co.uk/sites/default/files/resources/Acorn%20User%20Guide%202020.pdf.

Cairncross, F. 1997. *The Death of Distance: How the Communications Revolution Will Change Our Lives.* Boston: Harvard Business School Press.

CFRA (Center for Financial Research and Analysis). 2021. "United Parcel Service." MarketScope Advisor, New York.

Cheng, J. 2021. "Analysis of Integrated Report Adoption for Natura Cosmeticos." *Open Journal of Business and Management* 9 (2): 489–95.

Chiappinelli, C. 2017. "Buzzwords, Hidden Dimensions, and Innovation: A UPS Story." *WhereNext* (Esri), September 7, 2017. https://www.esri.com/about/newsroom/ publications/wherenext/buzzwords-hidden- dimensions-and-innovation-a-ups-story/.

Chiappinelli. C. 2018. "The Business Value of Sustainability." *WhereNext* (Esri), December 11, 2018. https://www.esri.com/about/newsroom/publications/wherenext/ sustainability-and-location-intelligence/.

Chiappinelli, C. 2020. "Think Tank: How to Reopen the Workplace during COVID-19." *WhereNext* (Esri), May 12, 2020. https://www.esri.com/about/newsroom/ publications/wherenext/reopening-the-workplace/.

Chostner, B. 2017. "See & Spray: The Next Generation of Weed Control." *Engineering and Technology for a Sustainable World* 24 (4): 4–5.

Church, R. L., and A. T. Murray. 2009. *Business Site Selection, Location Analysis, and GIS.* Hoboken, NJ: John Wiley & Sons.

City of Santa Rosa. n.d. Fire Aerial Photo Comparison App. https:// santarosa.maps.arcgis.com/apps/PublicInformation/index. html?appid=478994a6534e486db5fb2e6313fe213c.

Collis, D., and M. Rukstad. 2008. "Can You Say What Your Strategy Is?" *Harvard Business Review* 86 (4): 82–90.

Cooper, L. 1963. "Location-allocation problems." *Operations Research* 11 (3): 331–43.

CoServ. 2020. CoServ corporate website. https://www.coserv.com/.

Council of Economic Advisers. 2020. *The Impact of Opportunity Zones: An Initial Assessment.* https://trumpwhitehouse.archives.gov/wp-content/uploads/2020/08/The-Impact-of-Opportunity-Zones-An-Initial-Assessment.pdf.

Dalton, C. M., and J. Thatcher. 2015. "Inflated Granularity: Spatial 'Big Data' and Geodemographics." *Big Data and Society* 2 (2): 1–15.

Dangermond, J. 2019. Comments in "Enterprise GIS: Strategic Planning for Success," by A. Carnow (video). Esri Events (website), Esri, April 8, 2019. https://www.esri.com/videos/ watch?videoid=xaF6yBEvMj4&title=enterprise-gis-strategic-planning-for-success.

Dangermond, J. 2021. "GIS: Creating a Sustainable Future." Keynote presentation. Esri User Conference, Esri, Redlands, CA, July 12, 2021. https://www.youtube.com/ watch?v=1rtC_ZK74H0.

Davenport, T., and J. Harris. 2017. *Competing on Analytics: Updated,* with a new introduction, "The New Science of Winning." Boston, MA: Harvard Business Review Press.

Davenport, T. H. 2018. "From Analytics to Artificial Intelligence." *Journal of Business Analytics* 1 (2): 73–80.

Deere (John Deere). 2020. *Sustainability Report*. John Deere. https://www.deere.com/en/ our-company/sustainability/sustainability-report/.

Deere. 2021. *Annual Report, 2021*. John Deere. https://s22.q4cdn.com/253594569/files/ doc_financials/2021/ar/Deere-Co_Annual-Report-2021.pdf.

Deere. 2022a. *Innovation & Technology*. John Deere. https://www.deere.com/en/ our-company/innovation/.

Deere. 2022b. Deere Operations Center. John Deere. https://www.deere.com/en/ technology-products/precision-ag-technology/data-management/operations-center/.

De Pietro, Y. 2019. "Nespresso: The Business Value of Sustainability through GIS."

Geo Business Seminar, Amsterdam, Netherlands, March 19, 2019.

De Souza, R., and L. Iyer. 2019. "Health Care and the Competitive Advantage of Racial Equity: How Advancing Racial Equity Can Create Business Value." PolicyLink. https://www.policylink.org/sites/default/files/Health%20Care%20and%20the%20 Competitive%20Advantage%20of%20Racial%20Equity.pdf.

DiBiase, D., T. Corbin, T. Fox, J. Francisca, K. I. Green, J. Jackson, G. Jeffress, B. Jones, J. Mennis, K. Schuckman, C. Smith, and J. Van Sickle. 2010. "The New Geospatial Technology Competency Model: Bringing Workforce Needs into Focus." Special GIS Education issue, *URISA* 22 (2): 55–72.

Direct Relief. 2020a. *About Direct Relief*. https://www.directrelief.org/about/.

Direct Relief. 2020b. *Facebook AI Research (FAIR) Model of COVID-19 Spread*. Accessed December 28, 2020. https://directrelief.maps.arcgis.com/apps/ dashboards/2b329f0ef76246568511292df89fc2ac.

Dong, E., H. Du, and L. Gardner. 2020. "An Interactive Web-Based Dashboard to Track COVID-19 in Real Time." *The Lancet Infectious Diseases* 20 (5): 533–34. https://www. thelancet.com/journals/laninf/article/PIIS1473-3099(20)30120-1/fulltext.

Dresner. 2019. *Wisdom of Crowds Business Intelligence Market Study*, 10th Anniversary Edition. Dresner Advisory Services LLC.

Dresner. 2021. *Wisdom of Crowds Business Intelligence Market Study*, 12th ed. Dresner Advisory Services LLC.

Duckham, M. 2013. "Location Privacy." In *Information Resources Management Association, Geographic Information Systems: Concepts, Methods, Tools, and Applications*, vol. 1, chap. 3, 24–29. Hershey, PA: IGI Global.

Economic Innovation Group. 2021. EIG Opportunity Zones Activity Map. eig.org/ oz-activity-map.

Economic Innovation Group. n.d. EIG Opportunity Zones Activity Map. eig.org/ oz-activity-map.

Edward Jones. 2021. "Our History." https://www.edwardjones.com/us-en/ why-edward-jones/about-us/our-history.

Elliott, C. 2019. "Finding the Confidence to Grow a Business." *WhereNext* (Esri), March 5, 2019. https://www.esri.com/about/newsroom/publications/wherenext/ confidence-in-new-markets/.

Elliott, C., and C. Nickola. 2021. "Spotting New Business Opportunities in Consumer Data." *WhereNext* (Esri), July 6, 2021. https://www.esri.com/about/newsroom/publications/ wherenext/spotting-new-business-opportunities/.

Endsley, M. R. 1988. "Design and Evaluation for Situation Awareness Enhancement." In *Proceedings of the Human Factors Society Annual Meeting* 32 (2): 97–101. Los Angeles, CA: Sage Publications.

Esri. 2015a. "Savvy Businesses Share a Secret." *ArcWatch* (Esri), September 2015. https://www.esri.com/about/newsroom/arcwatch/savvy-businesses-share-a-secret/.

Esri. 2015b. "Supporting Sustainability through the Supply Chain." https://www.esri.com/library/casestudies/natura.pdf.

Esri. 2016a. "The New ArcGIS: It's All About the Portal." *ArcNews* (Esri), Spring 2016. https://www.esri.com/about/newsroom/arcnews/the-new-arcgis-its-all-about-the-portal/.

Esri. 2016b. "Urban Planning Scenario: Fictive Redevelopment of a City Block in Philadelphia (web scene)." ArcGIS CityEngine®. https://www.arcgis.com/apps/CEWebViewer/viewer.html?3dWebScene=86f88285788a4c53bd3d5dde6b315dfe#.

Esri. 2017. "GIS and Research: The Heartbeat of The Shopping Center Group." *ArcWatch* (Esri), February 2017. https://www.esri.com/about/newsroom/arcwatch/gis-and-research-the-heartbeat-of-the-shopping-center-group/.

Esri. 2018a. "John Deere: Data Science and the Future of Agriculture" (audio podcast). https://www.esri.com/about/newsroom/podcast/john-deere-data-science-and-the-future-of-agriculture/.

Esri. 2018b. "Location Intelligence: Powering the Next Wave of Supply Chain Performance." Esri (webinar). https://www.youtube.com/watch?v=iJMWDm0ERmI (13:19 mark).

Esri. 2019a. *ArcGIS the Foundation of Digital Twins for Utilities* (video, 25 min.). https://www.esri.com/videos/watch?videoid=jzn_u6uBRi4&title=arcgis-the-foundation-of-digital-twins-for-utilities.

Esri. 2019b. "Enterprise GIS: Strategic Planning for Success" (video). Esri Events (website), Esri, April 8, 2019. https://proceedings.esri.com/library/userconf/proc18/tech-work-shops/tw_2494-121.pdf.

Esri. 2019c. *Expanding Beyond Traditional Borders* (video, 10 min.). https://mediaspace.esri.com/media/t/1_11pdlrph.

Esri. 2020a. "John Deere: How Data Science Drives Business Growth" (audio podcast), January 24, 2020. https://www.esri.com/about/newsroom/podcast/john-deere-how-data-science-drives-business-growth/.

Esri. 2020b. "Spatial Analytics and Data Diminish Tree-Related Outages 60 Percent." Accessed May 31, 2020. https://www.esri.com/en-us/industries/electric-gas-utilities/segments/electric/mid-south-synergy-removes-tree-hazards.

Esri. 2021a. "ArcGIS Hub." https://www.esri.com/en-us/arcgis/products/arcgis-hub/overview.

Esri. 2021b. *Sustainable Development Report 2021.* https://storymaps.arcgis.com/stories/5387a3d2041c4773b4b1d70d9f981b65.

Esri. 2022. Node Capacity Analysis Node Utilization Dashboard. ArcGIS Dashboards. https://insights.arcgis.com/index.html#/view/2e009ad4a92c4b4b810c80d17f589728.

Fadda, E., L. Gobbato, G. Perboli, M. Rosano, and R. Tadei. 2018. "Waste Collection in Urban Areas: A Case Study." *INFORMS Journal on Applied Analytics* 48 (4): 307–22.

Fekete, E. 2018. "Foursquare in the City of Fountains: Using Kansas City as a Case Study for Combining Demographic and Social Media Data." Chap. 7 in *Thinking Big Data in Geography*, ed. J. Thatcher, J. Eckert, and A. Shears, 145–66. Lincoln, NE: University of Nebraska Press.

FEMSA. 2018. *Annual Report, FEMSA*. https://femsa.gcs-web.com/financial-reports.

FinSMEs. 2018. "RapidSOS Raises $30 million in Series B Funding." London: FinSMEs. https://www.finsmes.com/2018/11/rapidsos-raises-30m-in-series-b-funding.html.

Frankiewicz, B., and T. Chamorro-Premuzic. 2020. "Digital Transformation Is about Talent, not Technology." *Harvard Business Review*, May 6, 2020.

Fu, P. 2022. *Getting to Know Web GIS*, 5th ed. Redlands, CA: Esri Press.

Gans, J., E. L. Scott, and S. Stern. 2018. "Strategy for Start-ups." *Harvard Business Review*, May/June, 44–51.

Gao, S., J. Rao, Y. Kang, Y. Liang, and J. Kruse. 2020. "Mapping County-Level Mobility Pattern Changes in the United States in Response to COVID-19." SIGSpatial Special, 12(1), 16-26. DOI: 10.1145/3404820.3404824

Gardner, H. 2006. *Multiple Intelligences: New Horizons*. New York: Perseus Books Basic Books.

GeoComm. 2021. "Putting the Right Location Data, on the Right Map, for the Right People, at the Right Time: Introducing Public Safety Location Intelligence." GeoComm.com.

GeoTech Center. 2020. Geospatial Technology Competency Model. GeoTech Center. GeoTechCenter.org (website). https://www.careeronestop.org/competencymodel/competency-models/geospatial-technology.aspx.

GMC (Geospatial Media and Communications). 2019. *GeoBuiz: Geospatial Industry Outlook and Readiness Index.*

Government of Ireland. 2018. *The Changing Patterns of Unemployment and Poverty in Ireland, 2011–2018*. ArcGIS StoryMaps story. Dublin: Government of Ireland. https://irelandsdg.geohive.ie/apps/the-changing-patterns-of-unemployment-and-poverty-in-ireland-2011-2018/explore.

Grand View Research. 2020. *Location-Based Advertising Market Size, Share & Trends Analysis Report by Type (Push, Pull), by Content (Text, Multimedia), by Application (Retail Outlets, Airports, Public Spaces), by Region, and Segment Forecasts, 2020–2027*. Report GVR-4-68038-869-4. July 2020.

Gray, M. 2017. "Future of ORION, Our Powerful Route Optimization System." Address at UPS investors' conference, UPS, Atlanta, GA.

Green, A. 2020. "Complete Guide to Privacy Laws in the US." *Inside Out Security Blog*, Varonis Systems, New York. https://www.varonis.com/blog/us-privacy-laws/.

Grieves, M., and J. Vickers. 2017. "Digital Twin: Mitigating Unpredictable, Undesirable Emergent Behavior in Complex Systems." In *Transdisciplinary Perspectives on Complex Systems*, ed. F. J. Kahlen et al., 85–113. New York: Springer International Publishing.

Handly, B. 2019. "Getting Started with Location-Based Marketing." Forbes Technology Council Post, June 27, 2019. https://www.forbes.com/sites/forbestechcouncil/2019/06/27/getting-started-with-location-based-marketing/?sh=36c2b78657ba.

Harvard Business Review Analytic Services. 2020. "Rethinking Digital Transformation: New Data Examines the Culture and Process Change Imperative in 2020." *Pulse Survey.* Cambridge, MA: Harvard Business Review.

Harvard Business School. 2021. US Cluster Mapping Project. https://www.isc.hbs.edu/about-michael-porter/affiliated-organizations-institutions/Pages/us-cluster-mapping-project.aspx.

Harvey, F. 2001. "Constructing GIS: Actor Networks of Collaboration." *URISA Journal* 13 (1): 29–37.

Heimer, M. 2017. "How JPMorgan Chase Is Fueling Detroit's Revival." *Fortune*, September 7, 2017. https://fortune.com/2017/09/07/jp-morgan-chase-detroit-revival/.

Hitt, A. 2017. "Making Room for Innovation with GIS Strategic Planning." *ArcNews* (Esri), Spring 2017. https://www.esri.com/about/newsroom/arcnews/making-room-for-innovation-with-gis-strategic-planning/.

Hitt, M., R. D. Ireland, and R. E. Hoskisson. 2016. *Strategic Management: Concepts and Cases.* Mason, Ohio: South-Western Publishing.

Horner, P. 2016. "ORION delivers success for UPS." *ORMS Today*, INFORMS. https://pubsonline.informs.org/do/10.1287/orms.2016.03.10/full/.

HUD (Department of Housing and Urban Development). n.d. Map of Opportunity Zones. https://opportunityzones.hud.gov/resources/map.

Huff, D. L. 1964. "Defining and Estimating a Trading Area." *Journal of Marketing* 28 (3): 34–38.

Hwangbo, H., J. Kim, Z. Lee, and S. Kim. 2017. "Store Layout Optimization Using Indoor Positioning System." *International Journal of Distributed Sensor Networks* 13 (2): 1–13.

Investopedia. 2019. *The 4 Ps.* Investopedia. www.investopedia.com.

IPE (Institute of Public and Environmental Affairs). 2022. Green Supply Chain Map. http://wwwen.ipe.org.cn/MapBrand/Brand.aspx?q=6 [wwwen.ipe.org.cn].

Jacobides, J. G. 2019. "In the Ecosystem Economy, What's Your Strategy?" *Harvard Business Review*, September-October, 129–37.

Jacobs, T. 2019. "Digital Transformation at BP Is Starting to Add Up to Billions." *Journal of Petroleum Technology*, May 15, 2019. https://pubs.spe.org/en/jpt/jpt-article- detail/?art=5495.

Johns Hopkins University. 2020. COVID-19 Dashboard. Accessed December 28, 2020. https://coronavirus.jhu.edu/map.html.

Joseph, L. 2019. Interview, University of Redlands, Redlands, CA, January 24. 2019.

Kane, G. C., D. Palmer, A. Nguyen-Phillips, D. Kiron, and N. Buckley. 2017. "Achieving Digital Maturity." *MIT Sloan Management Review* 59 (1).

Kantor, M. 2018a. "Burgers for a Penny, and the Power of Location Intelligence." *WhereNext* (Esri), December 10, 2018. https://www.esri.com/about/newsroom/publications/wherenext/burger-king-marketing-campaign/.

Kantor, M. 2018b. "Business Advantage through Location Intelligence: The CEO's Guide." *WhereNext* (Esri), November 6, 2018. https://www.esri.com/about/newsroom/publications/wherenext/ceo-guide-to-location- intelligence/.

Kantor, M. 2018c. "How Social Media Could Improve Targeted Marketing." *WhereNext* (Esri), February 6, 2018. https://www.esri.com/about/newsroom/publications/ wherenext/social-media-and-targeted-advertising/.

Kantor, M. 2020. "A Lifelong Learner Brings a Data Science Edge to Fruit of the Loom." *WhereNext* (Esri), January 21, 2020. https://www.esri.com/about/newsroom/publications/ wherenext/a-lifelong-learner-brings-a- data-science-edge-to-fruit-of-the-loom/.

Kantor, M., and F. van der Schaaf. 2019. "How Data-Driven John Deere Wins the Market." *WhereNext* (Esri), October 8, 2019.

Kantor, M., and J. Peters. 2020. "A Blueprint for the New Era of Corporate Social Responsibility." *WhereNext* (Esri), February 25, 2020. https://www.esri.com/about/ newsroom/publications/wherenext/csr-and-location-intelligence/.

Kaplan, A. 2018. "Social media." In *The SAGE Encyclopedia of the Internet,* ed. B. Warf, 809–13. Los Angeles: SAGE Reference.

Kapur, M., S. Dawar, and V. R. Ahuja. 2014. "Unlocking the Wealth in Rural Markets." *Harvard Business Review,* June, 113–17.

Kazemi, Y. 2018. "How GM Maps and Manages Supply Chain Risk." *WhereNext* (Esri), November 15, 2018. https://www.esri.com/about/newsroom/publications/ wherenext/gm-maps-supply-chain-risk/.

Kazemi, Y., and J. Szmerekovsky. 2016. "An Optimization Model for Downstream Petroleum Supply Chain Incorporating Geographic Information System (GIS)." *International Journal of Integrated Supply Management* 10 (2): 151–72.

Kiron, D. 2017. "Why Your Company Needs More Collaboration." *MIT Sloan Management Review* 59 (1): 17–19.

Kouzes, J. M., and B. Z. Posner. 2017. *The Leadership Challenge,* 6th ed. Hoboken, NJ: John Wiley & Sons.

KPMG. 2020. *The Time Has Come: The KPMG Survey of Sustainability Reporting.* December 2020. https://home.kpmg/sustainabilityreporting.

Kumar, R. 2011. "Environmental Scanning." SlideShare (website), August 16, 2011. Accessed 2019. https://www.slideshare.net/rajworship/ environmental-scanning-8870811.

Lai, J., T. Cheng, and G. Lansley. 2017. "Improved Targeted Outdoor Advertising Based on Geotagged Social Media Data." *Annals of GIS* 23 (4): 237–50.

LAWA. 2019. *2019 LAWA Design and Construction Handbook.* https://www.lawa.org/lawa-businesses/lawa-docu- ments-and-guidelines/lawa-design-and-construction-handbook/ archives/2019-design-and-construction-handbook.

Le, M., M. Ibrahim, L. Sagun, T. Lacroix, and M. Nickel. 2020. "Neural Relational Autoregression for High-Resolution COVID-19 Forecasting." Facebook AI, October 1, 2020. https://ai.facebook.com/research/publications/ neural-relational-autoregression-for-high-resolution-covid-19-forecasting.

Leventhal, B. 2016. *Geodemographics for Marketers: Using Location Analysis for Research and Marketing.* London: Kogan Press.

Levis, J. 2017. "How UPS Strengthens Customer Connection with Spatial Analytics." Interview on October 10, 2017, of Jack Levis by Marianna Kantor (podcast), Esri. https://www.esri.com/about/newsroom/podcast/how-ups-strengthens-connection-with-spatial-analytics/.

Lewin, M. 2021. "Strategy for GIS: The Three Essential Steps to Creating Enterprise Value." Esri Canada. https://resources.esri.ca/news-and-updates/strategy-for-gis-the-three-essential-steps-to-creating-enterprise-value.

Lim, K. Y. H., P. Zheng, and C.-H. Chen. 2019. "A State-of-the-Art Survey of Digital Twins: Techniques, Engineering Product Lifecycle Management, and Business Innovation Perspectives." *Journal of Intelligent Manufacturing* 31:1313–37.

Litt, R. S., and S. M. Brill. 2018. *Location Information Is Protected by the 4th Amendment, SCOTUS Rules: Socially Aware.* San Francisco, CA: Morrison Foerster.

Lodge, A. 2016. "What Is a GIS Strategic Plan and Template?" *Farallon Geographics* (blog), August 30, 2016. https://fargeo.com/blog/what-is-gis-strategic-plan/.

Longley, P. A., M. F. Goodchild, D. J. Maguire, and D. W. Rhind. 2015. *Geographic Information Science and Systems.* New York: John Wiley & Sons.

Lowther, A. M., and D. Tarolli. 2020. "Cushman & Wakefield Clients Get 3D Tours and Market Insight." *WhereNext* (Esri), June 16, 2020. https://www.esri.com/about/newsroom/publications/wherenext/cushman-wakefield-3d-digital-transformation/.

Macy's. 2020. *Annual Report, Macy's.* https://www.macysinc.com/investors/sec-filings/annual-reports.

Marble, D. F. 2006. "Who are we? Defining the geospatial workforce." *Geospatial Solutions,* May 2006. www.geospatial-online.com.

Marks & Spencer. 2022. M&S Interactive Map. Accessed March 7, 2022. https://interactive-map.marksandspencer.com/?sectionPID=56c359428b0c1e3d3ccdf022.

Marr, B. 2017. "What Is Digital Twin Technology—and Why Is It So Important?" *Forbes,* March 6, 2017.

Marshall, P. 2016. "LA GeoHub: A Model for 'Datafying' Communities." *Government Computer News* 35 (2): 47.

Martonik, A. 2019. "After a Disaster, Imagery Gives Insurance Companies a Clear Picture." *Claims Journal,* July 25, 2019. https://www.claimsjournal.com/news/national/2019/07/25/292162.htm.

McGrath, R. G., and R. McManus. 2020. "Discovery-Driven Digital Transformation." *Harvard Business Review,* May/June.

McKinsey & Company. 2020. *Adapting to the Next Normal in Retail: The Customer Experience Imperative,* May 14, 2020.

MIT. 2021. "Amazon Last Mile Routing: Research Challenge." https://routingchallenge.mit.edu/.

MMA Global. 2019. *Heineken: Heineken@WhereNext.* New York: Mobile Marketing Association. www.mmaglobal.com.

Morningstar. 2021. *Walgreens Boots Alliance Inc.* Chicago, IL: Morningstar.

Munnich, L., T. Fried, J. Cho, and T. Horan. 2021. "Assessment of Spatial Location and Air Transport Patterns of Minnesota's Medical Device Industry Cluster." *Journal of Strategic Innovation and Sustainability* 16 (2): 106–18.

National Research Council. 2006. *Learning to Think Spatially*. Washington, DC: The National Academies Press. https://doi.org/10.17226/11019.

Natura. 2020. *Annual Report—2020*. Natura (website). https://www.naturaeco.com/en/.

Nelson, M. 2021. "Outsmarting Fraudsters with Advanced Analytics." Visa (website). https://usa.visa.com/visa-everywhere/security/outsmarting-fraudsters-with-advanced-analytics.html.

Nespresso. 2021a. "Our Business Principles." Nespresso (website). Accessed August 8, 2021. https://nestle-nespresso.com/our_business_principles.

Nespresso. 2021b. "The Positive Cup." Nespresso (website). https://www.sustainability.nespresso.com/.

Nespresso. 2022. *Facts and Figures*. Nestle-Nespresso (website). https://nestle-nespresso.com/our_company/facts_figures.

Newton Nurseries. 2022. Newton Nurseries web app, from Streetwise Retail Advisors. https://ccim.maps.arcgis.com/apps/webappviewer/index.html?id=1ac1f9c535834123b6e9d091d86af9a2.

NTIA (National Telecommunications and Information Administration). 2021. *Next Generation 911*. Washington, DC: National Telecommunications and Information Administration, US Department of Commerce. https://www.ntia.doc.gov/category/next-generation-911.

O'Sullivan, D., and D. Unwin. 2014. *Geographic Information Analysis*. John Wiley & Sons.

Pavate, V. 2021. "Why Warehouses Are Becoming Spatially Intelligent." *Material Handling & Logistics*, January 6, 2021. https://www.mhlnews.com/technology-automation/article/21151717/why-warehouses-are-becoming-spatially-intelligent.

Peppard, J., and J. Ward. 2016. *The Strategic Management of Information Systems: Building a Digital Strategy*, 4th ed. Chichester, UK: John Wiley & Sons.

Perez, J. 2017. Address at UPS investors' conference, UPS, Atlanta, GA.

PESA (Petroleum Exploration Society of Australia). 2020. "PESA Delegates Get Insights into BP's Digital Data Transformation." *PESA News* (Perth, Australia), First Quarter, 31-33.

Peters, A. 2017. "How John Deere's New AI Lab Is Designing Farm Equipment for a More Sustainable Future." FastCompany, September 11, 2017. https://www.fastcompany.com/40464024/how-john-deeres-new-ai-lab-is-designing-farm-equipment-for-more-sustainable-future.

Piccoli, G. and F. Pigni. 2022. *Information Systems for Managers in the Digital Age*, 5th ed. Burlington, VT: Prospect Press.

Pick, J. B. 2008. *Geo-business: GIS in the Digital Organization*. New York: John Wiley & Sons.

Porter, M., and M. Kramer. 2011. "Creating Shared Value." *Harvard Business Review* 89 (1 & 2): 2–17.

Porter, M., and M. Kramer. 2016. "The Ecosystem of Shared Value." *Harvard Business Review*, October 2016. https://hbr.org/2016/10/the-ecosystem-of-shared-value.

Porter, M. E. 1998a. "Clusters and the New Economics of Competition." *Harvard Business Review* 76 (6): 77–90.

Porter, M. E. 1998b. *The Competitive Advantage: Creating and Sustaining Superior Performance*, 2nd ed. New York: Free Press.

Porter, M. E. 1998c. *The Competitive Advantage of Nations*. San Francisco: Free Press.

Porter, M. E. 2008. "The Five Competitive Forces that Shape Strategy." *Harvard Business Review* 86 (1): 78–93.

Porter, M. E. 2021. *Cluster Mapping*. Cambridge, MA: Harvard Business School.

PricewaterhouseCoopers. 2020. "Welcome to the Crisis Era. Are You Ready?" Accessed May 1, 2020. https://www.pwc.com/gx/en/ceo-agenda/pulse/crisis.html.

Raad, M. 2017. "A New Business Intelligence Emerges: Geo.AI." *WhereNext* (Esri), April 18, 2017. https://www.esri.com/about/newsroom/publications/wherenext/new-business-intelligence-emerges-geo-ai/.

Radke, S., R. Johnson, and J. Baranyi. 2013. *Enabling Comprehensive Situational Awareness*. Redlands CA: Esri Press.

Rainforest Alliance. 2021. *The Birth of the AAA Sustainable Quality Program*. https://www.sustainability.nespresso.com/rainforest-alliance-insights.

RapidSOS. 2020. "Esri, GeoComm, and RapidSOS Partner to Improve First Responder Situational Awareness." https://rapidsos.com/.

RapidSOS. 2021. *The Ultimate Guide to Integrating Your Business with Public Safety* (e-book). https://rapidsos.com/ultimate-guide-integrating-business-with-911-ebook/.

Reid, A. 2021. "SecureWatch and Artificial Intelligence Fuel Safer, More Effective Monitoring of Real Estate Development during the COVID-19 Pandemic." MAXAR Corporation (blog), April 7, 2021. https://blog.maxar.com/earth-intelligence/2021/securewatch-and-artificial-intelligence-fuel-safer-more-effective-monitoring-of-real-estate-development-during-the-covid-19-pandemic.

Ricker, B. 2018. "Location-Based Services." In *The SAGE Encyclopedia of the Internet*, ed. B. Warf, 613–18. Thousand Oaks, CA: SAGE Publications.

San Diego Regional Economic Development Corporation. n.d. "Building San Diego's Talent Pipeline." https://sd-regional edc.maps.arcgis.com/apps/Cascade/index.html?appid=97fc15fd9df04152aa41d009a87ed8eb.

Sandino, T., G. P. Cavazos, and A. Lobb. 2017. "Oxxo's Turf War against Extra (B)." Harvard Business School Case 117-022. Boston: Harvard Business Publishing.

Sankary, G. 2020. "Inside Bass Pro Shops' Path to Business Continuity during COVID-19." *WhereNext* (Esri), May 14, 2020. https://www.esri.com/about/newsroom/publications/wherenext/inside-bass-pro-shops-path-to-business-continuity-during-covid-19/.

Sarkar, A., M. Koohikamali, and J. B. Pick. 2020. "Spatial and Socioeconomic Analysis of Host Participation in the Sharing Economy: Airbnb in New York City." *Information Technology & People* 33 (3): 983–1009.

Sarkar, A., H. Ramakrishna, N. Shin, J. Pick, B Hilton, and D. Farkas. 2022. "Adoption of Location Analytics and GIS in MIS Research: Current Trends and Opportunities." Unpublished manuscript. Microsoft Word file.

Sarlitto, D. J. 2020. "Evolution of Earth Observation." In *Encyclopedia of GIS*, ed. S. Shekhar, X. Hui, and Z. Xun. New York: Springer International Publishing.

Schroeder, A. 2017. "Humanitarian Aid and Spatial Technologies in Crisis." Presentation at the University of Redlands, Redlands CA. https://www.redlands.edu/csb-speakers/.

Semprebon, A. 2021. "Our Favorite Stories of 2021." *ArcGIS Blog* (Esri). December 19, 2021.

Shah, A. 2021. "Walgreens Brings 122 Apps to the Cloud." *CIO Journal* in the *Wall Street Journal*, August 11, 2021.

Sharda, R., D. Delen, and E. Turban. 2018. *Business Intelligence, Analytics, and Data Science*. New York: Pearson.

Shipt. 2022. "About Us." Home page. https://www.shipt.com/about/.

The Shopping Center Group. 2021. "About Us." Home page. Accessed August 8, 2021. https://www.theshoppingcentergroup.com/about/.

Simchi-Levi, D., P. Kaminsky, and E. Simchi-Levi. 2004. *Managing the Supply Chain: The Definitive Guide for the Business Professional*. New York: McGraw Hill Education.

Singh, C. 2017. "Nike Segment Analysis." Case study, April 5, 2017. Essays 24 (website). https://www.essays24.com/essay/Nike-Segment Analysis/75704.html#:~:text=Nike%20is%20unique%20in%20the,%E2%80%9D(Nike.com).&text=Thus%20segmenting%20to%20more%20precisely%20define%20various%20market%20segments%20is%20necessary.

Smith, N. 2020. "AI Predicts Highest Risk US Counties during Covid-19 Surge." Direct Relief (website), November 20, 2020. https://www.directrelief.org/2020/11/ai-predicts-highest-risk-u-s-counties-during-covid-19-surge/.

Solem, M. 2017. "Geography Education, Workforce Trends, Twenty-First-Century Skills, and Geographical Capabilities." In *The International Encyclopedia of Geography*, ed. D. Richardson et al., 2739–47. Chichester, England: John Wiley & Sons Ltd.

Somers, R. 1998. "Developing GIS Management Strategies for an Organization." *Journal of Housing Research* 9 (1): 137–78.

Sreedhar, B., and S. Bhatnagar. 2019. "Location Analytics Market: Global Forecast to 2024." MarketsandMarkets Research.

Stanley, J. 2017. "Space, Time, and Groceries." tech-at-instacart (website), June 13, 2017. https://tech.instacart.com/space-time-and-groceries-a315925acf3a.

Statista. 2021. "Statistics on Big Data." Statista (website). www.statista.com.

Stenmark, J. 2016. "Indoor Mobile Mapping Takes Off at LAX." *Geospatial World*, October 17, 2016. https://www.geospatialworld.net/article/indoor-mobile-mapping-lax/.

Swiss Re. 2021. "The Economics of Climate Change: No Action Not an Option." Swiss Re Institute (website), April 2021. https://www.swissre.com/dam/jcr:e73ee7c3-7f83-4c17-a2b8-8ef23a8d3312/swiss-re-institute-expertise-publication-economics-of-climate-change.pdf.

Tabrizi, B., E. Lam, K. Girard, and V. Irvin. 2019. "Digital Transformation Is Not about Technology." *Harvard Business Review*, March 13, 2019.

Tang, W., and J. Selwood. 2005. *Spatial Portals: Gateways to Geographic Information*. Redlands, CA: Esri Press.

Tao, F., H. Zhang, A. Liu, and A. Y. Nee. 2019. "Digital Twin in Industry: State-of-the-Art." *IEEE Transactions on Industrial Informatics* 15 (4): 2405–15.

Tate, N. J., and C. H. Jarvis. 2017. "Changing the Face of GIS Education with Communities of Practice." *Journal of Geography in Higher Education* 14 (3): 327–40.

Thompson, S. A., and C. W. Warzel. 2019. "Twelve Million Phones, One Dataset, Zero Privacy." *New York Times*, December 19, 2019. https://www.nytimes.com/interactive/2019/12/19/opinion/location-tracking-cell-phone.html.

Tobler, W. R. 1970. "A Computer Movie Simulating Urban Growth in the Detroit Region." *Economic Geography* 46 (sup1): 234–40.

Tomlinson, R. 2013. *Thinking About GIS: Geographic Information System Planning for Managers*, 5th ed. Redlands, CA: Esri Press.

Travelers Companies. 2019. *The Travelers Companies Inc. 2019 Annual Report*. http://investor.travelers.com/Annual-Reports.

Travelers Insurance. 2022. "Geospatial Intelligence Informs Safer, Smarter Business Decisions." https://www.travelers.com/resources/business-topics/internet-of-things/geospatial-intelligence.

Turner, A. 2018. *The Business Case for Racial Equity: A Strategy for Growth*. W. K. Kellogg Foundation report, July 24, 2018. https://wkkf.issuelab.org/resource/business-case-for-racial-equity.html.

UN (United Nations). 2022. Sustainable Development Goals Communications Materials. https://www.un.org/sustainabledevelopment/news/communications-material.

United Health Foundation. 2021. *America's Health Rankings: Health Disparities Report 2021*. https://assets.americashealthrankings.org/app/uploads/2021_ahr_health-disparities-comprehensive-report_final.pdf.

University of Redlands. 2018. "Charting Spatial Business Transformation." In *Spatial Business Initiative*. Redlands, CA: University of Redlands.

US Bureau of Labor Statistics. 2020. *Occupational Outlook Handbook*. Washington, DC: US Bureau of Labor Statistics.

Valentino-DeVries, J. 2018. "Five Ways Facebook Shared Your Data." *New York Times*, December 19, 2018. www.nytimes.com.

Valentino-DeVries, J., N. Singer, M. H. Keller, and A. Krolik. 2018. "Your Apps Know Where You Were Last Night, and They're Not Keeping It Secret." *New York Times*. December 10, 2018.

Van der Heijden, K., R. Bradfield, G. Burt, G. Cairns, and G. Wright. 2002. *The Sixth Sense: Accelerating Organizational Learning with Scenarios*. John Wiley & Sons.

Venables, M. 2019. "Change of Culture Reaps Rewards for BP's Digital Transformation." *Forbes*, January 31, 2019. https://www.forbes.com/sites/markvenables/2019/01/31/change-of-culture-reaps-rewards-for-bps-digital-transformation/?sh=27fa36306199.

VFC (VF Corporation). 2018. *We Are Made for Change: Sustainability and Responsibility Report 2018*. https://d1io3yog0oux5.cloudfront.net/vfc/files/documents/Sustainability/Resources/VF+2018+Made+for+Change+report.pdf.

VFC. 2020. Traceability Maps. https://www.vfc.com/responsibility/product/traceability-maps.

Walgreens. 2018. Interview with Walgreens. October 5, 2018.

Walgreens. 2021. Interview with Walgreens. July 23, 2021.

Wells, J. 2018. "FreshDirect Takes Aim at Amazon and Walmart with New Fulfillment Center." *Retail Dive* (online publication), July 23, 2018. https://www.retaildive.com/news/freshdirect-takes-aim-at-amazon-and-walmart-with-new-fulfillment-center/528069/.

Westberg, T. 2015. UPS presentation. 2015 Broadband Tech Summit, Provo, Utah, October 29, 2015. https://www.slideshare.net/UtahBroadband/2015-broadband-tech-summit-todd-westberg-ups-presentation.

Woodward, J. R. 2020. *Enterprise GIS: Concepts and Applications*. Boca Raton, FL: CRC Press.

Yaffe-Bellany, D., and M. Corkery. 2020. "A Wendy's with No Burgers as Meat Production Is Hit." *New York Times*, May 5, 2020. https://www.nytimes.com/2020/05/05/business/coronavirus-meat-shortages.html?auth=login-email&login=email.

Yunes, T. H., D. Napolitano, A. Scheller-Wolf, and S. Tayur. 2007. "Building Efficient Product Portfolios at John Deere and Company." *Operations Research* 55 (4): 615–29.

Zlatanova, S., and U. Isikdag, 2017. "3D Indoor Models and Their Applications." In *Encyclopedia of GIS*, 2nd ed., ed. S. Shekhar, X. Hui, and Z. Xun. New York: Springer International Publishing.

Index

About Esri Press

At Esri Press, our mission is to inform, inspire, and teach professionals, students, educators, and the public about GIS by developing print and digital publications. Our goal is to increase the adoption of ArcGIS and to support the vision and brand of Esri. We strive to be the leader in publishing great GIS books, and we are dedicated to improving the work and lives of our global community of users, authors, and colleagues.

Acquisitions
Stacy Krieg
Claudia Naber
Alycia Tornetta
Craig Carpenter
Jenefer Shute

Editorial
Carolyn Schatz
Mark Henry
David Oberman

Production
Monica McGregor
Victoria Roberts

Marketing
Sasha Gallardo
Beth Bauler

Contributors
Christian Harder
Matt Artz
Keith Mann

Business
Catherine Ortiz
Jon Carter
Jason Childs

For information on Esri Press books and resources, visit our website at **esri.com/en-us/esri-press**.